OBJECTIVE PROSPERITY

How Behavioral Economics Can Improve Outcomes for You, Your Business, and Your Nation

Roger D. Blackwell, Ph.D.

Retired Professor, The Ohio State University

Roger A. Bailey, Ph.D.

Clinical Assistant Professor, The Ohio State University

Print – ISBN: 978-1-944480-77-6
EPUB – 978-1-944480-78-3
PDF eBOOK – 978-1-944480-79-0

ROTHSTEIN
PUBLISHING
A Division of Rothstein Associates Inc.

i

OBJECTIVE PROSPERITY

How Behavioral Economics Can Improve Outcomes for You, Your Business, and Your Nation

Print – ISBN: 978-1-944480-77-6

EPUB – 978-1-944480-78-3

PDF eBook– 978-1-944480-79-0

Library of Congress Control Number: 2022936498

A Division of Rothstein Associates Inc.

4 Arapaho Road
Brookfield, Connecticut 06804 USA
203.740.7400
info@rothstein.com
www.rothsteinpublishing.com

What Your Colleagues Are Saying About Objective Prosperity

"This book will make you think. What factors influence the chances for individual success and national prosperity? How does behavioral economics help us understand who is financially rewarded? How can you prosper even if you were born poor? What is the best way to manage your savings? The authors cite the thoughts of many profound thinkers on how to live a rewarding life."
- *Philip Kotler, S.C. Johnson & Son Distinguished Professor of International Marketing, emeritus, Kellogg School of Management, Northwestern University*

"I really connected with the chapter that discusses the effort that must be put into those things that we find worthwhile or valuable to move us forward in our lives – mentors, discipline, education, personal responsibility and individual responsibility."
- *Deborah M. O'Brien, BS, RN, MPA, President, and Chief Executive Officer Community Resources for Justice*

"This book is a profound analysis of the roles of business, government, education, and personal responsibility in growing prosperity for everyone.'
- *Loretta Berryhill, California Business Owner*

"You will enjoy reading this book. The authors "colorize" principles with real-world examples from the individual (micro) level to that of nation-states (macro). Examples of successful (and less so) country policies are truly telling. They apply to political, business, and civic leaders not only at the federal but also at the state and local levels as well. The "solutionist" thread weaving its way through the book presents a unique perspective on how to approach issues on a broad range of topics."
- *The Hon Sunil Sabharwal, former US board member to the International Monetary Fund, global Olympic sports leader, investor, and champion fencer.*

"This book is one of the first that I could not put down the first read and enjoyed reading it the 2nd and 3rd times even more. Each time I found new thoughts expanding through my head. One is that we can no longer broad brushstroke economic models with the multi-layered behavioral changes around us in this hyper-informational age. This book is a must-read for any entrepreneur, like me in the automotive industry, to keep our eyes open to the rapidly changing consumer environment and how to think ahead."

-    *Rhett C. Ricart, Chief Executive Officer and Dealer Principal*
     2020 Chairman National Automobile Dealers Association

"There are few things more powerful than understanding why people behave the way they do. Here, the leading teacher of consumer behavior for the past half-century, with an accomplished marketing and economics colleague, explains it. This book is a virtual treasure chest of knowledge and understanding, about how behavioral economics helps people reach their ultimate objective – prosperity."

-    *John Mariotti, President & CEO, The Enterprise Group*

Dedicated To

Highly-Intelligent Readers Who Appreciate Facts More than Opinions

Foreword

STOP reading! Now, do I have your attention? NO – DON'T STOP reading!

Don't make the mistake I almost made of being put off by "Economics" in the subtitle. At first, I questioned, "who wants to read a 250-page book on economics?" Then I read a little more, skipped and skimmed based on the Preface. My first impression was wrong, as I found when I got deeper into the book's content.

I kept on reading, often peeking ahead to see where the book was going. The more I read, the more I liked it. I quickly realized that "prosperity" could also describe success, survival, happiness, and a host of other desirable outcomes. I also learned a lot along the way because the book is very rich in wisdom, and experience. I've known Roger Blackwell for 40 years and I've learned that when he has something to say – I listen!

I soon realized that the combination of "consumer behavior" and "economics," (i. e., "behavioral economics") is very powerful. Each of us will find our own treasures in this book. When I wondered how to stay on the path to prosperity, the "Keys" kept helping me.

There are few things more powerful than understanding why people behave the way they do. Here, the leading teacher of consumer behavior for the past half-century, with an accomplished marketing and economics colleague, explains it. I saw that not only individuals but also groups (companies, organizations, and even countries) were made up of people behaving in ways that serve their self-interest, seeking the rewards and prosperity.

Few books contain and explain so much content to help readers understand this. Everyone has similar objectives: success, gratification, recognition, and, ultimately, prosperity – each defined in their own unique context and terms. As I read further, chapters describe how diverse people learned and earned, or fought, to achieve prosperity (including enduring unintended consequences of even good ideas). This book is a virtual treasure chest of knowledge and understanding, about how behavioral economics helps people reach their ultimate objective – **prosperity**.

Suddenly, I found myself at the end, reading "Roger's Rules for Success." I was gratified, wiser, and far more aware of many things that I didn't understand as well before. Above all, I was happy I didn't take my own opening advice and STOP reading. I hope you will not stop but keep on reading. FYI: I found this book so rich in content, that it deserves a second or third reading.

John Mariotti

President & CEO, The Enterprise Group

Former Chairman, World Kitchen

Former President, Rubbermaid, Office Product Division
Former President, Huffy Bicycles
Former Chairman & Director, World Kitchen LLC
Powell, Ohio

July 2022

Preface

If you have ever heard Economics called "The Dismal Science," prepare to reset and propel your thinking about economics at quantum speed. Would you call it "dismal" to know how poor people of diverse racial, ethnic, and educational backgrounds escape poverty and become prosperous? Do you know how the ironic inequality paradox allows some people born in the bottom twenty percent to elevate themselves to the top twenty percent? Would you call it dismal or exciting to learn how, starting around age 45, to gradually become very prosperous with nothing more than what you have earned and learned working many years in a retail store?

Do you know how to grow up in one of the poorest nations in the world, called by some a "malaria-infested swampland" and see it become a nation more prosperous than the United States? Do you believe people in the Netherlands or Saudi Arabia are more prosperous? Do you know how the United States started equal in per capita income with the rest of the world to become one of the wealthiest nations in the world (but not *the* wealthiest)?

If you already know the answers to these questions, you probably don't need to read this book other than, perhaps, to have facts that will help you explain to friends who may not know them. But if you choose to read the rest of the book, you will find these answers and more about how to increase your own prosperity as well as understand why nations are poor or prosperous. And, perhaps, you will conclude the study of Behavioral Economics is not dismal, maybe even delightful.

Behavioral Economics is considered a new field of study by some, but as you will see in Chapter Two, it has many of the attributes of traditional wedding attire, "something old, something new, something borrowed, something blue." If you already know a lot about economics, you can skip Chapter One, but you may want to review it to be sure you understand two concepts essential to understanding how you prosper and contribute to national prosperity.

You may be tempted to go straight to the two most practical chapters in the book, "National Prosperity" (explaining why some nations are rich and other nations poor) and "How to Be Prosperous Instead of Poor." (Chapters 5 and 6). If you want to read those chapters first, that is reasonable, maybe to apply those principles to your life immediately. But if you want to know who controls future prosperity, perhaps it will be profitable to read Chapters Three and Four which document who controls future prosperity for both nations and individuals like yourself. Spoiler alert! It is not the President of the United States or even the Chairman of the Federal Reserve.

Is inequality getting better or worse? You may find the discussion of that issue in Chapter Seven ironic and paradoxical. You will probably also find that Chapter Eight raises issues you may not have considered in the past but that are critical to your future. And please don't read Chapter Nine until you have fully considered all the earlier chapters. Finally, when you arrive at the concluding chapter, the content of this book is summarized in Ten Rules that helped me survive and sometimes thrive in a life spanning many decades. They are not presented as suggested rules for you but perhaps as motivation to write down your own rules for the rest of *your* life.

After forty previous books, there was only one good reason for me to write another – to help you understand your own prosperity and typical income as well as wealth of people living in the nation. While this book is based on empirical research – the kind that helps people receive promotions as a professor and accumulate enough wealth to donate my career salary back to the university where I taught for forty years – it is also based on practical lessons growing up in the Missouri Ozarks, learning the only people who do not work on a farm are those who do not want to eat.

When I was in high school, at age 16, I began working at a local radio station as a janitor and progressed to higher positions, working full time while attending Northwest Missouri State before transferring to Missouri University to receive my bachelor's and master's degrees and a Ph.D. from Northwestern University, all without financing from parents or accumulating debt myself. You can read more details in the concluding chapter of this book, but from life and parents, I learned you do not have to have money to obtain a quality education. Where there is a will, there is a way for poor people to achieve a good education. This book describes how.

While reading this book, you will observe something different than most books: no footnotes. Some books include numerous citations at the bottom of pages, slowing reading substantially. To solve this problem, reader-oriented authors began putting citations at the end of chapters or the end of the book. Even with this improvement, printed citations were sometimes out of date or limited in scope.

When reporting national data, we generally reference the year 2019 rather than covid years of 2020 and 2021. Variations in managing the pandemic and collecting data vary so greatly between nations that reporting 2019 data provides more reliable comparisons than later years. Of course, you can always place different years in your browser to examine other years.

I have taken a behavioral approach, omitting footnotes in this book. If there is a term such as a demand curve or an author such as Daniel Kahneman about which you would like to learn more, you are encouraged to use your favorite search engine to get a recent explanation with as much detail as you prefer.

At The Ohio State University, I had the incredible learning experience of teaching over 65,000 students, mainly in the business school but also courses in Thanatology and Health Care Economics for the Medical School. I was also a member of the Black Studies faculty for a few years, reflecting a life-long interest in cross-cultural research, civil and human rights, and upward mobility among under-served minority groups.

My primary research area was behavioral aspects of marketing, co-authoring *Consumer Behavior*, a text translated into Russian, Portuguese, Spanish, French, Korean, and other languages used in universities and organizations in many countries. The success of that and other texts was the catalyst for being invited to teach and do research in 39 countries on six continents, learning from personal observation what makes some people poor and some prosperous.

After retiring from Ohio State, my understanding of poverty and prosperity was enriched further while teaching General Educational Development (GED) classes for almost six years to inmates at the Federal Correctional Institution in Morgantown, West Virginia. There is nothing quite as educational about how people escape (or do not escape) from project housing in the hood and other dysfunctional backgrounds as the daily teaching of former drug dealers. The GED students were often members of gangs, cartels, and other diverse occupations (including a former Mafia hitman) studying economics, math, government, grammar, and literature. In prison, when you teach math, explaining the metric conversion of grams to ounces, it is not unusual to be asked, "Is that with or without the bag?"

I taught students in prison how to obtain a GED and, when they left prison, how to get a job, but the GED students in prison taught me even more about the realities of poverty, crime, and injustice. Nelson Mandela was correct when he said no one understands a nation as well as people who spend time in its prisons. You can read additional details of my life, in both prosperity and prison, in *You Are Not Alone and Other Lessons a Teacher Learned from Parents, Professors, and 65,000 Students.*

While writing this book, I asked Dr. Roger Bailey for advice and help. His insights as a marketing professor at Ohio State and his strong background in Economics and Quantitative Methods were invaluable to improving and extending many areas of the book. I asked him to join me as co-author, which he graciously accepted. We might not agree on every detail in the book, but hopefully his addition will make it more useful to you.

Roger Blackwell, Ph.D.

Columbus, Ohio

July 2022

Additional Comments by Roger Bailey

First, I want to reiterate that this book is the brainchild of Dr. Blackwell, and I was very happy to join him and contribute my ideas and perspectives along the way. It is our sincere belief that every reader will take away something useful from the concepts and examples presented in the following chapters.

To point out another perspective that complements Dr. Blackwell's, I'll return to his comment about economics being called "the dismal science." This term for economics was coined in the 1800s by Thomas Carlyle. One view of economics at that time, proposed by Thomas R. Malthus, was that food would always be scarce and that poverty and hardship were unavoidable. Subsequently, many concluded that the "dismal science" phrase described the bleak outlook of economics for humanity.

This general view is consistent with many people's views of economics, business, and prosperity today. Most humans care about the well-being of other humans. It is easy to see the vast differences in wealth and prosperity across the globe and conclude that financial success requires a person (or a nation) to treat others poorly. In other words, prosperity appears to come from ill-gotten wealth. If this is your view of the world, this book will challenge that perspective.

The reality is that becoming more prosperous does not require you to mistreat others. Moreover, being a compassionate person does not require you to forgo successful strategies and sound business practices to improve the prosperity of you and your country. However, improving prosperity does require careful thought, planning, and methodical consistency toward your goals.

This book presents the view that economics, specifically behavioral economics, can be combined with an objective view of a situation to identify solutions for improving prosperity. The views in this book are consistent with fairness, empathy, and a desire to confront the problems in the world. On the other hand, this book will also objectively present the traits and characteristics of both individuals and nations that have consistently led to prosperous outcomes in the past.

Going back to Thomas Carlyle's view of economics, a brief investigation of his history reveals that he was anti-Semitic, racist, and had contempt for the notion of equal rights. Also, note that some of the first abolitionists in history were economists. In the 1770s, Adam Smith used economic theory to present a strong argument against slavery. Given Carlyle's pro-slavery views, it is widely believed that Thomas Carlyle's labeling of economics as "dismal" was a way to discredit a field that confronted his own bigoted beliefs. We hope you will agree that there is nothing dismal about the recommendations of this book!

In closing, the goal of this book is for you to come away with a "solutionist" perspective. Regardless of your political persuasion or your current financial situation, this book will provide you with tools for improving your own situation as well as for evaluating solutions and policies to improve the prosperity of your nation. After all, as you will see in the coming pages, your success can very much depend on the prosperity of those around you!

Roger Bailey, Ph.D.

Clinical Assistant Professor
Fisher College of Business
The Ohio State University
July 2022

Contents

Introduction

Regardless of how you earn a living, you have likely taken time during the pandemic to take stock of where you are and where you want to be in the future. These evaluations inevitably lead to the question: "How do I get there?" The answers may seem hard to find at times, and for a good reason. Every person comes from a different background, with different skillsets, constraints, weaknesses, and strengths. Identifying ways to increase your prosperity is made even more challenging by the reality that the success of your nation's economy can have a dramatic effect on your own success. Politicians, prickly pundits, and pompous TV personalities will promise answers for you and your nation, but consider this: Are there really one-size-fits-all answers to improve prosperity?

To be clear, this is *not* a book of simple answers to all of the world's problems. There are certainly enough "expert opinions" on the planet to go around. Instead, this book provides a method for you to arrive at your own answers not driven by upcoming elections and TV ratings. Throughout the text, there will be a number of explanations, recommendations, and examples to identify solutions to improve your own prosperity and to evaluate the policies that seek to improve the economy around you.

If you want to get the most out of this book, consider a few ground rules. First, try to approach the examples with as little bias as possible. Consider that this is far easier said than done. Biases, positive or negative, are learned predispositions to the environment around us. Just like every person has different strengths and weaknesses, every person also comes with different biases. Strong beliefs about the way things should be should not stop you from being able to evaluate a situation thoroughly and carefully. This book provides a behavioral-economics-based (data-based) view of prosperity that avoids the pitfalls of using preformed opinions and subsequent biases. In short, drop the dogma and dig into the data!

Second, this book will walk you through the opinions of multiple sources. Evaluation of the authoritative opinions of others allows you access to valuable information you may not otherwise consider. However, like every person, these sources will frequently have a slant to them (politically or otherwise), and yes, some may even include false or misinterpreted information! To help maintain objectivity, you should consider sources from different perspectives, not just those you are most comfortable with. The frequent quotes and references in the text provide further resources, but also highlight the importance of evaluating expert opinions in drawing conclusions for yourself.

In addition to the above, each chapter includes a few "Keys to Prosperity." These examples, quotes, and discussions are provided as practical insights from the authors. Consider these a base point to work from as you evaluate your own situation, the situation of those around you, the current state of your nation's economy, and how you might take action to improve your prosperity in light of these things!

Chapter 1

Essential Topics of Economics

Why are some people prosperous and others not? If you know the answer to that question, you increase your chance of being prosperous instead of poor. If you understand how to objectively analyze the world using economics, and more specifically behavioral economics, you also have tools to increase your chance of becoming wealthy, because high wealth has a different cause than high income.

There are many factors that contribute to wealth and poverty, some of which are very complex or may not be easily known in advance. However, the economic principles determining poverty and affluence for both you and a nation are as predictable and understandable as physical laws determining sunrise and sunset. Objective solutions from economic analysis are grounded in the reality that it takes no more effort to plan than it does to dream. However, planning is more likely to create the future you desire than dreaming. Just because the principles of economics are knowable does not mean that most people know them, and if you do not know the cause of prosperity, you will not know the cure for poverty.

Some parts of this book may challenge your beliefs about the economy. For example, here is a question you may not have considered before:

Which of the following is true regarding prosperity?

a) **When other people increase their income, my income must decrease.**

b) **When other people increase their income, my income can increase too.**

c) **I don't know.**

To determine your answer, you can simply choose which of the following statements best states your belief about income.

If you believe statement a) is true, you believe the economy is a zero-sum game. That means what any one person earns is subtracted from what other people earn because the total available in the economy is static or fixed. If you believe that when other people increase their income or wealth, an opportunity is created for you to earn more income and wealth yourself, you align with statement b) wherein the economy is *not* a zero-sum game. If you selected statement c), you will be able to understand the correct answer by the end of this book.

Make no mistake – it is important for you to understand which of the above statements is true. Your answer to this question can impact everything from your view of the economy, to how you spend your income, to the way you view the successes of those around you, and even your satisfaction with your current situation. Knowing the truth could enable you to reevaluate where you live, your best career, how many children you can afford to raise and educate, the kind of car you drive and who wins your vote in the next election.

Keys to Prosperity

"Life is 10 percent what happens to you and 90 percent how you respond to it."

-Charles Swindoll, *Attitude*

People live in a variety of economic systems. If you fail to understand them, you face a barrier to prosperity. The better you understand economic systems, the greater your probability of prosperity based on your individual response to economic realities. Be sure you understand the economic system that confronts you.

As one of the authors, I experienced eventual prosperity, but also near-death experiences and troubling times relating to economic challenges and injustices. Some of them are described in my previous book, *You Are Not Alone: What a Teacher Learned from Parents, Professors and 65,000 Students*. But instead of being destroyed by events that happened to me, I learned that my response determined eventual outcomes. In the book you are currently reading, examine closely how values determine consequences to understand the values that will lead to long-term success in your own life.

– Roger Blackwell

So how do you know which statement is true? You could read textbooks or take courses about economics. You could listen to politicians or celebrities express their opinion about economic topics. Or you could take the *Dragnet* approach.

The older you are, the more likely you are to have watched the classic TV police program, *Dragnet*. If not, you can still see episodes on YouTube and other media platforms featuring reruns of classic TV. In either case, you will see Sgt. Joe Friday interviewing witnesses who express their opinions about crimes. The laconic detective Sgt. Friday always confronts their opinions with a phrase attributed to him, "Just the facts, ma'am (or sir). Just the facts."

The fact-based *Dragnet* approach that identifies the way things are is more likely to help you achieve prosperity than beliefs or theories based mostly on the way things "ought to be." Life may not be fair, but much of it is predictable. And it is not easy to find the Dragnet approach when watching current news outlets as the accompanying Prosperity Key indicates.

Keys to Prosperity

News with a "Dragnet" approach

Where do you find a "Just the Facts" approach to the news? That is the stated mission of News Nation in an age of TV news competing for ratings with Fox News' Tucker Carlson and MSNBC's Rachel Maddow. Anchoring its nightly news program *Dan Abrams Live* is a reporter bringing to the show credentials of a *cum laude* undergraduate degree from Duke University and a J.D. from Columbia University as well as extensive experience at both ABC and NBC and formerly the host of the highly-rated TV show *Live PD*. Abrams is also the CEO and Founder of Abrams Media claiming over 20 million unique visitors per month across its digital properties

"Joining NewsNation is a welcome, natural fit for me," said Abrams, who has been publicly labeled "center-right" by Don Lemon of CNN and "center-left" by Megyn Kelly. "Too much of cable news is polluted by partisanship with shows focused on indoctrinating viewers, unabashedly cheering for one side or another. We are committed to presenting independent-minded analysis and opinion on politics, media, and the most important stories of the day, exposing hypocrisy on all sides so viewers can make up their own minds.

Abrams' approach to the news is designed as a neutral alternative to the opinion and commentary featured on Fox News, MSNBC and CNN in the evening hours. Abrams commented, "Being identified as a Republican doesn't make you a racist and voting for a Democrat doesn't make you a Communist. We just focus on facts seeking answers that are right."

In the chapters that follow, you will find discussions of various important issues using objective analysis from a combination of conventional economic theory and behavioral study. A traditional textbook in economics would present models designed to help you to understand and predict behavior with rigorous logic (and often supported with rigorous mathematics). These classical models are infamous for making unrealistic assumptions about human behavior. Ironically, it is precisely these oversimplifications of complex human behavior that allow traditional models to produce predictions of what might happen in a given situation. Surprisingly, the predictions of these models perform quite well in many situations. Hence, traditional economics has become an important mainstay of education across the globe.

 With that said, economists can now collect data and draw conclusions about human behavior that differ from the unrealistic assumptions of traditional models. This led to the development of a new field in economics, called *behavioral economics*, which investigates the psychological, sociological, and other factors that may amplify or alter predictions from traditional economic models.

Behavioral economics, also called descriptive economics or neoclassical models (NM), provides a way to consider more realistic human behavior in situations where traditional economic models perform poorly. Traditional economics, or standard economic models (SEM), emphasize mathematical models and provides valuable "benchmark" insights while behavioral economics (NM) emphasizes empirically-derived data, providing additional insights and realism. The purpose of this book is to draw from these insights to provide an objective application of economics that lays the foundation for understanding how to achieve prosperity.

Before jumping into chapters describing behavioral economics, it is useful to review some basic concepts needed to appreciate both the traditional and behavioral fields of study. The objective of the rest of this chapter is to understand a few essential economic principles you can recognize and apply to everyday life.

What is the "Economy"?

If you ask people what they mean by "the economy" you will hear different answers from different people. Some will say "jobs." Others may say "income" or perhaps "wealth." Perhaps you might hear someone say, "being able to afford all the things I need." Those variables are all affected by the economy and demonstrate the importance of considering the economy when thinking about how to improve your own prosperity. However, if you are to understand the relationship between the economy and prosperity it is important to be more specific about the meaning of the economy.

The "economy" refers to the *production and consumption* of *all goods and services produced in an area* such as a nation, region, or city. To make comparisons over time, between areas, or among groups of people, the metric normally used to measure goods and services is Gross Domestic Product (GDP) which refers specifically to the *money value of all goods and services produced in an area*. Sometimes it is also useful to measure Gross National Product (GNP) which refers to *money value of goods and services produced by firms domiciled in an area*, regardless of which area or nation in which the goods and services are produced. GNP is sometimes reported with a more recent, but similar term, GNI (Gross National Income). Frequently, it is useful to compute such metrics per person in the area. *Per capita GDP or GNP* can be considered the "average production" per person, convenient measures that can be compared across nations of varied sizes and over time when populations are changing.

An example of goods included in GNP would be when General Motors opens a plant in China making Cadillacs (as it did) or Honda operates a factory in Marysville, Ohio, as it does. The Cadillac factory is counted in the U.S. GNP, but the Chinese GDP. The Honda plant is part of Japan's GNP but part of the U.S. GDP. GNP may be important if you own shares in a company such as GM, but workers are more interested and affected by GDP because it has a direct effect on jobs. That is why most of the time when analyzing economics of an area, it is more useful to analyze GDP rather than GNP or GNI.

Neither GDP nor GNP is the same as happiness about *your* economic situation. To this end, sometimes people talk about GNH or Gross National Happiness, a concept so controversial and difficult to measure it is rarely used in creating government policies except in the nation of Bhutan. Of course, the GNH of a nation is related to GDP and GNI. Recent research by Matthew Killingsworth in *Proceedings of the National Academy of Sciences* indicates that life satisfaction and experienced well-being increases with income. However, when considering the topic of happiness from income, it is always useful to remember an old Italian proverb, "After the game, the King and the pawn go into the same box."

GDP is the metric you see most often used as a measure of how well an economy is doing. Keep in mind that GDP does not buy happiness for either an individual or a nation, although it allows people to look for happiness in interesting places (and sometimes choose interesting forms of misery).

Remember that both GDP and GNP refer only to the *money value* of goods and services – products for which money is exchanged (and reported to the government). When you mow your own lawn or teach your children to read, those are services produced by the economy, but since no money is exchanged, they are not part of GDP. If you pay someone to mow your lawn (other than a neighborhood kid not reporting earnings to the government) or if you pay a day care center, that is part of GDP. This is an important detail in determining the growth of GDP as you will read later. This also highlights the interest in other economic metrics, such as GNH, that might include the value created by stay-at-home parents, volunteers feeding the hungry, and goods donated to others. However, while these forms of non-market production have obvious value, they can be difficult to quantify, leaving GDP as the standard measure of economic performance.

Since everything included in GDP is measured in money value or prices, GDP will grow when the price of the goods increases (inflation). When the year-over-year (YOY) growth of GDP is greater than year-over-year (YOY) inflation, the economy is considered "good" or at least growing. When GDP declines two or more quarters in succession, the economy is considered "in recession." The movement between growth and recession and back again is called the business cycle. This is important, because if you do not understand how and when recessions occur, you could lose your job.

If you do understand how recessions occur and prepare for them, you may even do well in a recession. Recessions can be an opportunity for people who understand and prepare for them as they can buy goods and services at bargain rates, attract customers from other firms, or buy stocks at reduced prices. If you do not understand and prepare for business cycles, recessions could cause a personal economic disaster for you. If you are a politician or economist working for the government, you may be interested in how to eliminate or "smooth out" business cycles entirely.

Keys to Prosperity

Bringing it Home

The idea of expecting and preparing for recessions can be easily described using a household as a model of the economy. Occasionally, a single household might experience a positive boost to their total income, an unexpected promotion, a high-paying new job, or a household member entering/reentering the workforce by choice.

Unfortunately, almost every household will inevitably face negative shocks as well. Time off work due to injuries and other health issues, being laid off from a struggling firm, or coming upon a large, unexpected expense can all have dramatic consequences on a household's finances. Occasionally, a household might see these changes coming, but not always. The current wisdom of having an "emergency fund" and carrying insurance to protect against large financial losses is analogous to a nation preparing for changes in the business cycle. The key to prosperity here is that negative shocks and failures are inevitable; prosperity is just as much about planning for failures as it is about achieving success!

Warren Buffet, one of America's oldest and most successful investors, was asked a couple of years ago if he thought we would have another recession. His answer was, "I hope to see several more recessions in my lifetime." Depending on your age, you will also see several recessions in your lifetime, a reason to *always* save enough to establish an emergency fund allowing you to take advantage of recessions and avoid the disasters that occur to people who are unprepared. If you want to know an effective method to prepare for recessions, read the biblical book of *Genesis* and examine the advice Joseph gave Pharaoh when Egypt was facing an impending recession, that is, save for the future! Whether recessions occur because of predictable events such as economic mistakes or catastrophic events such as the Covid-19 pandemic, or "black swan" events such as the unexpected and sudden collapse of a country's financial system, recessions have occurred for centuries and will continue to do so. Be as ready for them as you can.

Who Gets How Much?

Two major concepts to consider when studying economics are *production* and *distribution* of goods and services. Production refers to how many goods and services are created in an area, and distribution refers to who gets them.

Production of *goods* refers to how many cars, homes, clothes, food, computers, and other *physical goods* are produced in a nation. Production of *services* includes such things as education, health care, day care, restaurants, home repairs, entertainment (including sports) and a myriad of other services people pay others to perform instead of making or doing those things themselves.

A Sunday afternoon tag football game with friends does not contribute to GDP. The NFL does. With that said, if you live in a state such as Ohio, home of both the Bengals and Browns, tag football games the past few years probably produced more happiness than the NFL.

Until the early 1800s, *production* in the United States was largely agricultural with more than 80 percent of the population involved in farming. Most manufacturing was centered on raw materials such as lumber from sawmills with products such as textiles, boots, and shoes as the primary manufactured goods. By 1860, the share of the farm population in the U.S. had fallen from over 80 percent to roughly 50 percent; today it's less than 2 percent. Data from the 1950 Census show that 32 percent of non-farm jobs were in manufacturing. Today it is less than 9 percent of total nonfarm employment and headed toward the same level as agriculture. Services, however, have soared to over 80 percent of all jobs.

Who cares how production is changing, you might ask? You, if you care about your job in the future! No one should assume that what they do today is what will be needed to prosper in the future. Unions cannot guarantee your job will be needed in the future. Neither can big corporations or small ones. Nor the government. The only person in the world determining whether you have a prosperous job in the future is YOU, and what you do now to change or improve your skills to be ready for the future. The more you know about economics and objective analysis of behavior, the more likely you are to identify a path to prosperity.

Distribution of goods and services is the process of determining who gets the cars, education, homes, computers and TVs, health care and all the other goods and services produced in an economy. A basic tenet of traditional economics that is fairly robust is the *insatiability of demand*. History and empirical data reveal that demand always increases faster than the required supply for everyone to have everything they want. Illustrating this concept, John D. Rockefeller was once asked "How much money is enough?" and he answered, "just a little bit more." There has never been an era or geographic location with enough goods and services to satisfy everyone to have everything they want or need.

And you should avoid getting into arguments about what is a *need* and what is *want* because you will probably lose that argument, regardless of what position you take. This is because there is a fine line between needs and wants, especially when they are characterized by quantities, quality, speed-of-service, etc. For example, everyone would consider food a need, but the minimum amount of food required to survive is most certainly not enough to be comfortable. At what point does the desire for more food become a want instead of a need? Similarly, most people would agree that reliable transportation is a need. However, even the most reliable mode of transportation can break down. What is the acceptable rate of failure where need is met, and additional reliability becomes a want? Moreover, and perhaps more importantly, who chooses these thresholds?

 It would certainly be nice if everyone could get everything they want, especially for goods and services such as homes, cars, clothing, food, education, and medical care, but that is not what occurs in reality. Unfortunately, because of the insatiability of demand, no economy produces enough of every good to fully satisfy all consumer wants. So, the big question is who gets what? Allocation methods determine not only who gets cars and who does not, but also whether the cars they get will be Fords or Ferraris and whether homes will have one bedroom or five.

The three basic methods of allocating goods and services all have advantages and disadvantages. When most of the people in the U.S. lived on farms, the question of allocation of goods and services was simple. For most goods and services, you got what you produced yourself whether it was food, medical care, or clothing. The source of medical care in most families was a grandparent and it was not unusual in the rare instances you needed to pay a physician it would be with a chicken or a bushel of corn.

In the rural Agrarian economies of long ago, the only people who did not work on farms were people who did not want to eat. In 1900, most of the U.S. population lived on farms, 46 million out of the 76 million total population. The 1920 census marked the first time in which over 50 percent of the U.S. population was defined as urban, and it took a few more decades before the majority grew up in urban environments. By 1950, only 16 percent of the population – 23 million people – lived on farms. In modern economies, most of the goods and services people consume are produced by someone else. So, in contemporary society, which of the three primary methods of distributing goods and services do you believe is best? *Lottery, need, or merit*?

One possible method of determining who gets new cars, homes and all the other stuff consumers want is by *lottery*. Since the economy typically produces about 17 million new cars a year in the U.S., everyone who wants one could register their name and let a computer randomly select who gets a new car. This method of distribution is currently used for certain types of organ transplants where the number of people wanting organs is far greater than supply. Given the vast need for these organs, there is little alternative except for medical facilities to register everyone qualifying who needs them and then allocate by lottery.

Some consumers vote with their wallet for a lottery system when they buy Mega Millions or Powerball tickets, paying a few dollars in the hope they will receive millions of dollars to buy everything they want. However, doubt may arise about the efficacy of lotteries. According to the National Endowment for Financial Education, about 70 percent of people who win a lottery or get a big windfall end up broke in just a few years.

Keys to Prosperity

Financial Wind-Fails

A brief internet search will reveal dozens of examples of lottery winners who were broke in a few short years. The common argument for why this happens is that winners are unfamiliar with handling large sums of money, and subsequently ignore sound financial advice surrounding saving, investing, and spending large sums of money. Of course, there is merit to this argument as the behavior of lottery winners frequently includes quitting one's job, lavish spending sprees, and a lack of wise saving and investment. However, note that not every case includes someone suffering from a lack of "financial literacy."

In 2002, Andrew Whittaker won an astounding $315 million from the interstate Powerball lottery. Whittaker is a unique case in that before he won the lottery, he had already amassed a fortune of $17 million through his construction/contracting firm. Nevertheless, while Whittaker made large donations to charities and others, he also made many poor financial decisions and found himself in legal trouble. Some of these legal problems resulted from gambling and other self-created problems, but according to an interview with ABC in 2007, he faced over 400 frivolous lawsuits against his him and his contracting business by people desiring a portion of his winnings. Unfortunately, Whittaker lost multiple members of his family to tragic deaths and eventually filed bankruptcy in 2007. In his interview, Whittaker was famously quoted as saying "I wish I'd torn that ticket up." The behavioral difficulties of dealing with a large windfall are certainly documented, regardless of your background.

Nevertheless, the principles in this book can be helpful in case you are the "victim" of a large windfall. Make sure you plan more than you dream and be careful in anticipating the behavior of yourself and others when they discover your newfound wealth!

A reasonable conclusion based on lottery data is that people who fail to earn their income through effective application of economic principles are likely to fail at spending it effectively as well, a valuable lesson based in behavioral study. There is an underlying truth in the adage about giving a person a fish to eat and they will be hungry the next day but teach them how to fish and they will never be hungry again.

Fishing in contemporary economies may not be that helpful in feeding you and your family, but we can adapt the same concept to a modern skill. For example, studies indicate that in contemporary economies workers from entry level to top management who understand how to write computer code earn substantially higher incomes than those who do not know how to code. Even if "coding" is not a job skill you might choose or like, it most certainly appears to be connected with prosperity.

One form of lottery in which people receive goods and services is the birth lottery. If you are lucky enough to be the child of wealthy parents, you get more goods and services than children of poor parents. If you do not win that lottery, you will have to obtain cars, homes, clothes and goods and services from one of the other two ways of distributing what the economy produces. But here is a secret that prosperous people learn: It is better to have parents that give you *values* that help you to become prosperous than parents who give you money or capital. You will see why in later chapters.

A second way of distributing goods and services produced in an economy is by need, called *collectivism*. Food, clothes and homes and all other goods and services could be distributed "to everyone according to their need, from everyone according to their ability to pay." Many people defend that method of distribution, as did Karl Marx and Vladimir Lenin. From a philosophical or moral perspective, collectivism is difficult to refute, but there is a difficult question to answer with this method. Who decides what you need or do not need?

Do not get into arguments with people about collectivism, because they have an attractive perspective. If you want to achieve political power, it is also a perspective likely to win votes.

But remember the admonition attributed to Sgt. Friday: "Just the facts." The ultimate way to evaluate a collectivist philosophy is with data. And remember, distrust or denial of data is often the beginning of tyranny. There is plenty of evidence to determine what happens to an economy when the collectivism philosophy of distribution is followed. You will see some of those data in a later chapter when you examine what happened when the collectivist principle was applied in Russia, Cuba, and other countries and after the collectivist principle was modified in China.

Keys to Prosperity

Communal Systems

Each Thanksgiving season, people celebrate the Pilgrims and their early settlement at Plymouth in 1620, essentially founded as a socialist commune. The settlers received their clothing, food, and supplies from the colony's "common stock," all farmland was collectively owned, and each family received provisions according to their needs, with the profits of labor being divided equally rather than by what was earned through their own work.

The system quickly led to discontent: The healthy and able-bodied colonists who worked in the fields all day began to resent the colonists who claimed to be ill, frustrated they received the same amount of food and supplies as those who performed zero labor. The socialist system was also harmful to the health of the Pilgrims: nearly half of the colonists died of starvation during their first winter, unable to feed themselves and stay healthy with the colony's shrinking harvest sizes.

The best way for a society to prosper is through hard work and personal responsibility, not through promises of equal outcomes. The Pilgrims saved their settlement by abandoning socialism and embracing the free market. Property in Plymouth was privatized. The housing and cattle were assigned to separate families, and provision was made for the inheritance of wealth. The colony flourished.

There are examples of success in socialism, however, such as those of a kibbutz, a type of settlement unique to Israel, traditionally agrarian. The first kibbutz was Deganya Aleph, founded in 1910, but today, there are over 270 kibbutzim in Israel. They have diversified since their agricultural beginning and are often now private, mostly in manufacturing, with many highly successful. Kibbutz Degania's diamond cutting factory now grosses millions of dollars a year. Kibbutz Hatzerim's company Netafim was the global pioneer in drip irrigation equipment with a flagship factory on the kibbutz and others around the world. In recent decades, the trend has been privatization of the kibbutzim, participating in the prosperous wider economy of Israel.

The third method of distributing goods and services in an economy is *meritocracy*. The difficult question here is in determining who is meritorious. This could most easily be defined as people who contribute most to the *production* of goods and services. When land was the principal determinant of production, the families who owned land received the most goods and services, usually produced by people who lived on that land. That form of "meritocracy" became "aristocracy" in Europe and remains one of the reasons economic mobility in Europe, even today, is more constrained than in nations such as Canada, the United States, Australia, New Zealand, Singapore, and other countries with substantial intergenerational economic mobility.

Who decides who contributes most to production and therefore gets the largest amounts of goods and services? It is not aristocracy in nations such as the U.S.

and Canada. It is not banking or other financial institutions on Threadneedle or Wall Street. In the U.S., it is not even the government, although the government has some influence on distribution of goods and services with progressive taxation and inheritance rules. Those that get to be prosperous, perhaps even billionaires, in the U.S., China (especially Hong Kong), Singapore and other nations is controlled by an entity called "The Market" (assuming you can participate in the market and reap the benefits of that participation).

You will find data to support your decision of the best method of distribution in the next few chapters where you will see data disclosing that a major factor determining the *quantity* of goods and services *produced* in an economy is the method of their *distribution*.

You can take a closer look at "meritocracy" as a method of distribution in Chapter 5 after you examine why some nations are wealthy and some are poor, and plenty of insights about why some people within nations are prosperous and others are poor in Chapter 6. Remember, most billionaires started out with nothing or nearly nothing, a fact disclosed in annual *Forbes* billionaire issues, sometimes surprising people who have not studied which entrepreneurs are successful and which ones are not. You will observe that what happened in the U.S. in the past is also happening today in China, Hong Kong, Canada, Singapore, Nigeria, and other nations. If you want to understand why these changes are happening, stay tuned!

But resist the temptation to skip to Chapter 5 and 6 or you will miss important history lessons about Behavioral Economics in Chapter 2, the answer about who controls the economy in Chapter 3, and how people buy goods and services in Chapter 4.

Discussion Questions

- The people of every democratic country have the important responsibility to vote upon proposed policy changes, sometimes by directly voting on the policy, and other times by voting for representatives that support a policy. Consider what you believed the economy to be before reading this book. How might misunderstanding the economy, such as believing the economy to be only about jobs, lead someone to make poor decisions when evaluating proposed government policies?
- Recessions are inevitable, even with best efforts to "smooth out the business cycle." When do you believe the next recession will occur? What are you personally doing to prepare for it?
- Consider the three methods of distributing income and wealth discussed in the text (need, lottery, and merit). Which do you believe is best? Why? Are there any other alternatives to these three?
- Which method of distribution does your nation primarily use? How might changing the method of distribution of goods and services in your economy affect the resulting supply of goods and services?

Chapter 2

Behavioral Economics:

Something Old, Something New

To understand the causes of prosperity, you need to understand how people are likely to respond when presented with choices. To begin, consider the following question:

Which is the best way to predict how people will respond to something?

a) Use assumptions about how all people behave in general.

b) Use data on how people have behaved in the past.

c) Use your beliefs about how people should behave.

d) Some combination of the above.

Your answer to this question is likely to result from how you approach understanding the behavior of others. Given that economics and prosperity are heavily dependent on the choices and actions of people, the way that you identify the likely behavior of people is critically important for success.

"Something old, something new, something borrowed, something blue." You probably have heard that expression describing traditional attire at weddings. It is also true about the wedding of behavioral economics to traditional economic principles.

Behavioral economics does not "throw out the baby with the bath water" but it does explain the importance of "something old, something new" with respect to understanding a nation's economic growth. Much of the substance, probably most, behavioral economics espouses is "old" in that it retains essential principles from the past that still apply today. In traditional economics, a demand curve is simply a line that maps out the quantity of a good that would be sold at different prices. In behavioral economics, a demand curve is still a demand curve, and many other properties of traditional economics are still foundational.

But behavioral economics contains much that is new, sometimes explaining anomalies found in traditional economics, such as how a lottery winner might quickly spend all of their money or how a demand curve might slope upward. Is it rational that when a product is priced higher, the quantity demanded is greater instead of less? Yes, it is rational if you understand the "price-quality relationship." Consumers often do not know the quality of different options, and upward-sloping demand curves are revealed by objectively studying the behavior of consumers that typically believe higher-priced goods are of higher quality. Such behavioral insights become an important piece of understanding how to shift a demand curve (moving it to the right so that the same quantity is sold at higher prices), a common goal of marketing strategists.

Keys to Prosperity

Don't "Wine" About Upward Sloping Demand

One of the difficulties with the rational actor paradigm is the assumption that consumers have full information about the alternatives in front of them. Obviously, this is rarely the case. Consider the purchase of wine at a restaurant. Unless you are a connoisseur of wine, you are unlikely to have the information to know which wines are better. If you're like me, you may not have the palette to be able to discern good wine from great wine even when you drink it. In such situations, people will often take the price of the wine as signal of the quality. Instead of carefully evaluating the options, you might act similar to me and simply pick a middle-priced wine believing that this is likely to be a safe bet compared to the cheapest and likely "worst" wine. Such behavior often leads to middle-priced options being the most popular choice in purchases when few consumers have full information.

Situations like this bring up a problem for the assumption of downward-sloping demand curves. If there are 3 wines, and two are priced very low with a third priced very high, consumers may randomly pick one of the two lowest-priced wines. However, if the price of one of the low-priced wines was a few dollars more, it suddenly becomes the middle option. This might signal a higher quality to uninformed consumers and demand could actually increase!

The point here is not to toss away the first law of demand (downward sloping demand curves). Rather, consider the information available to potential consumers and the availability of alternatives when considering purchase behaviors. Another key is to always have a few friends that can recommend good wines!

- *Roger Bailey*

A substantial amount of behavioral economics is also borrowed, sometimes from quaint coffee shops in Vienna, Austria. These coffee shops are known for excellent coffee, tasty pastries, and as the historical hangouts for the economists known as the "marginal revolutionaries." These economists are responsible for laying some of the groundwork for many ideas in behavioral economics.

However, you will have to be the judge about whether objective solutions resulting from behavioral economics should be considered mostly "blue" (politically progressive) or mostly "red" (politically conservative).

The Original Economists

The "old" part of economics is often linked to a book that served as the foundation for economic thought, *The Wealth of Nations,* written by Adam Smith in Scotland in the 18th Century. Among other economic realities, Smith described the negative effects of monopolies on economic growth and prosperity and the positive effect of competition in driving progress in a "market-driven economy." He described market forces as "the invisible hand" that guides the economy to achieve the most progress and prosperity. Smith is also credited with creating the theory of rational choice (described later), but Smith was not the first economist; he was reacting to earlier economists' theories of "mercantilism" and influenced by philosophers dating back to Aristotle's *Politics.*

Problems faced by individuals and societies are the catalysts for applying economic analysis in order to find solutions. A key personality in the thrust to find solutions to world-wide economic malaise and depression was British economist John Maynard Keynes, notably in his book, *The General Theory of Employment, Interest and Money,* published in 1936. Keynes believed classical economic theory did not provide a way to end depressions. His solution to depressions, defined as multiple years of sustained reduction in GDP, was a belief that the government should step in and spend money to get the economy back on track.

The problem of business cycles is an economic problem existing for centuries, and Keynes' solution was more or less the same as Joseph's recommendation to Pharaoh in ancient Egypt. Simply stated, the solution to smoothing out business cycles by both Joseph in *Genesis* and Keynes was for the government to increase taxes during the boom phase of the business cycle (with grain when that was the currency of Egypt) and stimulate the economy by increasing expenditures and cutting taxes or using other stimuli to create spending during the bust or downturn part of the business cycle. If this solution worked perfectly, business cycles would be eliminated, as would recessions and depressions, and the economy would sail along smoothly from year to year.

Eliminating business cycles and preventing depressions provided the impetus for Keynesian economic analysis. Keynes' approach leads away from the notion of the "invisible hand" of the market guiding the economy, toward an increased role of government in determining economic growth and prosperity. In this framework, the government achieves prosperity through the use of policy tools. This includes monetary policy such as interest rates controlled by the Federal Reserve and fiscal policy controlled by Congress for expenditures on projects such as infrastructure.

Keys to Prosperity

Pay Attention to the Details

Infrastructure is critically important to the economy of a nation, and federal spending on infrastructure is most certainly necessary. With that said, when evaluating proposed legislation be sure you examine the details to determine which portions are for the stated purpose, such as infrastructure, and which portions are inserted to achieve other purposes. For example, a refund might be proposed to encourage consumers to buy electric vehicles to reduce carbon emissions. Look carefully, however, and you may find that the refund is significantly larger if the vehicle is produced in a union organized factory, a purpose different than the stated purpose. And remember the adage, "the devil is in the details."

Keynesian economics became a major part of the standard economic model (or SEM) for managing the economy throughout much of the world, thanks to the textbook *Economics: An Introductory Analysis*, first published in 1948 by MIT Professor and Nobel Prize winner Paul Samuelson. He emphasized that changes in demand are more likely to cause recessions than changes in supply. The emphasis on understanding and predicting changes in demand is one of the reasons the two chapters that follow will help you to analyze why people buy (or do not buy) and the determinants of what they buy; valuable information for anyone seeking success in business.

Samuelson's *Economics* is one of most successful textbooks on any subject in the history of publishing. It is translated into nearly every language in the world where economics is taught and has been the text of choice by economics professors throughout the world, selling millions of copies through multiple revisions. It is the reason Keynesian economics dominated economic thinking until recently. One of the goals of Samuelson and traditional economics (SEM) is to express economic relationships in mathematical equations providing precise predictions of results expected by changes in causal variables.

One of the problems with these mathematical models is they deal only with the most important variables and rely on assumptions that other non-measured variables are "constant." A demand curve, for example, predicts "demand as a function of price… holding constant all other variables such as consumer preferences and income." Other assumptions greatly simplify consumer decision-making. One reason that these assumptions are necessary is because data for these assumed constants and/or regarding more complex behavior were not historically available.

If you studied economics in universities of most every country in the world or read *Economics* by Samuelson, some of the assumptions you would have discovered include the following:

1. Consumers make rational choices, carefully evaluating all options.
2. Consumers make choices that maximize the total benefit (total utility) they receive from the goods they purchase, and firms make choices that maximize profits.
3. Consumers act independently with full and relevant information.

Do you believe these "assumptions" are true? Are there data to support or challenge these assumptions? Keynesian economics contains more restrictive assumptions than traditional economics, but if you reflect on these assumptions, you begin to understand why behavioral economics emerged to challenge or relax these and many other assumptions of traditional economics.

Something Borrowed

Many economists challenged the assumptions and predictions of traditional economists. Many of them were in Austria beginning in the late 19th century, where they heard lectures by Austrian (and other) economists at the University of

Vienna during the day and discussed them at length in the coffee shops of Vienna, often late into the night.

The Austrian school of economics emphasizes the organizing power of markets. It differs from traditional and Keynesian economics in the basic approach to solving problems in determining the value of a product, emphasizing the importance of utility to individual consumers rather than an inherent value based on inputs of commodities, labor and capital required to produce the product. Keynesian and traditional economists consider consumers all the same in deriving utility from products, a theory as questionable as assuming fingerprints of all consumers are the same.

Austrians were troubled with what they called apparent paradoxes, like the classic water-diamond paradox discussed by Adam Smith. The paradox is that water is necessary to life, and diamonds are shiny hard rocks with little intrinsic value except sometimes to cut harder things. Yet diamonds are much more expensive than water.

The answer to the paradox is explained by marginal analysis which says that a person will not trade all their water for diamonds; they are trading a rare shiny diamond for a common glass of water. Even though diamonds are not especially useful, on the margin they are valuable because they are scarce. Even though water is essential, on the margin it is cheap because it is abundant. In other words, people who are buying diamonds have more than enough water to meet their needs. But the value of products varies from one consumer to another depending on the context of the decision. If you were dying of thirst and offered the choice of a 5 carat diamond or a 5 liter jar of water, you are likely willing to pay more for the water than for the diamond.

Because the value of a product varies so greatly between individuals, under various circumstances and over time, it is difficult for an organization such as the government to decide what products should be produced and who should receive what is produced. Austrians believe that nature should be allowed to run its course and the less government interferes in free markets, the better it is.

You will see a lot of ideas borrowed from the Austrians when you examine behavioral economics. You can also understand why Austrian economists had to flee during the rise of fascism and the Nazis in that part of the world prior to World War II.

The most influential of the Austrian economists was Joseph Schumpeter who left Vienna in 1932 to take a position at Harvard University, becoming a U.S. citizen in 1939. Other Austrians went to the U.S., U.K., and Switzerland. Schumpeter's teaching and scholarship influenced many while he taught at Harvard. One of those was Clayton Christensen, a professor at Harvard Business School whose book on innovation and competition *The Innovator's Dilemma* became one of the most influential on business management in the world, demonstrating why some firms succeed and some fail. When Christensen taught seminars for executive groups on the topic of innovation, he sometimes acknowledged that his books were mostly up-to-date research on Schumpeter's concept of Creative Destruction.

Another famous economist, F.A. Hayek, grew up in Vienna. Hayek chose to study economics not for its own sake, but because he wanted to improve social conditions, influenced heavily by the poverty after World War I. Socialism seemed to provide a solution to some Europeans, but its failures were the subject of the book *Socialism* by fellow Austrian Ludwig von Mises. This book is often called the most important critical examination of Socialism ever written and had a major influence on Hayek. Mises argued that economic calculations require a market for the means of production. Without such a market, there is no way to establish the values of those means and, consequently, no way to find their proper uses in production. Mises's devastating attack on central planning converted Hayek to *laissez-faire* economics.

Hayek left Vienna for the London School of Economics before World War II and went on to the University of Chicago in 1950 where he worked with Milton Friedman, George Stigler, and others. For Hayek, market competition generates an order that is the result "of human action but not human design" (a phrase borrowed from Adam Smith). This "spontaneous order" is a system that comes about through the independent actions (behavior) of many individuals (such as you), producing benefits to the total society unintended and mostly unforeseen by those whose actions bring it about and often contradicting Keynes' mechanistic analysis of business cycles.

Keys to Prosperity

Net Benefit?

Hayek considered the market itself an example of spontaneous order, but there are more recent examples in society. One example that is relevant to everyone is the internet. The internet as we see it today spans borders, languages, and economic systems. While any one government can dictate (to some degree) how the internet operates within its borders, no single authority has control over it. The internet has become what it is today through enterprising individuals and entrepreneurs incentivized to build and create content for their own purposes. New innovations continue and the resulting system is far more complex than a single government or firm would have been able to design or predict. Instead, like the market, we all play a role in the existence, function, and growth of the internet.

Obviously, not everything on the internet is beneficial to society. However, much of it can be understood through a behavioral lens. Consider the incentives and behaviors you see on the internet every day, and it's not surprising that so many people have been able to build large fortunes by using and contributing to it.

Hayek became a household name in post-World II America because of his 1944 book *The Road to Serfdom*, remaining a best-seller for decades. *The Road to Serfdom* is an accessible source to understand Schumpeterian (Austrian) economics and was pivotal in Hayek winning the Nobel Prize for Economics in 1974.

Most of the Austrian economists dispersed from Vienna in a manner reminiscent of the von Trapp family in *Sound of Music*. If this thumbnail sketch of their ideas and the culture that created them intrigues you enough to know more, an excellent source for the rest of the story is a recent book *The Marginal Revolutionaries: How Austrian Economists Fought the War of Ideas* by Janek Wasserman.

Something New: Behavioral Economics

How do you blend the theories of Adam Smith, Keynes, and the Austrians? The reality is to collect empirical data about behavior instead of predictions based on mathematical equations and assumptions. Behavioral economics focuses on what people do in response to changes in economic and other variables, not assumptions based on the more simplified models of traditional economics.

How does demand change in response to changes in personal preferences, income, supply, quality variations, and a host of other variables affecting and affected by human behavior? Answers to these questions based on empirical data incorporating the conceptual foundations found in all three approaches is called behavioral economics (or NM for Neoclassical Model). Understanding how objective analysis with behavioral economics can contribute to individual and national prosperity is the purpose of this book, which could even be called "Prospernomics."

Behavioral economics can be described as a method of economic analysis that applies psychological insights, neuroscience, sociological variables, and demographic realities affecting human behavior to explain economic decision-making. Traditional economics assumes that all people and organizations act rationally in their own self-interest. In contrast, behavioral economics emphasizes additional variables, including the possibility of altruism.

Behavioral economics also allows for bounded (or limited) rationality, wherein people are not always "fully rational" when making decisions. Moreover, the context in which a decision is made can have a significant effect on the decision or preference. The variables that traditional economists assume as "constants" in a demand curve may (in some cases) be even more important than traditional price-quantity relationships.

The most likely candidate for the title "father of behavioral economics" belongs to Dr. George Katona and his 1951 book *Psychological Analysis of Economic Behavior*. A Hungarian-born Gestalt psychologist, Katona brought realism to economic analysis through psychological concepts, beginning with his early days studying hyperinflation in Germany and extending these concepts from macro-economics to micro-economics, as you will see in Chapter 4.

Daniel Kahneman

If Katona is responsible for the birth of behavioral economics, Daniel Kahneman is responsible for its rebirth. Kahneman and his colleagues' findings countered assumptions of traditional economic theory that people make rational choices based on their self-interest by showing that people frequently fail fully to analyze situations where they must make complex judgments. Instead, people often make decisions using rules of thumb (heuristics) rather than rational analysis, and they base those decisions on factors economists traditionally do not consider, such as fairness, past events, and aversion to loss.

Keys to Prosperity

"Braking" the Rational Actor Paradigm

A nice example for understanding the behaviorist's view of rationality is the frequently encountered decision of a driver facing a yellow light at an intersection. What do you typically do? Would you consider this a fully rational decision?

Before we completely disregard the value of the rational actor paradigm, think again about what you actually do when deciding whether or not to press the brake or the gas pedal. Do you evaluate how far you are from the intersection? Do you consider your current speed and whether or not you will make it into the intersection before the light turns red? Do you consider (from past experience) how long this particular light takes to turn from yellow to red? Do you glance around to see if there is a vehicle close behind you or speeding in cross-traffic?

Might you look for pedestrians, consider the weather conditions, or even the possible presence of a camera or law enforcement? Even in such a time-constrained choice, the amazing human brain is quite capable of considering all of this and more before making this decision! Turns out, the usefulness of the rational actor paradigm may not be quite so surprising.

However, a behaviorist would note that your careful evaluation and consideration of these factors will depend upon *context*. In some situations, you may be distracted and not make the decision carefully. Your decision could be affected by your emotions or being recently reminded of the dangers of running a red light.

You may depend upon simple rules (heuristics) such as "always stop when there is other traffic present." In any case, we need not disregard the rational actor paradigm. Understanding what the "rational" decision would be can serve as a benchmark to consider how behavioral variables or bounded rationality might change our conclusions!

Behavioralists have found that peoples' decisions can be swayed by how the situation is framed. When Kahneman and (co-researcher) Amos Tversky asked people to decide hypothetically what procedure to take to cure a disease, most preferred a procedure that saved 80 percent of people compared to one that killed 20 percent.

Behavioral economists developed an economic model, described as *prospect theory*, to explain analogous economic behavior that is difficult to account for using traditional models. For example, why are there large, seemingly unprovoked fluctuations in the stock market? Why do people drive to a distant store to save a few dollars on a small purchase, but not for the same discount on an expensive item? The theory now forms the basis for a significant amount of the applied research in economics.

Kahneman, a Princeton University professor, won the Nobel Prize for Economics in 2002 for research included in his book *Thinking, Fast and Slow*. From that book you will learn about how the brain works and how you can use that understanding to improve your own decision-making.

Among other ideas, Kahneman expanded the deductive or theoretical methods of traditional economics to include controlled experiments, often in a laboratory, to describe how people and markets really operate. How many courses in economics would someone such as Kahneman need to take as a student to achieve the Nobel Prize in Economics? Zero is the answer, if media reports are correct. His Ph.D. was in Psychology. It appears he was never a student in an Economics class.

Kahneman was driven throughout his career to find ways through research to predict real-world behavior. It started when he served in the Israel Defense Forces (IDF) with the task of predicting which officers would become the best combat leaders. His contributions progressed by studying and teaching in a variety of U.S. universities and research institutions. You could learn much about predicting human behavior by studying his life story.

Perhaps after you read this chapter, you will be sufficiently intrigued to do a web search on Kahneman's progression from predicting military leadership to winning the Nobel Prize in Economics. Much of Kahneman's research was undertaken starting as a student in Israel with his lifetime colleague Amos Tversky.

After teaching at Michigan, Harvard and Hebrew University, Amos Tversky joined the Stanford faculty in 1978, winning the American Psychological Association's award for distinguished scientific contribution in 1982 and the MacArthur and Guggenheim fellowships in 1984. He once said that much of what he had studied was "already known to advertisers and used car salesmen." However, simply knowing that these behavioral realities exist may not be useful if you do not know how consumer response may vary in different contexts.

One of the dilemmas when analyzing economic problems is the observed variability in how the same consumer responds depending on the situation. These differences are often due to latent (unobserved) variables that the economist has not controlled for because they have not been measured or considered. Statisticians call this "noise" when interpreting data. The reason it occurs and what to do about it is described in the 2021 book *Noise: A Flaw in Human Judgment* by Daniel Kahneman, Olivier Sibony, and Cass R. Sunstein.

Kahneman's Nobel Prize was not the only Nobel prize for behavioral economics. That honor in 2017 went to Richard Thaler, professor at the University of Chicago's Booth School of Business, after publication of his book *Misbehaving: The Making of Behavioral Economics*. If you want an overview of how behavioral economics evolved, that book is a good place to start. Perhaps the most engaging and insightful book for the average reader, however, is *Predictably Irrational: The Hidden Forces That Shape Our Decisions*, by Dan Ariely, professor at Duke University and researcher at other institutions. Ariely cites and explains many of the experiments in consumer behavior that form the basis for the next two chapters in this book.

The purpose of this book is to apply objective analysis of behavior to find solutions for prosperity, and a great deal of research has been done. For example, if you are concerned about reducing poverty, do not pay much attention to what politicians describe as simple answers or even what well-intentioned government and non-governmental organizations (NGOs) proclaim as the answer. You will find more effective answers in *Poor Economics: A Radical Rethinking of the Way to Fight Global Poverty* by Abhijit V. Banerjee and Esther Duflo, both professors of economics at MIT. Using a behavioral approach, they studied how those in poverty make decisions on such matters as education, healthcare, savings, entrepreneurship, and a variety of other issues.

Much more useful than deductive conclusions by non-behavioralists, Banerjee and Duflo demonstrate how to use rigorous randomized controlled testing to reduce poverty by improving consumer decision-making. They advocate listening to what the poor have to say to discover answers which are often startling and counterintuitive from those of non-empirical economists or philosophers. You should also know that Banerjee and Duflo, a wife and husband team, won the Nobel Prize for Economics.

So, who is right? Traditional economists? Austrian (Schumpeterians)? Or behavioral economists? In making your decision, consider some of the differences between traditional (Keynesian) economists and behavioral economists. Traditional economists make conclusions relying mostly on logic and mathematical predictions, with little interest in empirical data. Behavioral economists challenge many of the assumptions in traditional models, relying more on data from psychology, anthropology, history, sociology, and other empirical sciences. Behavioralists seek realism with observable data, something of little concern in Keynesian economics.

A basic difference between the two streams of economic analysis is assumptions about human behavior. Traditional economics assume full rationality, that is, people can acquire and completely process all relevant information to make a decision. Behavioralists believe rationality is "bounded," or limited in knowledge of relevant facts, the ability or desire to process the information, or the ability to understand the consequences of different decisions. In short, behavioral economics accepts that consumers (and firms) make decisions as well as they can, sometimes with limited information and/or with incomplete or "irrational" analysis of the possible outcomes.

Product failures can cause people to regret a purchase. However, consider some of the purchases you have made in the past, such as a car or a home. Have you ever made a purchase, then later regretted it even though the product was everything you expected it to be? Maybe you realized that there were better options, or that you did not really need it as much as you had thought. Maybe the lessened size of your bank account caused you some guilt for spending so much. These are all common examples of regret that are outside the realm of "rationality" but perfectly consistent with behavioral economics.

Note that traditional economic analysis also assumes that the motivating cause of individual behavior is limited to your own income and wealth maximization, and for firms, profit maximation. In other words, it does not matter how much income your neighbor has; the only thing that affects your decisions is what you have.

Behavioral analysis concludes that people are also motivated by things that could be more important than income and wealth. This include things such as being fair to others, doing the right thing, maintaining a good reputation, and pleasing family, friends, neighbors, and stakeholders in a firm even if the result is less income and wealth. Ethics and reputation matter in the real world but are not frequently considered in the deductive world of traditional economic analysis.

Traditional economists usually define the purpose of a corporation to be maximization of profits. Behavioral economists are more likely to define the purpose of a corporation like Microsoft CEO Satya Nadella on CNBC's Mad Money when he explained, "The social purpose of a company is to find profitable solutions to the problems of people and planet." He added the two key words are *profits* and *problems*. In Chapters 3 and 4, you will encounter an analytical framework that helps you to do *exactly* that.

Another difference is that markets are assumed to be efficient in the Keynesian world of economic policy. Behavioralists challenge that assumption at its core, believing empirical data indicate markets often look inefficient, and sometimes sloppy. If markets look inefficient, that is probably because they are – and people who understand that (such as Warren Buffet, and maybe you) will prosper more from understanding these inefficiencies and the opportunities they create than the Keynesian assumption that they do not exist.

The most fundamental issue separating traditional economics and behavioral economics is the question of whether humans are basically all pretty much the same in their economic behavior or all quite different. Are all buyers – whether consumers or business organizations – all seeking the same benefits when they part with their money in a purchase, or are they all different? Do all consumers make purchase decisions in the same way? Think about the last time you were out with friends trying to decide where to have dinner, and the answer is clearly no. The pursuit of understanding when and why these differences occur has given rise to a whole new stream of research and scholarship called Consumer Behavior, the focus of the next two chapters.

Discussion Questions

- Can you think of examples of purchases you have made that were different than predicted by traditional economic assumptions that all decisions are rational, made with complete information, and without influence from other people?
- Consider the role of a business leader attempting to use economics to make decisions. How would understanding behavioral economics change the way you approach a problem compared to principles taught in traditional economics courses?
- Compare the Keynesian economic view centering on the actions of a social planner (government official) to the view of Hayek that centers around the importance of markets. Which of these two views do you believe is most beneficial for the support of a healthy economy? Under what circumstances might the alternative view be beneficial?
- Consider the discussions of the famous economists in the text. What lessons did you observe that can be applied to your personal life?

Chapter 3

Who Controls the Economy?

To learn about how to improve the prosperity of a nation, you can start by understanding who has the power to improve it. To this end, here is an important multiple-choice question:

Who is most responsible for the size and growth of the U.S. economy?

a.   The President of the United States

b.   The Federal Reserve

c.   U.S. Congress

d.   CEOs of large corporations

e.   None of the above

To answer that question correctly, remember from Chapter 1 that the primary method measuring an economy is GDP. You may wonder how GDP is calculated; after all, there are many different sources of production in a nation. To see how these components of GDP stack up, we can turn to a simple formula from macro-economics:

$$GDP = C + I + G + (X-M)$$

Where C = Consumption, I = Private Investment (business), G = Government purchases, X = Exports, M = Imports

As an example, consider the US economy. When you examine the data for each of the GDP components, you see the total economic pie in a recent (typical, non-pandemic) year is made up of slices in the proportions of the following table:

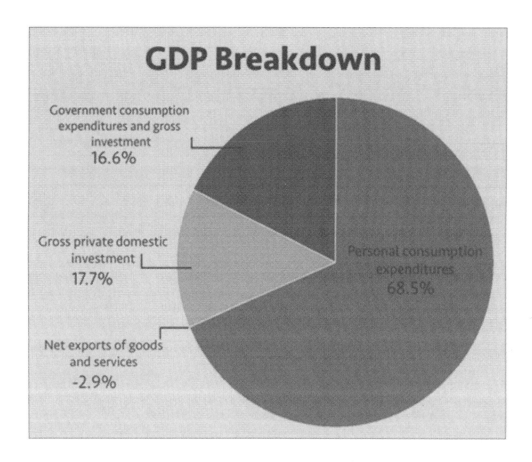

Political pundits often reference the economy when discussing the performance of the President of the United States, but how much of the above chart is within their direct control? Yes, the President's influence is represented in the "Government Consumption and Investment" piece of the pie, but in the USA the only money available for the President to spend is whatever is voted on by Congress, and more specifically, the House of Representatives. Even still, total government consumption and investment is less than 17% of total GDP.

Discussions of economic performance in the USA will also frequently include the Federal Reserve, but where is this represented in the graph? The Fed does not have money to spend other than its own salaries when Congress appropriates them. The Federal Reserve can change interest rates and the supply of available currency, adjusting monetary policy to improve the economy. For example, lower interest rates can induce businesses to invest private capital for new buildings, technology, research, and other expenditures. But this effect is not as strong as people might assume. Lower interest rates may provide incentives, but the Fed cannot force anyone to invest, and business investment is only about 17% of GDP.

Politicians and economists alike will sometimes discuss the "trade imbalance." This occurs when X (for exports) is less than M (imports), with the net result represented in GDP by the quantity of (X-M). If (X-M) is zero, the effect of trade on GDP is zero. In nations where people have enough money to purchase a large number of imports, the total imports are usually greater than exports. This results in a negative value of (X-M), but the net effect on GDP is small and often close to negligible.

For some nations, X is greater than M, but usually this occurs in developing nations that rely upon commodities and cheap labor to sell exported items to improve their nation's prosperity. If you understand economics, you probably recognize that despite the negative effect on GDP, when imports are greater than exports, this indicates that a nation is so prosperous it can afford to buy a lot of stuff from other nations.

So, returning to the question at the beginning of the chapter: Who is most responsible for an economy's size and growth? Presidents and Prime Ministers from developed economies around the globe do have some control over the varying amounts of government spending from country to country, but the bulk of economic growth comes from another source. If you want to know who is responsible for an economy's success, look no further than the producers and consumers engaging in voluntary transactions.

Successful businesses create and sell goods and services that consumers value. If a good or service is more valuable to a consumer than the cost of producing it, then both the producer and the consumer can benefit from a transaction. The chart reveals that this accounts for about 70 percent of GDP. This means that understanding GDP requires knowledge of how many consumers there are in a nation, how rapidly the population is changing (population growth or decline), how much income they have to spend and their interest in spending it (called "propensity to buy"), and the proportion of their goods and services they make themselves (called "non-market production of goods and services") compared to what they purchase from business owners.

From a practical perspective, when you understand what really determines the future of the economy, you understand it is *consumers'* wants and needs and *producers'* ability to understand and deliver goods and services that satisfy them.

Yes, government and business have some direct effect on GDP (about 30 percent combined) but what producers make and what consumers buy (or do not buy) determine the other 70 percent. Thus, facilitating an environment for consumers to engage in transactions is a key role of government. Actions and policies that negatively affect consumer confidence can have a negative effect on GDP, but even the most positive environment for consumer transactions cannot force producers to make things or consumers to spend their money.

And what of the role of the President? Consider cheerleaders in a Super Bowl. Cheerleaders in a football game are highly visible (as is the President) and have a role in the feelings of the fans and the environment surrounding the game, and that may encourage what players do on the field ("home field advantage"). The President may convince Congress to appropriate a bit more or tax less and may criticize the Federal Reserve when he or she does not like what his or her appointees at the Fed are doing. However, the President has as much direct control of the success of the economy as cheerleaders have in determining the outcome of the Super Bowl!

Time and Money Budgets

People have two types of resources to spend: Time and money. The way that consumers spend both time and money determines not only the prosperity of a nation, but which consumers are more prosperous than other consumers. An extreme example of this principle is "996 workers" in China – workers who work from 9 am to 9 pm, six days a week, mostly in technology firms. Not only are 996 workers more prosperous than people who work fewer hours, but they contribute to an accelerating GDP for the nation of China.

It is useful to remember that something similar occurred in the high growth era of the U.S. when nearly all employees (including managers) worked long hours, six days a week. When Henry Ford offered a wage twice the typical rate for something like "996 workers," people moved to Detroit from much of the rest of the U.S. seeking those jobs producing cars, a product that eventually changed much of the rest of the economy. Of course, another question is what "996 workers" are sacrificing for this additional prosperity. There is an interesting relationship between a consumer's budget, how they allocate their time, how their time is valued by others, and how they value their own time.

When analyzing money budgets of consumers, the facts reveal wide variations between consumers. Some consumers earn $25,000 a year (or less) to allocate for food, shelter, and other necessities. They do not have much left over for products and services they might desire to buy. While some wealthy consumers squander their money budgets on frivolous luxuries or recreational drugs, the Nobel Prize winning book, *Poor Economics*, discloses that some consumers in poverty will choose to spend their meager money budgets on sugary drinks or recreational drugs instead of basic food and shelter. In other words, empirical data reveal that many people spend their income on the things that they desire, regardless of whether other people believe their purchases should be spent on other "needs."

In fact, beliefs about which products and services are "needs" compared to "desires" vary so greatly between individuals (and people who may judge these decisions) that it can be frustrating to try to define the difference between desires and needs. Nutritionists calculate that a diet that will sustain life can be purchased for a few hundred dollars a year. It might satisfy basic needs, but not many "desires." Moreover, whether consumers choose to buy groceries at Aldi, Costco, or Whole Foods can be a major determinant of their ability to buy basic food "needs" and whether they have any money left to buy "desires."

Of course, wealth and poverty vary greatly from country to country. In many countries most consumers earn less than $25,000 a year, but in the U.S. most consumers earn more than $25,000, and sometimes a lot more. The majority of U.S. households meet the definition of middle income. Using 2019 data from the Pew Research Center for a four-person household, this was in the range of $46,960 to $140,900 in annual income. Based on median income around $61,000, this means half of U.S. households made more than $61,000 in income in 2019. Average income for U.S. households is even higher than $61,000 because many households earn a great deal more than this amount. So, this begs the question, where do these differences in prosperity come from?

People who work more hours in paid jobs are also usually more prosperous, a simple fact observable when a family has more than one member earning income, whether a spouse or another family member. However, an increase in prosperity does not necessarily require a lifetime of long work weeks. People whose time is more valuable in making the economy prosperous are usually more prosperous themselves compared to people with less valuable skills. The traditional structure of supply and demand determines the price of workers in nearly every type of economic activity. Therefore, increasing the value of your skillset in order to increase demand for your time often requires significant up-front investment in time, money, risk-bearing and other short-term sacrifices.

Physicians typically earn around $200,000 to $400,000 on average but those with even more highly valued time, such as cardiologists and plastic surgeons, may earn a million dollars or more per year. Many plastic surgeons are able to earn high wages without the option of accepting insurance for their services. While this may improve the surgeon's ability to charge higher rates, this also means that patients may pay completely out-of-pocket. This certainly demonstrates the value patients place on skillsets of these surgeons.

According to the 2019 annual report from the American Association of University Professors, the average salary for professors in U.S. universities is about $121,000. However, the top 10 professors in the U.S. earn between 1 and 4.33 million dollars, depending on their value in increasing the reputation of the institution, winning research dollars, and attracting talented students. That compares to €186,000 (over $200,000 in USD) in Switzerland, according to Swiss news service NZZ. The best paying college in the U.S. is Columbia University in New York, with average full professors there earning $259,700 a year followed by Stanford, Princeton, Harvard, and the University of Chicago. While this may seem to suggest that the road to prosperity requires years of education and advanced degrees, note that athletic coaches at major universities are usually paid more than both professors and the CEOs of all but the largest corporations.

Of course, money budgets are not solely determined by single salaries. It is not unusual for physicians, professors, and coaches to make as much or more income than their salaries in their "second jobs" as consultants, directors, or endorsers. In these situations, people are trading extra time for increased prosperity. Few make as much "other income" as Mark Zuckerberg whose salary at Facebook/Meta is only $1 a year, but his additional income since dropping out of college was reported by Forbes to be $8 million a day (despite recent questions surrounding the behavior of Facebook). An infamous example of this phenomenon comes from schoolteachers that work evenings and weekends as waitstaff in restaurants or as bartenders. This increases their money budget but does not leave much in their time budget for grading papers or enjoying time with friends or family.

The sector in which people work can also impact their money budget. Government employees may average less than $100,000 a year, but in most states, top government employees earn over $500,000 (usually more than the governors to whom they report.) If you want to know the number of high-income workers in your state's government, ask Siri, "How many state employees earn more than $100,000 a year?" The answer in Pennsylvania recently was 9,751. In California, the answer was 220,000 and 598 of the employees in the University of California system earned over $500,000. It is not unusual for state government employees to average twice the median income of all people in the state.

When understanding how an economy works, it is critical to understand the difference between money and time budgets. There is no upper limit of what a consumer's money budget may be, but everybody gets an equal time budget – 24 hours per day. So, how would economists analyze consumer time budgets? A chart below shows how traditional economics portrayed time budgets (although, for the most part, traditional economists gave little attention to the topic of time). From the traditional perspective, part of a consumer's 24 hours is spent on work and the balance is considered "leisure."

This conception of non-working hours was due partly to Thorstein Veblen, an economist and sociologist best known for coining the term "conspicuous consumption" in his 1899 book *The Theory of the Leisure Class*. Veblen was critical of an economic system focused on the accumulation of capital that allows business leaders a life of leisure, displaying their wealth in conspicuous consumption. Veblen believed that "lower classes" strive to climb up to a "higher class" in which they can display wealth in their own consumption. This was in contrast to Karl Marx who described the "historical struggle" of classes, where lower classes fight to overthrow the upper classes. Veblen's influence was negated considerably by his personal lifestyle, causing the loss of his job at several major universities, but he did introduce ideas from anthropology and sociology to the study of economics, especially regarding how people spend time.

CHANGING VALUE OF TIME: ANALYZING TIME BUDGETS

Traditional Concepts of Time and Leisure (24 hours)

Work	Leisure

Contemporary Concepts of Time and Leisure (24 hours)

Work	Non-Discretionary Time	Leisure
"Paid Time"	"Obligated Time"	"Discretionary Time"

A more realistic analysis of consumer behavior introduced contemporary concepts of time and leisure, shown in the chart as Work (paid time), non-Discretionary time (such as home, family, and societal obligations and sleep), and Leisure (discretionary time when consumers do what they enjoy doing, which might be nothing.) Understanding each of these categories could be useful in determining your own prosperity, as well as explaining differences in prosperity within and across nations.

Keys to Prosperity

Work-Life Balance and the Great Resignation

The Covid-19 pandemic has most certainly been a disruptive shock to the economy, and especially to the labor force. In the U.S., massive layoffs at the beginning of the pandemic were followed by the largest number of employee resignations in the history of the country. While there are myriad reasons for employees quitting their jobs, including concern over Covid-19, better employment opportunities, and rising costs for childcare, there also appears to be a shift in how employees are viewing the value of their time in the post-Covid world.

According to Prudential's recent Pulse of the American Worker Survey, 87% of the employees that worked remotely during the pandemic would like to continue working remotely at least one day per week. Moreover, 68% of all US workers surveyed described the flexibility to work both in-person and remotely as the ideal employment model. If you are wondering why the majority of employees are suddenly more desirous of remote work options, there are answers in behavioral economics.

A consistent behavioral finding is that when a person possesses something, they tend to value it more than if they do not possess it. This is called the endowment effect. From the survey, saving time, saving money, and spending more time with family were the three most commonly stated benefits of remote work.

Note that during covid, many remote workers were able to experience these benefits for the first time. Having been "endowed" with these benefits during the pandemic, workers value these benefits more now than when they had not yet possessed or experienced them. Therefore, employees would be unwilling to give them up for the same salary they received before the pandemic. This could be a sea-change in how people value their leisure time versus their work time and is supported by the survey finding work-life balance as the number one reason for employees changing careers.

Again, there is no limit to how much money a consumer can make – any amount from a few thousand to many thousands or even millions of dollars per year. However, unless they are flying west through time zones, even people with large money budgets have only 24 hours a day to spend. As a result, when consumers increase their money budgets, the value of their time also increases.

Most people would agree that more education affects how high your income is likely to be. MDs, Ph.D.s, JDs, MBAs, and top-level coaching pedigrees require a lot of time and effort to complete, but often yield much higher pay rates for those that complete them. Part of that extra income may be spent on leisure, but a significant amount of their income is spent on "buying time" by hiring other people to reduce obligated time expenditures for activities such as home maintenance and childcare. This also includes the purchase of products that reduce non-discretionary time obligations such as automatic dishwashers, microwave ovens and robotic sweepers.

Prosperous consumers purchase these goods and services because the amount of time it would take for them to complete these activities is valuable. Highly skilled workers create value by doing these activities much faster or by producing better results, thereby incentivizing prosperous consumers to hire them. This also allows high-skilled workers to become prosperous themselves.

Highly skilled welders and house painters can earn over $100,000 a year and are able to hire other high-skilled workers to mow their lawns, clean their homes or walk their dogs. Skilled dog handlers can be paid $100-150 per hour to train dogs for physicians, lawyers and business owners who earn $1,000 or more per hour. People earning thousands of dollars per day hire pilots and support staff to fly private airplanes that increase their hours available for work or leisure.

Demand for such skills is typically high, but all these skills take years to develop, which means that the supply of such highly skilled workers is low. Hence, these skills typically lead to high wages. A straightforward way to consider the income potential of a skillset is ask yourself 1) is it valuable to others now; 2) is it likely to be valuable to others in the future; 3) is it relatively rare; and 4) is it difficult for others to develop this skill and imitate you. If your answers are all yes, this is quite likely to be a profitable skillset. Note that this is similar to the questions a firm can consider when reviewing their competitive advantages against competitors by estimating a firm's value, rareness, imitability, and organization (called VRIO analysis).

You can likely see from the above that there are many ways to earn high income. Whether through years of academic education, or through diligent practice of a craft, high income requires valuable skills. Surgeons are paid well to save lives, but highly skilled craftsmen and craftswomen can earn very high incomes by allowing other high-income workers to buy time.

Today, there are window washers earning $1,000 per day washing windows for people whose time is valuable enough to afford hiring people more efficient than themselves to clean windows. But the window washers who earn high rates are people highly skilled and incredibly fast at disassembling, washing, and reassembling double-pane windows for people earning enough to afford those skills. You can be sure that dog trainers earning $150 per hour and window washers earning $1,000 a day are not doing that very often for families earning low or middle-income wages.

The more high-income households in an economy, the more opportunities for people with high skills (perhaps with only limited years of formal education) to earn high incomes. Workers who are highly skilled at maintaining lawns, repairing air conditioning, painting houses, or flying airplanes for time-impoverished high-income workers can earn $100,000 or more per year. If you type in your browser "jobs paying $100,000 a year without degrees," you will find a substantial list including air-traffic controllers, salespeople, and plumbers. But only if they have skills needed to reduce time expenditures for other high skilled/high income workers.

If you analyze the value of time and its relationship to income, you understand why mature economies have evolved from making "things" (everything from crops and animals on the farm in an agrarian economy to manufactured products after the industrial revolution) to an economy dominated by services (80% currently in the U.S.). This also helps to explain some of the differences in nations' incomes mentioned above.

An interesting career path of high-income potential is that of entrepreneurs. These people have skills to provide valuable services but also tend to have interpersonal skills that give them the ability to manage other skilled workers. Unique combinations of skillsets and management ability can have extremely high income potential, sometimes millions and occasionally billions. If you do not believe that, just examine the careers of Mark Zuckerberg, Michael Dell, Bill Gates, or the estate beneficiaries of Steve Jobs. Given his untimely passing, you may wonder what happened to the wealth created by Steve Jobs' knowledge of technology and skills as an entrepreneur? In Chapter 6 you will learn the rest of that story.

So, what determines the services and products people buy and from whom they buy it? Understanding the answer to that question made major advances in the 1960s, as you will see in the next chapter.

Understanding the answer to what people will buy is also the answer to who oversees the economy. It is not the President or the Chairman of the Federal Reserve. It is not necessarily high-profile business leaders either, although the most successful of those leaders will start firms that create jobs giving consumers income to spend. Most (65% to 95% depending on which study you examine) of the new jobs in an economy are created by leaders of small firms, not large ones. These are the entrepreneurs who understand what consumers want to buy.

It is not business or government who control the future of the economy, but entrepreneurs who facilitate prosperity and growth by discovering improved ways to solve consumer problems. The entrepreneurs who run these small firms, especially the most successful, can reach remarkably high levels of prosperity, a topic discussed in the book *Saving America: How Garage Entrepreneurs Grow Small Firms into Large Fortunes*.

Business-to-Consumer (B2C) firms prosper because their leaders understand the minds of consumers. Business to-Business (B2B) firms prosper because their leaders understand the minds of their customers but also understand the minds of their *customers' customers* – consumers.

Remember, the future of the economy, and eventually your own prosperity, is determined by transactions between producers and consumers. Understanding what consumers will buy led to a new field of knowledge in the 1960s called consumer behavior. Turn to the next chapter to read how the birth of consumer behavior developed to understand why and how people buy, use, and dispose of goods and services.

Discussion Questions

- How valuable is your work time compared to other workers in society? What actions can you take now to increase the value of your time in the future?
- Suppose a business leader would like to increase the average income of their employees. In what ways could they make this happen without impacting their profitability?
- If a young person were to ask your advice on how to earn a high income in the future, what advice would you give that person?

Chapter 4

How People Buy Goods and Services

Production of valuable goods and services leads to the transactions that drive most of GDP, but this leads to a question:

How do consumers arrive at the decision to purchase?

Understanding the process of the consumer purchase decision is one area of study in the field of consumer behavior. Like the birth of behavioral economics, the birth of a body of knowledge called consumer behavior can also be traced to George Katona and his book *Psychological Analysis of Economic Behavior* and his later books such as *The Powerful Consumer*. Katona gets credit for starting behavioral economics, emphasizing macroeconomics, but his contributions also had significant influence on microeconomics, the study of individuals, households and firms' behavior in decision-making and allocation of resources. Katona brought needed realism to Keynesian consumption functions and consumption behavior, a topic of great interest to marketers and everyone else hoping to prosper in modern businesses.

The earliest marketing scholars were mostly professors with PhDs in economics. Textbooks such as *Elements of Marketing* by University of Illinois professors Converse, Huegy, and Mitchell defined marketing as "Business activities which have to do with the creation of place and time utilities. Marketing, to the economist, is then a part of production." This standard definition was amplified by describing the functions of marketing in Beckman and Davidson, *Principles of Marketing*. At Wharton, Wroe Alderson, with his interdisciplinary background, introduced behavioral realities in his book *Marketing Behavior and Executive Action*. He challenged traditional economics with his *Dragnet* approach ("Just the facts") of inductive research and practical experience, analyzing costs arising from the discrepancy in assortments caused by the typical heterogeneity of demand and homogeneity of supply. For these reasons marketing institutions have evolved to perform the functions of logistics, wholesaling, retailing, financing, and other functions. *Performing marketing functions* more efficiently reduces those costs, creating lower costs for consumers, higher profits for firms, and a more productive economy.

Alderson's scholarship pioneered the concepts of market segmentation and branding, important determinants of which firms prosper and disrupt previously successful firms. Those concepts are key to understanding the prosperity of Bezos, Jobs, Gates, Walton, Dell, and other entrepreneurs who started with nearly nothing, applying Alderson's concepts so well that they disrupted previously prosperous firms (such as Barnes & Noble and IBM). The success of many of these firms contributed significantly to the growth of the economy, a feat that is difficult for individual firms to accomplish.

Most earlier books and marketing courses emphasized what happened after goods were produced, opening the door for new research to determine what goods and services should be produced. The people in charge of what should be produced – consumers – became a new focus of marketing. In the past, some people considered marketing as attempts to influence consumers to buy what firms produce and want to sell. A more contemporary understanding of marketing is *the ability to understand consumers well enough to produce what consumers will buy at a profit*, a revolutionary approach compared to traditional economic models (SEM).

Keys to Prosperity

The Value of Academia

We typically think of academic institutions around the world as being the sources of knowledge, but it is often a question as to which direction this knowledge flows. In many cases these institutions are simply deepening understanding of knowledge found in industry and society. Case in point, the birth of the field of Consumer Behavior arose from the practical knowledge of managers and salespeople that had grown over decades of listening and responding to consumers.

One of the first analytical models of consumer decisions was *Consumer Decision Processes* by Francesco Nicosia at Berkley in 1966. A similar approach at Ohio State resulted in the 1968 book *Consumer Behavior* by Engel, Kollat and Blackwell. Howard and Sheth published *The Theory of Buyer Behavior* in 1969 at Columbia University. These three books were the catalyst for courses on Consumer Behavior in psychology departments and business schools throughout the world, forever changing the thinking about who determines production of goods and services and how they should be marketed.

Before this time, the teaching of concepts in consumer behavior was limited to highly theoretical discussions in psychology or the anecdotal learnings from salesmanship courses. As the field of consumer behavior grew, courses were created and textbooks on the subject (like those above) were adopted. Subsequently, a Workshop on Consumer Behavior was sponsored by the American Marketing Association in 1969. At that gathering of researchers, the Association for Consumer Research was formed which recently celebrated its 50th Anniversary as a professional group of 1,700 scholars in nearly every part of the world dedicated to generating scientific knowledge of how and why consumers buy products and services.

The reality of academic institutions is that knowledge flows are a two-way street. Even Amos Tversky, one of the founders of the field of behavioral economics, said that his findings were common knowledge to advertisers and salespeople. To provide value to the world, scholars must stay apprised of what is happening outside of colleges and universities. On the other hand, for knowledge to continue to flow, professionals should pay attention to what the academics are discovering.

If you're interested in the consumer behavior topics discussed in this chapter, you can keep up to date on this research in publications such as *Journal of Marketing Research, Journal of Consumer Research, Journal of the Association of Consumer Research,* and other similar scholarly journals.

As the author of one of the above textbooks used by millions of students in universities around the world, it has been gratifying to receive thousands of letters, emails and personal comments from students who reported how the study of consumer behavior and marketing changed their perspectives on business and improved their personal finances. If you have never taken a course on consumer behavior, it is never too late to find a nearby academic institution and take a consumer behavior course, or perhaps study one of the texts mentioned above. People who understand why people buy are in the best position to develop strategies that contribute to their own prosperity.

-Roger Blackwell

Why People Buy

You wouldn't walk into a store and say to the clerk, "I have an extra $100 dollars in my wallet. Just pick out something and sell it to me." When you enter the checkout lane or click "buy" on a website, you believe your decision is rational. These are voluntary transactions, so consumers must believe your purchase warrants parting with the charged price, otherwise you walk out or abandon the website.

An engaging book on this process reflecting knowledge from Behavioral Economics *is Predictably Irrational: The Hidden Forces That Shape Our Decisions* by Dan Ariely in which he describes experiments and asks readers to predict outcomes. You can test your own ability to predict how consumers behave with his book. What some people consider irrational is at least "predictably irrational." You will find most of the same experiments and conclusions in the many textbooks with the title of *Consumer Behavior*. You can also discover the practical applications of Behavioral Economics to many areas of life by reading Professor Ariely's weekend columns in the Wall Street *Journal*.

Decision process research, described by Engel, Kollat, Blackwell (EKB) and similar consumer decision process (CDP) models, reveals consumers move through stages in obtaining, consuming, and disposing of products and services. These stages can be described as problem (or need) recognition, search, alternative evaluation, purchase, and outcomes. Sometimes people move quickly through the stages (limited problem solving), perhaps drawing mostly on information stored in their memory from prior experiences. That is typical in the purchase of milk, toothpaste, and other products. Other decisions by consumers involve extended decision-making, usually taking more time on stages such as search and alternative evaluation. Computers, clothes, and cars usually fit that pattern. All these stages are influenced by many variables, shown in the chart below. Outcomes produce satisfaction or dissatisfaction, stored in consumers' memory, determining future product, brand, and channel decisions.

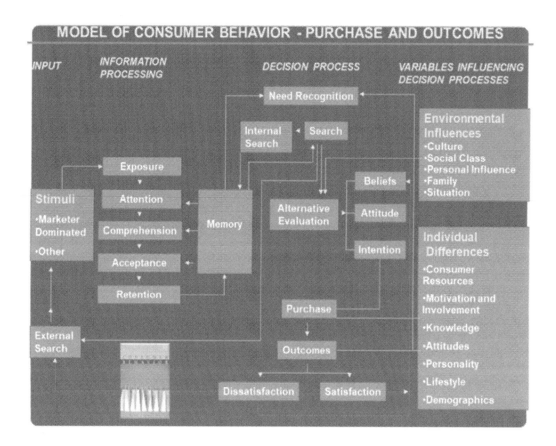

MODEL OF CONSUMER BEHAVIOR - PURCHASE AND OUTCOMES

Problem Recognition. Problem or need recognition occurs when consumers perceive a difference between what they desire and their perception of their current situation. This stage can be something as simple as squeezing a tube of toothpaste or pouring a glass of milk and making a mental note (or written list) to replace an almost empty tube or carton. If previous purchases have been stored in memory as "satisfied outcomes," future purchases will be similar unless something changes in perception of a problem, either by changed circumstances such as an increase or decrease in income or because of added information about available products and services. AI and other technologies are predicted to supplement such processes in the recent book *Quantum Marketing* by Raja Rajamannar.

Consumers may not acknowledge emotional or social needs to be relevant to their purchase even when those needs are strong motivators to buy things or affect where they shop and which brands they choose. Consumers may have needs but unless they perceive products or services as solutions to their problems (felt needs), there are no markets for the products and services.

"I feel your pain" is just the first step to solving problems for potential customers. If you are an aspiring entrepreneur using this model to attract customers, it is essential to recognize consumers' needs are not there to help you make a profit. Moreover, you will not make much profit unless there is a substantial segment of people who *feel* the problem or need you hope to satisfy. This was the key used by A. G. Gaston in becoming one of America's most successful Black entrepreneurs, as you will see in Chapter 6.

The way to think of your product is *the total utility of the bundle of attributes designed to solve a problem*. The more pressing a problem, the greater the opportunity to sell a product solving that problem. Your product must scratch where people itch!

To prosper as an entrepreneur, you must truly deliver the utility from solving their problem and do it repeatedly and consistently. That is why some people (both entrepreneurs and their employees) prosper – because their products continue to sell, grow revenues, and expand segments served. Selling a product is not the same as fulfilling a need.

To be a prosperous person, your business must be built on relieving felt needs. Most firms do not fail because their products do not function well; products fail because they do not fulfill functions for which consumers have a strong felt need. That is especially important to understand when introducing new products with innovative technology. The failure to do that explains why most (about 80%) of new products fail.

Search. Once problem recognition occurs, the search process begins, identifying methods and products to satisfy an unmet need.

Search may be internal, retrieving knowledge from memory, or it may be external, collecting information from the marketplace. At times consumers passively search, simply becoming more receptive to information about products and services, such as advertising or email blasts. Sometimes consumers engage in active search behavior, starting with search engines. Active search may provide enough information to proceed to purchase or may direct them to a location-based, brick-and-mortar firm.

If consumers know what they want, the Internet offers the potential to find a solution to their needs from firms of all sizes and located anywhere in the world. In B2B applications, such as looking for a specific machine part, grade of oil, or type of paper, the Internet shines, leading many supply chains to be global in nature.

Variables such as personality, social class, income, and the size of the purchase determine the amount and extent of the search. Past experiences and customer satisfaction also influence search. If customers are delighted with products they currently use, they do not search much for innovative solutions to their problems. That is why prosperous firms (and prosperous people within those firms) place a high priority on keeping customers satisfied and returning to the store or their website repeatedly. But if consumers are unhappy with current products or brands or experiences in existing stores or Web retailers, search expands to include alternatives. In a highly competitive market, it is not enough to have satisfied customers. Customers must be delighted, or they will search for alternative solutions.

Interestingly, some consumers even enjoy the search itself. Browsing through malls is fun for some consumers; for others it is a chore. Understanding when search is fun and when it is a chore provides valuable information in constructing marketing strategies. For example, the search for microwave oven information and alternatives does not excite many consumers. The most effective marketing channel in this instance minimizes time and effort required to obtain information.

The search for new clothing might be different. Browsing, trying on distinctive styles, and experiencing the store may be more important than the speed with which the clothing is compared and purchased. That is why stores emphasizing these experience attributes were hurt most by the 2020 pandemic that made those activities difficult. Similarly, for high-end restaurants the experience is as important, perhaps more so, than the food.

The Internet fits the search stage of consumption particularly well, while stores, catalogues, or other forms of selling may also lead to the purchase stage of consumer decision-making. Studies show, for example, that when consumers perceive the need for a car, a majority now search websites such as Consumer Reports, Carvana and others. Consumers use that information to buy the car at a price they learned on a website to be realistic. Searching where to buy a car also helps consumers find information about issues such as convenient service, an opportunity to test drive or evaluate appearance, or ability to talk to a real person when problems arise with the car. The website may be critically important to many consumers in searching for information, but for new cars the dealer is usually important in the transaction stage.

Consider your shopping habits for relatively basic products like breakfast cereal or shampoo. How do you "search" across the available alternatives? Perhaps you evaluate whether or not a cereal has genetically modified grains or too much sugar. Often, you may even learn about what is important to you as you identify what is available in the market. For example, you may have never considered how you would evaluate a gluten-free cereal with Açai berries until you see it on a website or on the shelf at your local store. In your search for exactly the right shampoo from the hundreds of available choices you may include judgment about whether the container is easy to grip in the shower and whether the aroma and color matches your needs.

You may be asking, why spend time and effort analyzing all of the ways customers process information during the search stage of the CDP? That is the way you decide whether a firm's communication program should be built on advertising, in-store information and experiences, salespeople, publicity, and third-party communications (such as *Consumer Reports*), the use of reference group role models and social influencers such as Taylor Swift or Michael Jordan, or the firm's webpage. Which one is the best way to get information disseminated about your product? The answer increasingly is "all of the above." If you analyze how people search and use the relative advantages of each media, you know a lot about developing a strategy that makes you prosperous in today's economy.

Alternative evaluation. How do consumers evaluate alternatives? They rely on specific criteria to select one manufacturer or retailer over others. Customers choose products, services, and stores based on the attributes most important to them. Some attributes are salient (most important) – things like does it function well, does it fit, and is it durable?

But if all the alternatives perform well on the salient attributes, customers make their choices on determinant attributes – the things, perhaps minor in nature, which differentiate one product or supplier from another. All cars within a category are likely to perform well on attributes such as providing reliable transportation, similar mileage and are usually about the same price for similar attributes. The determinant attributes causing consumers to buy one SUV instead of another may be appearance, exact color, and interior design or perhaps the number and design of cupholders. Toyota introduced minivans with dual sliding side doors, causing some parents unloading kids at schools to choose those brands over Ford or GM vehicles with doors that banged against other cars or could not easily be unloaded on the driver's side.

That is why the success of entrepreneurs is closely aligned with details. Get one detail wrong – even details like cupholders or sliding doors – and your competitor gets your customers instead of you. The genius that led to the prosperity of Steve Jobs was his ability to get more of the details right than his competitors.

Comparing alternatives requires consumers to compare and contrast a significant amount of information. Traditional economic analysis assumes that more information causes improved decisions (or that consumers have full access to all information), but behavioral research indicates it sometimes has the opposite effect. Too many choices and too much information often leads to worse decisions, delayed decisions, or no decision. Professor Jacoby, at Purdue University, demonstrated this with what he called *information overload* in a frequently cited 1984 article in the *Journal of Consumer Research*.

Given the potential difficulty in evaluating substantial amounts of information, consumers sometimes let situations or circumstances make the decision instead of making it themselves. This relieves them of the responsibility of making a bad decision. The most common response is for consumers to rely on brand loyalty or association with a retailer such as Costco or Lululemon rather than evaluating individual attributes that might improve their decision. In contemporary marketing, influencers in social media may also determine consumer decisions. If Michael Jordan or Kylie Jenner recommends a product, what else does a consumer need to know?

Have you ever made a purchase, then learned something later that suggested you made the wrong choice? When information is received after a purchase that conflicts with the consumer's decision (or sometimes no information), the result may be cognitive dissonance, more commonly called "buyer's remorse." The greater the consequences (or larger the purchase), the more likely cognitive dissonance (CD) occurs.

As an example, imagine that you have recently spent a great deal of money on a new car. Now imagine that an article is published that highlights the strong advantages of a different model that you had not considered. How would you deal with this new information? The unease that accompanies CD can cause interesting behaviors in consumers, possibly rejecting or discrediting new information to make their choice appear consistent with the information they accept. Textbooks on consumer behavior describe methods marketers use to reduce CD, and these details can be important in the design of a marketing strategy. These are important lessons for anyone seeking to retain their customers!

Purchase. The fourth stage of decision-making is purchase – buying the product. Customers move through the purchase stage in two phases. In the first phase, consumers choose one retailer over another retailer, or one supplier over others for industrial goods. Potential customers may also choose one form of retailing over another such as e-tailing, mailed catalogues, direct sales (by mail or direct response ad or from a person representing firms), TV informercials and buying channels, and location-based retailers.

A second part of purchase involves in-store choices, influenced by salespersons, product displays, kiosks, digital signage, and point-of-purchase advertising (POP) in location-based retailers. For online retailers, the purchase process includes finding sites (search engine optimization, or SEO), Web navigation, the influence of banners and other ads, payment systems (e.g., credit cards, Paypal), security issues and checkout procedures. Consumer expectations of and satisfaction with these issues greatly affect choices made in the purchase process.

A customer might move through the first three stages according to plan – perceiving a problem, searching for information, and evaluating alternatives. The consumer may intend to purchase a product or brand but end up buying something quite different, or perhaps does not buy at all because of what happens during the purchase or choice stage. A consumer may prefer one retailer but choose another because of a sale or a promotional event at a competitor, hours of operation, location, or traffic flow problems.

Inside the store, the consumer may talk with a salesperson and change their decision, see an end-of-aisle display or digital signage that switches the brand preference, use a coupon or price discount, fail to find the intended brand, or lack the money or right credit card to make the purchase. Successful entrepreneurs must manage the overall attributes and image of the supplier outlet to achieve preferred patronage among the target market and to manage, in micro detail, all aspects of the in-store shopping experience.

Whether by phone, tablet or computer, a consumer should easily be able to find what he or she is seeking on a website. How well the web site navigates and handles transactions is critically important in determining whether the purchase is made. Ads may pop-up or pop-down that lure the would-be buyer to another site, perhaps never to return. Perhaps the graphics and text do not provide enough information to be confident that the product will meet expectations.

Recent data reported by Jumpshot found that the majority of Google searches (50.33%) ended without a click on an organic or paid search result. Even if consumers enter the website, this doesn't necessarily mean that they will buy something. Consider your own online shopping habits – how often do you add something to your shopping cart, only to eventually leave the website without making a purchase? Why? Seeking to understand these behaviors is important for online retailers.

Many studies in academic and trade journals indicate that as many as two-thirds of customers end their website visit without buying due to slow loading times, unacceptable logistics issues, boring content, or requiring providing payment information too early in the search process. In fact, studies by Episerver, a provider of platforms to manage digital content, indicate a third of consumers who visit a brand's website or mobile app with the explicit intent of making a purchase rarely or never complete checkout. Further, 98 percent of shoppers report times they have been dissuaded from completing a purchase because of incomplete or incorrect content on a brand's website. Effective websites rely on a seamless integration of quality, informative, and credibility-boosting content into the overall fabric of the site.

Consumers who decide to buy on a website and move to the checkout portion of the purchase process often terminate without buying for many reasons. Perhaps it was because the credit card was not close by or the process evoked concerns about security or other issues. Perhaps the website could not change quantities, sizes, and colors well with multiple purchases. Maybe the total included delivery charges or sales tax the customer finds unacceptable. Perhaps the only thing the customer really wanted was a printout of the price and product details to use for reference and negotiation at a location-based retailer. Or maybe, someone in the household said, "Dinner's ready. Put down your phone!"

Keys to Prosperity

"Just Be Nice"

Dave Thomas was born in Atlantic City, NJ, adopted soon after birth by a Michigan couple who experienced hardships. His adoptive mother died at age 5, leaving his father, who struggled for years to find work, with the responsibility of raising Dave. Frequent moves caused him to attend twelve different schools in a 10-year period and he knew frequent hunger living with his itinerant father.

The stability in Dave's life came from Grandmother Minnie Sinclair, a strong and loving woman who worked hard to provide for her own four children after her husband died. It was from her Dave learned the value of hard work, which she always told Dave was "good for the soul." When Dave's father remarried and moved away, Dave dropped out of school to work full-time in an Indiana restaurant. The decision to drop out haunted Dave until he went back to school 45 years later and received his GED from Coconut Creek High School in Ft. Lauderdale. Long after he built a restaurant chain of more than 6,500 stores named after his daughter, Wendy, he said getting his GED was one of his greatest accomplishments. The graduating class voted their 60-something classmate, "Most Likely to Succeed."

At Wendy's, attention to consumers' changing wants and needs is at the center of its vision and strategic direction. For example, Wendy's was the first national chain to add salad bars (1979), the first to offer baked potatoes (1983), and establish a specific Value Menu (1989). When consumers became more concerned about cholesterol and fat, Wendy's took a leadership role in formulating and offering chicken items, eventually adding a skinless, grilled chicken sandwich in 1990, and other items over the years in response to changing lifestyles and preferences. In 2021, Wendy's introduced a new French fry designed to retain heat and crispness for between 15 and 30 minutes to optimize freshness for Wendy's growing drive-thru and carry-out sales during the Covid pandemic.

Thomas built the Wendy's restaurant chain on values he learned from his adoptive grandmother that included *quality, integrity, respect, pride, and responsibility*. When he spoke to a class of university students, one of the students asked him why he made the effort in his sixties to go back to school and spend the time and work to achieve a GED. He explained, "Because I was adopted, I work with a lot of young people. I realized I was telling them to get an education, but I wasn't a good role model for them to do that. That's why I thought I needed to get a GED." Values tell you much about why some people prosper and others do not. When one of the students asked him about his values, his answer was, "Just be nice."

Dave often said he was lucky to have been born in America. "Only in America," he said, would a guy like me, from humble beginnings and without a high school diploma become successful. America gave me a chance to the life I want and work to make my dreams come true. We should never take our freedoms for granted, and we should seize every opportunity presented to us."

It's Not the Product – It's the Benefit

Producers of valuable products and services can become prosperous, but where does value come from? The key to understanding value is to understand that a product or service's value is simply the total benefit that a consumer receives from owning or consuming it. This is important, as focusing on benefits desired by customers instead of physical products allows an entrepreneur to adapt to new and better methods of delivering those benefits. Entertainment, information, social acceptance, saving time, and a host of other basic problems do not go

64

away, but methods of satisfying those needs change constantly and often rapidly. Just look at what happened to Kodak when it dominated the globe with its analog cameras and film – until the world went digital.

Firms committed to a specific technology or product open the door for new entrepreneurs to confiscate their customers. Continued success can lead to a lack of interest in seeking out new ways to create and improve value. Such complacency has been the downfall of many successful firms. Be sure the firm where you work does not get "Kodaked." The future often arrives before previously prosperous firms are willing to give up the past.

All products are not equal in the minds of consumers. That is a different assumption than the one found in simple market analysis with supply and demand curves portrayed in traditional economics textbooks. Traditional economic theory can provide valuable insights by applying simplifying assumptions, such as all products in an industry having the same value and price.

However, these unrealistic assumptions limit the generalizability of the subsequent conclusions. In the real world, the value from different products differs dramatically depending on the context of usage, the social and cultural preferences and perceptions of individual consumers, the variations in both time and money budgets of consumers and other variables that have been researched since the birth of consumer behavior.

Coffee and tea drinkers provide a quick example. If you drink coffee, what drives your purchase decision? How do you choose between sizes, caffeinated and decaffeinated or whether you want sugar, cream, flavors, sizes, and other potential features? It is likely a combination of the time of day, the amount of sleep you have had recently, and your "mood" on that particular day. These "context effects" can significantly impact your decisions. Consumer preferences vary as much between consumers as their fingerprints and can vary even further with the context of the purchase, a key to understanding why behavioral analysis is often more practical in achieving prosperity than traditional economic principles alone.

The Road Map

Every result has a cause (or multiple causes). If you understand the causes of customer behavior, you can be more prosperous as an entrepreneur or employee in the future, regardless of what your role in a firm may be. Prosperity does not arise from "luck" in having the right product for the market. Prosperity arises from knowledge and the diligence to apply that knowledge, a reason the study of consumer behavior diffused so rapidly. Entrepreneurs that create products to consistently deliver value to customers at a price in line with that value are much more likely to find success.

A road map is useful in getting where you want to go when driving a car. Some people just ask directions about how to get to a desired location. That is what a lot of entrepreneurs do – just ask experienced observers or watch what customers do at successful firms. The problem with following directions based on the past arises when you need to go where no one has ever gone before, and that often is the situation for new products and services. This is where you need a road map.

Keys to Prosperity

Knowing What People Will Buy

Your probability of success in starting and operating a prosperous business begins with your ability to understand and predict what and how people buy from your firm. As an employee, your value and ultimately your pay is determined by your ability to delight customers of the firm at every stage of the decision. The chapter you are reading describes how this happens, but here is a simple diagram of the process. Analyze every stage to increase your contributions in helping customers move through each stage of the buying process.

How Consumers Make Decisions for Goods and Services

Need (Problem) Recognition

↓

Search for Information

↓

Alternative Evaluation

↓

Purchase

↓

Consumption

↓

Post Consumption Evaluation

↓

Divestment

Adapted from Blackwell, Miniard and Engel, Consumer Behavior.

The same is true in the study of consumer behavior. There is a lot of math, sophisticated models, and analytics useful in predicting consumer behavior but no GPS. The science of consumer behavior has evolved a lot since those early textbooks in the 1960s and now includes analytics, Bayesian statistics, stochastic modeling, AI, and other techniques that are far beyond this discussion. The simple model of the customer decision process in this chapter provides a roadmap you can use in designing marketing strategies to make you and your firm prosperous.

"Whew!" That may be your reaction to all the concepts in this chapter. It probably seems like a lot to understand, but it could be the key to understanding your own prosperity in the future as you will see in Chapter 6. The more you understand how consumers control the economy, the more you also understand the future size and growth of a nation's economy and what makes some countries prosperous and some countries poor, the topic of the next chapter.

Discussion Questions

- Consider the most expensive item you have purchased over the last year. What were the most important reasons for this purchase? How might knowing these reasons be helpful to the producer of the product?
- Think of an innovative product that was introduced within the last few years. How does this product create value for consumers? How did/will you decide whether to buy this product or not?
- Consider the idea of value creation. An old adage says, "Build a better mousetrap and the world will beat a path to your door." Is that true? Why or why not?
  In the firm in which you work, how important is the internet in decisions of consumers to buy from your firm compared to competitive firms? How would you change your firm's offering to improve your competitive position?
- When you read the Prosperity Key about Dave Thomas, what values or traits could be applied to your own personal prosperity?

Chapter 5

National Prosperity: Lessons from History

Only a quick glance at the value for per-capita GDP from nation to nation demonstrates there are vast differences in prosperity. Given this, consider the question:

What causes the differences in prosperity across nations?

If you were to ask those around you, a common answer you might receive is "natural resources." If someone gave that answer, you could follow up with , "How does the natural resource theory square with the facts?" or "What country has the most natural resources?"

"Russia" might be a common answer to the country with the most natural resources, and this is a plausible answer. Russia has substantial amounts of oil, gold, diamonds, and valuable minerals. Russia also has more land than any other nation, almost twice either of the next two largest countries, Canada, and the U.S. Yet, Canada's economy is larger than Russia's (1.74 trillion USD compared to 1.69 trillion USD in 2019. This is despite the population of Russia being nearly four times as large as Canada. In fact, Russia ranked 65th in the world in per capita GDP. Using statistics from the World Bank, the average GDP per person in Russia was $11,585 in 2019 compared to $46,195 in Canada and $65,281 in the United States. Russian leaders may be highly visible but Russian citizens are only just above the global per capita GDP ($11,436).

If natural resources were the cause of prosperity, Russia, and oil-rich countries such as Nigeria and Venezuela would be among the world's richest, but many nations rank higher than either of these according to the three primary data sources: the World Bank, United Nations, and International Monetary Fund. Moreover, oil-plentiful Venezuela a decade ago had per capita GDP over $11,000 but dropped continually to $2,500 by 2019. While the average price of oil may have fallen some over this time, there is certainly more going on than just the value of Venezuela's natural resources.

As another example, consider the Netherlands. Data from all three major data sources reveal the Netherlands is more prosperous than many other nations that have an abundance of land and other valuable natural resources. Even more telling is that the per-capita GDP of the Netherlands ($52,448 USD) is over four times larger than that of Russia, despite Russia being over 400 times larger in land area.

Perhaps you might hear someone suggest population as the primary driver of GDP. After all, a nation's GDP is directly influenced by its population (number of consumers and producers), as you read in Chapter 3. Both India and China, the two most populous nations in the world, have over 1.3 billion consumers. China is second only to the U.S. in the total size of its economy but ranks 70th with its per capita average of $10,262 in 2019. At $2,104 per person, India ranks 135th among the nations of the world. Population size matters, but not as much as you might guess.

Whether ranked on natural resources, land area or the size of the population, none of the world's largest nations are among the richest for the average person living in those nations. It might surprise you to know that the highest per capita GDP is found in some of the smallest nations. The rankings vary slightly among the various data bases, but the highest ones are usually Monaco ($190,512), Liechtenstein ($172,541), Luxembourg ($114,685), and Macau ($86,116).

So, what causes people in some countries to be prosperous and in other countries to be poor? That is the subject of the rest of this chapter. While you may not necessarily be interested in the wealth and prosperity of other nations, the answer to this question is important. When you understand the answer, you will understand a lot about what causes changes in the wealth of a nation. Hence, you will understand a key factor in improving your personal prosperity in the future.

Attempting to achieve prosperity in the future without understanding what causes prosperity is analogous to trying to blindly find a place that you have never been!

An Ancient Example

In a speech to House of Commons in 1948, Winston Churchill said, "Those who fail to learn from history are condemned to repeat it." This was a paraphrase of an earlier quote by philosopher George Santayana in 1905. This statement is as true when studying prosperity as it is in many other activities of life.

When economists analyze the prosperity of a nation, they will usually focus on labor, capital, and land. For many millennia, land was the most important of those determinants of prosperity, more specifically, the commodities produced on land. Whether in early cave dweller society, the landed aristocracies of Europe or pioneers on the American frontier, those with more land would generally have more wealth.

But land area alone was not the key. Children whose parents had the skill and diligence to produce more from the land they owned were more prosperous than children whose parents lacked those abilities. It is not simply luck that makes some farms more productive than neighboring farms, as people who grew up on a farm could attest. In a prior era when small farms dominated the U.S., it was possible to drive on country roads and observe that some farmers were more prosperous than others. While there is clearly a difference in the production capacity of the soil and climate from region to region, the difference in yields from neighboring fields could easily distinguish farms that planted crops earliest, kept weeds out best, and harvested most efficiently. After all, the rain falls equally on both sides of the fence separating prosperous farmers from others. *Knowledge and work ethic* created the most productive farms, a relevant lesson for everyone.

One of the first nations to develop land better than other nations was Egypt. A few thousand years ago, ancient Egyptians perfected the farming of wheat, barley, and other crops. The most important crop was grain for bread, the mainstay of daily Egyptian diets, as well as emmer wheat which went into the production of beer, the most popular drink. Around the same time, agriculture was also developing in the Far East, with rice rather than wheat as the primary crop in China. Maize was domesticated from wild grass in Mexico and potatoes, tomatoes, squash, and several varieties of beans became part of agriculture in early centuries of many nations, but usually they raised just enough of these crops to feed their population.

In contrast, Egyptian agriculture was more advanced than most others. Innovative technology, such as basin irrigation and hydraulic technology to control water flow in canals allowed Egypt to do something most previous economies had been unable to do – grow food so efficiently that most of its citizens had more food than needed to survive. Using technology to increase productivity above subsistence level provided Egypt enough food to employ part of the population in activities other than raising food. Two of those activities were armies and art.

Nations with the largest economies often become dominant military powers, as Egypt did. Egyptian society was highly stratified with a king/god (Pharaoh) at the top of the government pyramid and farmers at the bottom. At that time, a strong military could not only defend a nation, but could also conquer other nations to gain additional resources. Of course, an army large enough to exercise power and subdue enemies requires a substantial amount of food. Egypt had the technology but did not have enough of its own workers to grow the crops or build grand structures. Like many other nations before and since, Egypt resorted to the deplorable practice of slavery to acquire cheap labor.

What happens when wealthy rulers abuse, oppress, and enslave other people? The people rebel, in this case under the leadership of a man named Moses. This is a useful lesson from history that is relevant for the prosperity of a nation even today as you will discover at several points in this book.

Many practical economic lessons can be learned from studying Egyptian economics. First is the importance of using technology to grow a food supply beyond subsistence level. That lesson was not lost in the New World when the U.S. Congress passed the Morrill Act in 1862. The Morrill Land-Grant Acts used funds from the sale of federal lands to create new universities emphasizing research and education in agriculture and engineering. Until then, prestigious universities in the United States mostly emphasized liberal arts but Land-Grant universities became engines of growth establishing the world's largest agricultural industry and the U.S. as "breadbasket of the world," a title held by Egypt centuries earlier.

For individuals, a university degree in ag science or engineering at the nation's Land-Grant universities became an alternative path to prosperity rivaling a liberal arts degree at Ivy League schools. Because of research and education at Land Grant institutions, agriculture became one of the largest sectors of U.S.

exports (Food, beverage, and feed = $137 billion in 2019) and foundational to U.S. prosperity.

A second lesson from Egypt is the need for large quantities of food for governments seeking to support a strong military. Recall from Chapter 3 that national prosperity requires a stable and secure environment for consumers and producers to engage in transactions, an obvious call for strong national defense. Napoleon Bonaparte was correct when he said, "an army marches on its stomach." To be effective, an army requires good and plentiful food, and in contemporary society that requires a supply chain anchored in highly sophisticated logistics systems. That was a major reason for the success of the U.S., beginning in World War I and especially in World War II.

In 1990-91, Operation Desert Storm was a successful campaign by Coalition Forces, and much of the speed and success of that operation can be traced to U.S. logistics systems and their ability quickly to transfer troops, equipment, water, and food in record time. Following their military service, many of the junior level logistics officers from Desert Storm were hired by corporations such as Walmart, bringing their expertise to creating the supply chain of the world's largest retailer.

A third lesson to be learned from Egyptian agricultural prosperity is something else that happens when the economy supports citizens working at something other than growing their own food, such as employed artists. Affluence is essential for extensive support of the arts. That was true in Egypt, and the results can be observed at countless museums around the world. The "starving artists" stereotype is inevitable when artists attempt to support themselves by selling art to others that are not prosperous themselves. In contrast, "Follow the money" was a lesson learned well by artists such as Rothko, Warhol, Lichtenstein, and Koons. If you are the curator or director of art museums, you understand why they often carry the names of affluent citizens of the community, such as Whitney or Guggenheim.

The economic dominance of Ancient Egypt faded over the centuries, but there is one more lesson in economics to be gained from this story. According to the biblical book of *Genesis*, one of the slaves Egypt acquired was a bright young man named Joseph. Joseph served time in an Egyptian prison for a crime he did not commit but was released by Pharaoh because of his talents that other prisoners observed and reported. How did Joseph gain power with Pharaoh? As an economic forecaster! Joseph interpreted a dream Pharaoh had about the meaning of seven plump cows on the bank of the Nile and seven lean cows who destroyed the fat cows (and a similar scenario involving ears of corn).

When Pharaoh asked Joseph the meaning of the dream, Joseph's answer was that the economy would have seven good years (a boom in business cycle terms) followed by drought and seven bad years (a recession). Pharaoh's next question to Joseph was what to do about the recession. The answer was to tax people (grain was the currency of the time), store it in the cities to feed people and make it available to stimulate the economy in the lean years. Apparently, the theory was sound enough that Pharaoh put Joseph in charge of the commerce in Egypt, making him the second most powerful government official in the nation.

The lessons learned about business cycles align closely with the conclusions of John Maynard Keynes a few thousand years later. Although Keynes considered the marginal efficiency of capital the reason for business cycles (instead of drought) and interest rates the appropriate government intervention (instead of grain), the basic goal of smoothing out business cycles was the same. Keynes was most concerned with avoiding depressions but the principle of government intervention to control the economy became a permanent principle of traditional economics. Regardless of your opinion of Keynesian economics, the takeaway here is simply: to have prosperity in the future, you must be prepared for the ups and downs of the business cycle!

Keys to Prosperity

Life Lessons from an Economic Forecaster Named Joseph

A remarkable character and role model Is Joseph, described in the biblical book of Genesis. In addition to being considered the "first economic forecaster" by interpreting a dream for Pharoah, Joseph is an example of perseverance in overcoming personal life challenges.

Joseph was the favored son of the wealthy family of Jacob, an important figure in Abrahamic religions, such as Judaism, Christianity, Islam, and Baha'i. Life for Joseph must have seemed good as a youth—so good his father gave him an ostentatious coat, described as "a coat of many colors," probably because Joseph reminded Jacob of his favorite wife, Rachel.

What happens when one child receives special advantages compared to siblings? Answer: Envy and jealousy, triggered by the favored child's behavior. Who knows what would have happened if Joseph had shown more humility about his prosperity, but the result of his behavior was an ambush by jealous brothers who sold him into slavery to a traveling caravan who took him to Africa and sold him to Potiphar, the captain of Pharaoh's guard. Joseph's winning ways not only pleased Potiphar, but also attracted Potiphar's wife who had Joseph imprisoned when he resisted her sexual advances. In prison, Joseph gained the respect of his fellow inmates resulting in his introduction and service to Pharaoh.

Joseph's administrative skills resulted in economic recovery for Egypt during a drought-induced recession and reunion with his father and brothers who sought his help. Instead of taking revenge on them for enslaving him, Joseph welcomed and helped them.

Do you see any lessons for life in what Joseph learned about humility, perseverance through suffering, wisdom, loyalty to God, integrity when faced with temptation, willingness to help others, and forgiveness of people who mistreated him?

Economic Prosperity and Global Dominance

The nation with the largest and most prosperous economy usually fills the role of the world's dominant military power. That was true for Egypt. It did not last forever, replaced by the Greeks at first, then the Romans, and then the Ottoman

Empire. One thing great economic and military powers have in common is that each of them eventually fades as a world power.

Alexander became king of Macedonia upon his father's death in 336 BCE and went on to conquer most of the known world of his day, establishing Greek colonies throughout the empire. Greek became the language of business, learning, and government, and the drachma became the currency used in much of the world. Alexander's father enlisted Aristotle as a teacher for Alexander for three years. Although Aristotle's teachings about slavery are reprehensible, his analysis of how to achieve one's goals are informative. Alexander apparently learned well from Aristotle's teaching that "Excellence is never an accident. It is always the result of high intention, sincere effort, and intelligent execution; it represents the wise choice of many alternatives – choice, not chance, determines your destiny." A useful lesson, not only for Alexander, but anyone who desires to be prosperous.

What Egypt achieved by growing wheat, Alexander achieved with horses. Macedonians were known for horse breeding and riding expertise, and Alexander (learning from his father) used that expertise to employ cavalry instead of infantry as the decisive element in his army. His engineers used technology to perfect spear design which Alexander coupled with a tactic using the Phalanx military formation. Using a main phalanx as a holding force to lock up enemy infantry, Alexander's cavalry and elite infantry would break through at a weak point and flank the main phalanx. Apparently, the effort his father invested in education was productive. In 15 years of conquest Alexander never lost a battle. He named more than 70 cities after himself (and one after his horse) and established Greece as the intellectual and artistic center of the world. For observers today, the lessons from Greek history added the subjects of animal husbandry, technology, and behavioral understanding of military tactics.

Greece eventually lost its empire to Rome. As the unity of Greece declined, the constant warring between its city states weakened Greece and made it difficult to unite against a common enemy like Rome. Inequality was rampant and the poorer classes in Greece began to rebel against the aristocracy and the wealthy, yet another lesson for modern economic observers. Roman legions defeated Macedonia in 197 BCE, destroying and plundering the city of Corinth in 146 BCE as an example to other Greek cities. Greece today is no longer a major world power, a minor vestige of its former economic and military strength. However, the Greeks did bequeath lasting architecture, drama, and sculpture.

But here is the most important lesson for consideration of prosperity: there are still lots of Greeks living good lives with their families, operating small and large businesses, and living on exceptionally tasty food enjoyed with their national drink, ouzo. Whether the example is Egypt or Greece, it is not necessary to be the world's superpower to be a nation of people living prosperous and satisfying lives, a lesson that at some point in the future may be important for citizens of the U.S. when the economies of China (sooner) and India (later) become larger than the U.S.

If any nation can claim to conquering the ancient world, at least western portions of it, most people would agree that Italy came close, creating an empire and pioneering technological breakthroughs such as aqueducts, highways ("the Appian Way"), a worldwide currency, replacement of Greek as the world's standard language with Latin, and world peace ("*Pax Romana*") based on military control of conquered nations.

A major reason for the decline of the Roman Empire, however, was its economy. Government overspending, loss of trade with North Africa to pirates (because of declining military strength and the demise of *Pax Romana*), reliance on mercenaries instead of loyal Roman legions and widespread government corruption were all contributing factors in the decline of Rome's prosperity. Moreover, the exploitation of slaves and the abuse of the poor caused rebellion and chaos.

High tax rates caused the richest citizens to leave Rome and take their wealth with them beyond the reach of the government. Traditional economic theory predicts raising the tax rate on the rich increases revenues for the government. Behavioral economics (and historical data) reveal such a policy may reduce revenues for the government. Those economic realities and other changes brought barbarians to the gates – and the end of the Roman Empire. Do you observe any other lessons from history that might be applied to contemporary economies?

Details on how Rome rose to power and eventually fell have been thoroughly addressed by Gibbon in *Decline and Fall of the Roman Empire*, and other historians have done that as well with many volumes of data and analysis. On one dimension, Italy still rules the planet. Pizza seems to have conquered food preferences in just about every nation of the world. But Italy's economy is no longer a world power. With that said, like Egypt and Greece, the nation is still populated with millions of people living rewarding lives, providing for their families in small and large businesses and good food and wine. Again, a lesson to be learned by all nations temporarily occupying world power.

Rise of Nation States

Throughout Europe, areas emerged controlled by landowners capable of providing protection and stability to farmers in the region. Farmers brought grain to manor villages to be ground and milled. When marauding bands of thieves invaded farms (because there was no centralized government), the farmers fled to the strongest of nearby manors which built walls and large homes (castles) to offer a safe refuge. The farmers paid part of their produce as "liege" to the manor lord, providing that person funds to hire the fiercest fighters of the area to be something like a police force – providing weapons, horses, and titles ("knights").

When lords of one manor encountered resistance from greater forces, they formed alliances with regional lords in a system of fiefdoms that evolved into hierarchies with titles such as Duke or Baron giving allegiances to other leaders, with one of them eventually emerging as King. That is how nations formed throughout much of Europe from various Germanic groups, Austria, Poland, as well as Spain, France, England, Russia, and others.

Some of those nations embraced the British economic theory of mercantilism, also called commercialism, a theory of trade from 1500 to 1800 in which countries attempted to amass wealth through trade with other countries, exporting more than importing and increasing stores of gold and precious metals. Mercantilism motivated countries such as France, Portugal, Spain, and Britain to establish colonies that hopefully would buy high-valued goods from the mother country with lower-value commodities in the colonies. That goal motivated nations to send explorers to various parts of the known and unknown areas of the world, usually to the detriment of the native peoples of those lands. Britain competed with France in Canada and northern colonies and with Spain in Florida and the Caribbean Islands.

These intense rivalries sometimes caused wars between colonial powers. One nation already discussed in this chapter fought a different type of war – The Netherlands. Instead of warships, The Netherlands sent merchant ships, mostly making commercial transactions instead of war. You can observe how that turned out by visiting the Rijksmuseum in Amsterdam which is full of expensive "Old Master" paintings, but they are different in size than paintings by the same artists in other European museums.

The reason for the difference in size of Dutch-owned paintings by Vermeer, Rembrandt, and other lesser-known artists of the era? In Amsterdam, the commercial trading companies were successful at making friends instead of war, allowing many of the Dutch entrepreneurs and middle class to become wealthy enough to afford expensive paintings by the best-known artists. In Amsterdam, the paintings had to be small enough to fit into private homes instead of the large paintings for castles and churches that housed expensive art in the rest of Europe. Once again, we see that art and economics are intertwined, a result observed by comparing the Rijksmuseum with museums in other European nations. There is a clear lesson here for practical economics and prosperity.

The Netherlands also gave birth to a speculative bubble when tulip bulbs reached extraordinarily high levels and then dramatically collapsed in February 1637. Tulip mania is generally considered the first recorded speculative bubble, another lesson from which the rest of the world can learn. People who invested in dot.com stocks in 1999 and real estate speculation in 2007 probably wish they had paid more attention to lessons from Dutch economics.

Instead of sending ships of conquistadors as Spain and France did, the Netherlands sent ships of tulip bulbs, food, and other high-value cargo, a legacy of agricultural skill that remains today. The Netherlands is the second largest exporter of agricultural goods in the world after the United States and has some of the most advanced food industries on the planet. Twelve of the world's largest ag/food companies have major production or R&D sites in Holland, including Cargill, Heinz, Monsanto, Unilever, Mead Johnson, ConAgra, Mars, and many others.

The port of Rotterdam is Europe's largest seaport, largest in the world until 2004 when Singapore overtook it. Rotterdam's eminence in logistics creates direct and indirect employment for some 385,000 people in businesses throughout the Netherlands. The conclusion? Wars and military strength do not create prosperity as effectively as skill in high-value agriculture and commercial trade.

The Sun Never Sets

Britain established colonies not only in North America and Bermuda but also in Asia (India, Hong Kong, Burma), Africa (Nigeria, South Africa, Botswana, and other countries), the Caribbean (Bahamas, Virgin Islands, Barbados, Antigua, and others), the Mediterranean (Gibraltar), Australia, New Zealand and even a little in South America (Falkland Islands). The extent of British colonization was captured in the phrase, "The sun never sets on the British Empire."

To understand prosperity in the world today, consider the differences in how colonization occurred by Britain compared to other European countries. Spain, France, and Portugal colonies were mostly funded by the "Crown" – usually the king or queen in search of gold or other riches with which to accumulate wealth and fight wars. Although the authority of the Crown was required in Britain, the funding mostly came from entrepreneurs hoping to profit from crops grown in colonies ranging from lumber (to build ships needed for the British navy) to tobacco (especially in Virginia) and cotton in southern colonies. In Asia, the "crop" the British sought was usually "spices," sometimes another name for opium. British colonies were mostly founded from the bottom up (entrepreneurs) while other countries were founded from the top down (government).

An entrepreneur and successful steel merchant named Thomas Weston agreed to fund the Mayflower, enlisting poor, uneducated farmers motivated by a desire for religious freedom. In return for passage to America, the Pilgrims agreed to work as traders or fishers for seven years, sending back furs, lumber, and other resources so that Weston and the others could profit. By 1776, Weston made profits for his stockholders but most immigrants to America were more interested in personal prosperity and freedom than loyalty to the Crown.

In Australia, "bottom up" colonists were emptied from British prisons to create a penal colony. Starting in 1788 over the next 80 years, more than 160,000 convicts were transported to Australia from England, Ireland, Scotland, and Wales. Prisons in that era were mostly "debtors' prisons," with the result many of the original inhabitants of Australia had previous entrepreneurial experience along with plenty of ambition for a more prosperous future. In Australia, the inmates "ran the prison" and ran it so well, Australia soon was prosperous enough to hire wealthy people from Britain to work for the former inmates running the new nation. In the first part of the 21st century, Australia was one of the very few nations to have 20 years of economic growth without a single quarter of GDP decline, a lesson to be learned from the "bottom up" nation founded as a penal colony.

Hong Kong was acquired by treaty in 1841, because of a war over the right to sell opium. The combination of a densely populated mainland and 200 islands in the South China Sea, the small, strategic territory of Hong Kong was under British rule for 156 years before reverting to Chinese sovereignty in 1997. Today, of course, it is one of the most prosperous of the former British colonies and more prosperous than the rest of China on a per-capita GDP basis.

The British Empire began with overseas colonies and trading posts and ended up with dominions, protectorates, and mandates totaling 13 million square miles of land, more than 22% of the earth's land-mass. In 1922, the Empire had a population of 458 million people or about 20% of the global population but the financial burden of World War I was the beginning of the end for the British

Empire. Japan's occupation of British territories in the Second World War and the independence of India (and Pakistan) in 1947 brought a sunset to the British Empire. What was left after World War II, however, was a legacy of laws and language leading North America into a position of dominant economic and military power over much of the rest of the world. Some of the British "children" grew strong while watching the sun set on conquests of their aging parent.

Whether farmers, surveyors, army officers or inmates from debtors' prisons, most of the early migrants to British Colonies were looking for upward mobility more than military conquest. And from Hong Kong, New Zealand and Australia to Botswana and Gibraltar, many of them became the economic stars of a new world, eclipsing older economies of Europe and the Middle East.

By most criteria, the United States along with its North American neighbor, Canada, are now powerhouses of the world. But learning from lessons in Egypt, Greece, Italy, and Britain, believing the U.S. economy will dominate forever is a shaky proposition. With a projected combined population of 3.5 billion in 2050 compared to projected U.S. population of about 350 million, the stars of economic power traveled from Europe to North America but are now migrating to the far East.

The sun has set on the British Empire, but lessons learned linger. You probably made conclusions about some of those lessons as you read how colonies developed and prospered. A thoughtful analysis, however, should raise the question, "Why did the Industrial Revolution, which gave Britain the economy to finance a navy that created the most extensive empire the world ever experienced, occur in Britain instead of Europe or Asia?" That question has been answered and thoroughly documented in the book *A Culture of Growth: The Origins of the Modern Economy* by Joel Mokyr. Why Britain dominated the world is what Mokyr and other observers describe as culture, the values inculcated among inhabitants of a society.

The term describing Britain's economic supremacy was the Industrial Revolution. But why did the Industrial Revolution advance more in Britain than in Europe, the Middle East (the old Ottoman Empire), or Asia? Education and science were just as advanced or more so in Europe and China than in England. China, as an example, was highly advanced in areas of technology such as gunpowder, porcelain, the compass, paper making and other technologies. Over 350 years before Gutenberg was born, Chinese and Koreans were printing books with movable type.

Mokyr's book documents how scientists such as Francis Bacon and Isaac Newton, possibly because of their religious convictions, differed from others in Europe and Asia. Bacon and Newton believed knowledge and understanding of nature (through scientific experimentation they pioneered) can and should be for the purpose of advancing the material conditions of humanity. Moreover, the political structure of England at the time allowed entrepreneurs to reap the benefits of their investments via property rights protecting them from the ruling elite. In contrast, other countries like China that also produced technological innovations were still subject to the will of the ruling elite. In other words, property rights were key in allowing for economic growth.

Keys to Prosperity

Growth and Government

As discussed in Chapter 3, the role of government in economic growth is to facilitate an environment where producers and consumers can come together and transact. Political turmoil or uncertainty work counter to this goal.

Ironically, important ideologic innovations like the concept of property rights often come about through political turmoil. In the case of Britain, the formation of parliament and the subsequent reduction in the authoritative power of the monarchy came only after the glorious revolution of 1688. In a renowned paper in economic history, Douglas C. North and Barry Weingast argued that without the events leading to this fundamental change in the British government, it is unlikely that the monarchy would have yielded its' power willingly. Moreover, without a structure in place that could allow the government to credibly commit to upholding its promises, the outcome could have been very different.

For this reason, governments in the most successful free nations of the world tend to be built with clear rules defining the limits of power for various branches and institutions. As history has proven through countless coups and takeovers, lack of these balancing forces can result in the capture of power by tyrants of all forms that invariably lead to economic problems.

It is for this reason that most historians are very protective of constitutions and governmental systems like "checks and balances." Put simply, what may seem like a hindrance to getting things done is often put into place to prevent the growth of authoritarianism.

For any nation, and its citizens, the lesson here is to carefully consider policies and actions that roll back freedoms of citizens and/or remove limits on government power. This is especially true for policies, actions, and behaviors that ignore the rule of law or the will of the people.

Creating a Culture of Prosperity

You can observe the importance of culture on values in nations that have prospered for hundreds of years such as The Netherlands and Switzerland and some that are more recent, such as Singapore.

Switzerland has one of the highest levels of GDP per capita in the world and has held those levels for centuries. Why? You will not find oil or many minerals in Switzerland and most of the land is made of mountains. In the 18th century, Switzerland was known primarily for the Alps, cows, and sheep. Abundance of natural resources is clearly not the answer to Swiss prosperity.

Today, 200 years later, Switzerland is known for its innovative capacity and strong economy. It tops the major international rankings for innovation creating *value-added products* instead of commodities, allowing Swiss firms to sell steel for thousands of dollars per pound with brand names such as Rolex, Cartier, Patek-Philippe, and Swatch made by a highly-skilled work force. Agriculture is not such a big deal in Switzerland and the cows probably have shorter legs on one side than the other. Selling the commodity of milk would not be a good source of prosperity unless you convert it with great skill into a product with higher value, called cheese.

Financial services are a major source of prosperity but only in a nation with a well-educated work force, low inflation, a stable currency, and a strong work ethic – all found in abundance in Switzerland. It also has world-class universities, attracting students and professors from throughout the world. Although it has major corporations such as ABB, Roche, Nestlé and Novartis, most Swiss firms (over 99%) are small and medium-sized businesses (SMBs), companies with fewer than 250 employees. In terms of exports the largest shares of exported goods are chemical and pharmaceutical products (44.8 percent), machinery and electronics (14.8 percent) and watches (9.2 percent), all high-value products.

The official languages are German, French, Italian, and Romansh, reflecting ethnic variations among its 26 cantons. Creating and making laws or changing them is not as easy as in other countries and all laws that are passed are subject to overturn by popular vote. Laws do not make a country rich. The key to prosperity in Switzerland is the *values* of its people.

Mandatory military service is required for all males (and voluntary for females) allowing young people to see and learn to mingle with other people from completely different social backgrounds. Military service in the reserves continues until age 42 and it is customary to keep a rifle or pistol plus uniform and sealed ammunition at home, allowing Switzerland to mobilize an army of around 500,000 in 24 hours. Do not mess with Switzerland!

Social services in Switzerland are among the best in the world, accompanied with higher taxes needed to pay for them. Crime rates are among the lowest in the world, less than half the rate in the U.S. Switzerland welcomes workers and guests from many countries with about a 25% foreign-born population bringing a lot of talent, but citizenship does not come easily.

If you spend time in Switzerland, you might summarize the values that make Switzerland prosperous to include innovation based on education and research, value-added products produced by an educated and skilled work force, diligence in work ethic, dependability (the trains run on time!), non-alignment with other countries, ethnic and religious tolerance – and cleanliness everywhere. (Described in *From the Edge of the World: Global Lessons for Personal and Professional Prosperity*.) Switzerland is prosperous because of its values, not its natural resources.

The Netherlands exhibits similar values, creating prosperity for the past 300 years. Not only did The Netherlands lack oil, minerals, and other natural resources, it also lacked land. So, Holland created it with dykes and canals to produce fertile agricultural land.

Many years ago, the Amstel River flowed from central Europe to the ocean through the Netherlands, creating frequent floods. Using advanced technology, the Dutch constructed canals and a dam to control the flooding, converging in an area where ships could sail up to and have their goods unloaded. The wares were either sold there, carted to warehouses, or switched to smaller ships which then sailed onward. Sometimes people who control a logistics advantage such as that set the price for their services as high as possible. That is the answer from traditional economic theory (maximize profit), but the Dutch did something different based on behavioral realities. The Dutch provided superior quality service at low prices, based on a belief it is better to make a little on a lot than gouge customers with high prices.

The principle of "make a little on a lot" made Holland prosperous for hundreds of years and works well today for retailers such as Aldi, Costco, and Walmart. Retailers know the adage, "Sell to the class and you live in the mass. Sell to the mass, you live in the class." Aldi, Ikea, and Walmart sell very well to the masses. The originally poor families who started those firms now live (very well) in prosperity.

Neither Switzerland nor the Netherlands achieved prosperity based on military might. They treated customers (and rivals) fairly, dependably, with respect, friendliness, and confidentiality. Not bad values for an individual, a business firm or a nation desiring prosperity!

You might think this sounds good if you are raised in a prosperous nation with useful values, but what if you are poor with few resources? That question is answered by what happened in Singapore.

Singapore was a poor island nation of 1 million people in 1950, on land described by some as "malaria-infested swampland." In the rest of the world, the United States and Switzerland were ranked number 1 and 2 in 1950 with per capita GDP almost $10,000; Singapore was near the lowest in the world with per capita GDP of a few hundred dollars. Today, Singapore ranks higher than the

U.S. at $65,233 according to World Bank data from 2019, one of the most prosperous nations in the world. Singapore General Hospital is ranked third best hospital in the world by *Newsweek*, outranked only by the Mayo Clinic and the Cleveland Clinic in the U.S. How did Singapore get so rich?

The succinct answer is that Singapore changed its values. You can read how that was achieved in the book *From Third World to First* by Lee Kuan Yew, the leader responsible for rebuilding a nation around three values – survival, security, and success. Visit the Singapore Discovery Center in Singapore and you will see how values are taught to its citizens along with respect for racial and religious diversity. Walk or jog around Singapore and you will observe results of these values – no crime, no poverty and above all, no dirt! There are exceptions, of course, but Singapore's values helped it to achieve exceptional prosperity for both individuals and the nation. In the next chapter you will read what people do who are born poor but want to be prosperous. Singapore is a prime example of how that is accomplished.

Values do not happen without active programs to inculcate those values. In Singapore, children grow up attending daily assemblies reciting the Singapore Pledge right after singing the national anthem. The pledge is recited daily in multiple official languages (English, Chinese, Malay, and Tamil). People who grew up in Singapore report those values impact behavior throughout life.

In English, this is what every person growing up in Singapore learns by heart: "We, the citizens of Singapore, pledge ourselves as one united people, regardless of race, language, or religion, to build a democratic society based on justice and equality to achieve happiness, prosperity, and progress for our nation."

It would be difficult to find two nations more different in geography and weather than Switzerland and Singapore, but probably few nations more similar in values. If your mother ever told you, "Soap doesn't cost much," she was giving good advice. Prosperity is closely correlated with cleanliness, both national and personal. That is probably not something you will find in a traditional economics textbook but evident when you study Behavioral Economics or visit either Switzerland or Singapore (or the Netherlands).

Traditional economists describe inflows of capital into both Switzerland and Singapore, the immigration of highly-educated individuals to both countries and the high rates of consumer savings (46.1 % in 2019 in Singapore) but those metrics are results. For answers about how those highly desirable results are achieved, you find answers in practical economics.

You might want to see data about why countries similar in geography, language, climate, and natural resources are so different in prosperity. If so, they are available in *Why Nations Fail: The Origins of Power, Prosperity, and Poverty* by Daron Acemoglu and James Robinson.

Why is New Mexico more prosperous than Mexico and other South American nations? Why is Florida so much more prosperous than Cuba? Why is South Korea more prosperous than North Korea? And, in one of the most revealing comparisons, why is Botswana one of the highest income per capita in Africa (and least corrupt) and so much more prosperous than its neighbor Zimbabwe? In 1990, Botswana's income per capita was three times higher than its next door neighbor Zimbabwe; today, it is nearly six times higher.

You can find all those answers in *Why Nations Fail*. But here is a quick summary. Prosperous nations create incentives and reward innovation. Poor nations do not. Prosperous nations are inclusive and encourage everyone to participate in entrepreneurial activities while poor nations are dominated by government institutions mostly benefitting the extractive elite who control the government.

One word describes the cause of national prosperity better than any other word. That word is *values*. This is not to say that the nations noted above have had ideal value systems with respect to morality. European colonialism caused great suffering for non-European peoples around the globe. The Dutch East India Company was heavily involved in the slave trade, and all these countries (including the USA) have been guilty of injustices toward their citizens.

The point of this chapter is not to say that nations are perfect. Instead, this chapter highlights the historical evidence for, and great importance of, values that lead to national prosperity. Understanding these values can then be an integral part of the continuing improvement of national prosperity for all peoples.

For a deeper look at how values are formed and what they mean for nations, for firms and their workers and for you, turn to the next chapter.

Discussion Questions

- If someone asked you for a succinct explanation of why some nations are poor and other nations are prosperous, in a few words, what would be your answer?
- In the Prosperity Key about the biblical character of Joseph, what attributes of Joseph's character describe the evolution of his life? While you may not endure slavery or false imprisonment as Joseph did, what lessons from Joseph's character do you observe as useful for your own life and character?
- Consider the examples of Singapore and Switzerland discussed in the text. In what ways are these countries different and what ways similar? What might this indicate about the possible ways that a nation can achieve economic success? What might these characteristics suggest for improving your own future success?
- Consider the lessons about national prosperity from observing art in the Rijksmuseum in Amsterdam. Has this altered your view on national wealth, the wealth of individuals, and the success or artists? What are some examples of fine art that exist in spite of a lack of wealthy benefactors/buyers?
- Based on lessons from history, how likely is it that the United States will continue to be the most dominant economy for many more decades? How would your conclusion affect policies for the United States in the future?

Chapter 6

How to Be Prosperous Instead of Poor

The world is full of examples of both poverty and prosperity. The previous chapter discussed the differences between nations, but what about individuals? This might lead you to the following question:

Why are some people poor while others are prosperous?

If you do not understand why poverty occurs, you will not know the cure or how to move from poor to prosperous. Equally important is that if you are prosperous now and do not understand why, you risk becoming poor in the future. In a market-driven economy poor people can, and often do, become prosperous and prosperous people can, and sometimes do, fall from prosperity to something much less. Objective economic analysis, and especially analysis of behavior, provides answers to why this is the case.

Two books describing how poor people rise from poverty and dysfunctional family backgrounds are *The Other Wes Moore* by Wes Moore and *Hillbilly Elegy* by J.D. Vance. The books are different in that Moore describes how he overcame poverty in the African-American culture and Vance describes how he rose from Appalachian white culture. Read them both and you will discover the suggested solutions are similar from both perspectives. They include *mentors*, military-esque *discipline*, focused *education* and the importance of *personal motivation* and *individual responsibility*. Such values are key attributes in rising from poverty to prosperity because values drive behaviors.

A book full of principles analyzing inter-generational mobility for children from both generationally advantaged families and generationally disadvantaged families is *Sociopsychonomics: How Social Classes Think, Act, and Behave Financially in the Twenty-First Century* by Lawrence Funderburke. There are academic articles and economic data reporting the same conclusions, but Funderburke provides practical examples showing that while people are who they are for many reasons, this does not prevent them from changing and living out principles that lead to prosperity. Bad financial habits and self-sabotaging emotions around money can be broken with the right frame of reference.

Keys to Prosperity

Decisions, Decisions

When I was a teenager, a friend named Chuck Hebestriet told me: "Success usually requires a long sequence of good decisions, and failure often results from a single bad decision." Within this advice is an understanding that making decisions with an eye on the future is the more reliable method to achieve prosperity and considering the behavioral implications of these decisions is certainly a valuable addition.

Historical examples of bad decisions disrupting success are not hard to find. One such example is the tragic story of Tony Hsieh, the venture capitalist turned CEO who famously guided the online shoe company Zappos from just over one million in annual sales to over a billion in annual sales. A Harvard graduate in computer science, co-founder of LinkExchange, and CEO over a billion-dollar increase in growth would certainly exemplify a sequence of good decisions. Unfortunately, Mr. Hsieh's struggles with mental health led down the dark but well-worn path of addiction. Even worse, his untimely death in 2020 is rumored to be tied to the resulting problems he faced.

The heights and depths of Mr. Hsieh's life exemplify the importance of continued focus on good decision-making, especially in connection with your own health and well-being. The behavioral reality of the stigma around mental health should not stop anyone from seeking help when it is needed. The most important factor in your future is to make sure that you are there to see it!

A more light-hearted example of a bad decision comes from the A&W restaurants that peaked at over 2400 locations around the USA and Canada in the 1970's. At a time when fast-food competition was heating up, A&W launched a 1/3lb hamburger priced similarly to McDonalds' ¼lb offering. A&W hoped that having a better value would attract more customers. Unfortunately, marketing research would later find that many people believed that a 1/3lb burger was smaller than a ¼lb burger, turning A&W's strategy against them. A scholar in consumer behavior will tell you that numerical processing can affect perceptions of numbers in strange but predictable ways, valuable information for anyone seeking to successfully market a product.

-   *Roger Bailey*

In short, for individuals as well as nations, the path to prosperity is *values*. Even if everything goes according to plan, prosperity typically requires a long sequence of good decisions. In contrast, poverty can often result from just a single (very) bad decision. Given that the values you espouse will determine how you make decisions, your values will have a significant impact on the likelihood you will be prosperous in the future.

Data supporting that conclusion are found in books by Diedre McCloskey, who holds professorships at the University of Illinois in Economics, History and Literature. The most recent of McCloskey's analyses of prosperity is *Bourgeois Equality: How Ideas, Not Capital or Institutions, Enriched the World.* The other books in this encyclopedic trilogy documenting the relationship between values and prosperity are *Bourgeois Dignity: Why Economics Can't Explain the Modern World* and *The Bourgeois Virtues: Ethics for an Age of Commerce.* You will see McCloskey's conclusions throughout this chapter and the rest of the book. You will probably find it easier to read summary conclusions in the book you are now reading than all 1994 pages of the McCloskey trilogy, but each one of McCloskey's books is worth a read.

It's a Marshmallow World

The ability to pursue *delayed gratification* is an essential value separating prosperous people from those likely to be found in poverty, a lesson that applies to many dimensions of life beyond economics. Delayed gratification separates entrepreneurs building long-term fortunes from those choosing short-term salaries and perks. To understand this, consider the marshmallow study at Stanford University which examined the differences between those who delay gratification versus those that cannot.

The original marshmallow study was conducted in 1972 by psychologist Walter Mischel, who observed children aged four to six in a laboratory setting. After learning their preferred treat, a marshmallow was offered to the child and placed on the table by a chair. The children were told they could eat the marshmallow, but if they waited for fifteen minutes without giving in to temptation, they would be rewarded with a second marshmallow. Some children covered their eyes with their hands or faced the opposite direction while others simply ate the marshmallow as soon as the researchers left the room. Of the 600 children who took part in the experiment, about a third deferred gratification long enough to get the second marshmallow.

The results forecast success in many areas of life. In a follow-up study of the same kids in 1988, the ones who delayed gratification were significantly more competent. A second follow-up study, in 1990, showed the ability to delay gratification also correlated with higher SAT scores. These results have been replicated many times by researchers with chocolate bars and other variations. The conclusion: People who can delay gratification for a greater reward are more likely to be winners in most areas of life, including economics.

Delayed gratification also explains why some entrepreneurs build long-term fortunes, in contrast to entrepreneurs spending Too Much Capital (TMC) on corporate facilities, high salaries, and personal perks. Discovering what customers want and providing more value than competitors requires patience. People who fail in starting a business often cite the reason as being "under-capitalized." A behavioral analysis of what really happened usually shows they were "over-expensed." Winning entrepreneurs are *patient*. According to the book *The Everything Store*, instead of rushing to find funds to build swank facilities, Jeff Bezos moved from New York City across the nation to Seattle in his station wagon and worked in a garage on a desk made from a door on metal brackets.

In the early days of Amazon, Bezos endured the pain of hard work and low profits. Sales rose rapidly, but profits were still elusive. The company's investments in technology, physical plant and marketing were so extensive that in 2005, a decade after it began, the company's balance sheet still reported negative worth. For a decade, the firm reported a profit and loss statement with negative or minuscule profits, but this eventually turned into wealth measured in billions.

That is strong support for the conclusion that *delayed gratification* beats immediate. If Jeff Bezos had been one of the kids in the Stanford experiment, he probably would have chosen two marshmallows in the future instead of one immediately. But patience is not the only virtue commonly found in prosperous people. Bezos was still driving a Honda Accord as recently as 2013.

A related attribute that often separates prosperous people from poor is *frugality*. You may have heard people ask the question, "Why are wealthy people so stingy with their money?" Prosperous people often ask the more perceptive question, "How do you think wealthy people became wealthy?"

If you analyze firms such as Costco, Berkshire Hathaway, and annual lists by magazines of "America's Best CEOs," you will often find the best executives are in firms where top executives receive modest salaries. The payoff for these executives is in the growth in value of the company's stock rather than annual salary.

That has certainly been true at Amazon, which did not pay high executive salaries in its early days, and still does not. The highest-paid executive receives $175,000 and Bezos' salary was $81,840. He has also foregone stock options for years. This may seem shocking given that Bezos is the CEO of the world's largest e-tailer. However, note that his net worth has climbed to over $150 billion on *Forbes'* list of the world's richest people. With that said, he also lost almost half of this fortune when he was attracted to someone other than his wife. Once again, even a single bad decision can have a dramatic effect on your wealth.

Remember: Objective application of behavioral economics reveals that life is not the way it is supposed to be. It is the way it is. The way you cope with or improve upon your life is what makes the difference. Objective analysis is about identifying solutions!

Behavioral Antidotes to Racism

If there is a question of our time that deserves an objective, solutions-based approach it is the enduring burden of racism. Evident in nearly every nation, is it possible that there are antidotes? Are there solutions from psychology, cultural anthropology, sociology, and behavioral economics that can help the victims of racism move from poverty to prosperity? Yes, and one place to start is to study the actions of those who succeeded despite racism. People such as A.G. Gaston.

If you took a course in Black History, you may already be aware that A.G. Gaston was born in Demopolis, Alabama, heart of the segregated South, as the grandson of formerly enslaved individuals in 1892, the same year that saw the lynching of 165 black men, women, and children in America, reportedly the largest number recorded in a single year. If you have not studied the life of A.G. Gaston, you might want to learn how the evolution of his life reflects the lessons you are reading in this chapter.

When he was a teenager, his mother moved the family to become the cook for a wealthy Jewish department store owner in Birmingham. While his mother prepared food, Gaston observed how he could apply lessons of how the department store owner immigrant entrepreneur achieved success, permitting Gaston to achieve similar success. His mother, with help from the wife of her employer, enrolled Gaston in The Tuggle Institute, a school where students could earn a certificate after they completed the 10th grade. The school closely followed Booker T. Washington's teaching methods of "industrial education" in the skilled trades and business, led by "Granny" Tuggle, a formerly enslaved person, who drilled into students an unparalleled *work ethic*, the necessity of *saving part of everything earned*, no matter how small, and a *lifelong*

94

relationship with God, along with the philosophy that financial success could be achieved by *finding a need among people in the community and fulfilling it.*

After serving in the U.S. Army during World War I, the only job available to Gaston was working in the coal mines near Birmingham, which did not offer much money ($1.55 per day) for a great deal of (extremely dangerous) work. Gaston was frugal and while others spent their paycheck at local bars, Gaston's primary recreation was at a local African Episcopal Methodist Church, allowing him to save between 65 to 75 percent of his meagre earnings.

When other workers ran short of money, they turned to Gaston for loans – with interest – the embryo of an informal bank, and later a bank he owned. Gaston's mother prepared such excellent lunches for him the other workers expressed an interest in buying a similar lunch, so Gaston, with his mother's help in preparing the food, started a small business selling lunches to other workers. It was the first of many small businesses he started to meet the needs of the Black community. He followed the process you read about in Chapter 4, decades before books about consumer behavior were written.

Instead of figuring out what he could *sell*, he took a long look at what the community in which he lived *needed*. He soon discovered a major problem was paying for the many deaths the community experienced, leading him to start a successful burial insurance company. So successful, he negotiated discounts with the largest funeral firm in the area. Eventually, he bought the funeral firm – and later vertically integrated it with cemeteries and a casket company. It was so successful that Gaston was invited to become a member and leader in the previously all-white National Funeral Directors Association. You can read more about him at https://www.smithandgastonfuneralhome.com/history.

Perhaps the most interesting and important example of seeing and meeting a need was his observation that when Blacks visited Birmingham (and most of the South) their patronage was usually refused by white-owned hotels and motels. He built the Gaston Motel, where Dr. Martin Luther King stayed while leading civil rights activities in Birmingham. When Dr. King was arrested, it was Mr. Gaston who paid the $160,000 bail with personal funds for Dr. King's release from jail. The Gaston Motel was also where Secretary of State Colin Powell stayed with his wife Alma on their honeymoon, along with celebrities such as the Temptations, Stevie Wonder and Little Richard.

This very brief description of Gaston's life is only a minor account of his accomplishments helping other people achieve financial success, supporting institutions such as the Tuskegee Institute, NAACP and many other Black (and white) organizations including being selected as the U.S. delegate to the World Council of Churches. You can read these details in *Black Titan and the Making of a Black American Millionaire* written by Carol Jenkins and Elizabeth Gardner Hines, which a Dallas newspaper stated should be required reading for people of every color who seek success.

On pages 273-274 of *Black Titan*, you will find A. G. Gaston's Ten Rules for Success. Read them or Gaston's autobiographical book *Green Power: The Successful Way of A.G. Gaston.* Compare his life with the lessons you discovered in the book you are reading now, and you may come to similar conclusions regarding the cure for racism. He gave millions away to important causes, but when Mr. Gaston died at age 103, his estate was valued between $130,000,000 and $140,000,000. Any young person who wishes to achieve prosperity can benefit from a model of success, and it is difficult to find a better example than A.G. Gaston.

What Gaston learned from "Granny" Tuggle raises the question, what should be taught in today's schools? In a sense, the Tuggle Institute was an early model for schools that teach values as well as intellectual content. A contemporary example is the Charter School of San Diego serving grades 6 through 12 and recipient of the Malcolm Baldridge National Quality Award. According to the school's website, it is dedicated to creating equality and access for all children, made up of 73 percent disadvantaged students and graduating tens of thousands of students who otherwise might not have earned a quality high school diploma. The values of the school are oriented to education that motivates and inspires the disadvantaged to do great things. This is built around the philosophy that "Inclusion is nothing if not put into practice in a real, tangible way that produces results."

While A.J. Gaston provides a worthy example of overcoming racism and tearing down the barriers resulting from it, the burden of eliminating racism should not fall to those already burdened by its effects. If the detrimental results of discrimination are to be reversed, people in advantaged groups must take responsibility to recognize their advantages and extend those advantages to other groups.

Unlike traditional economics that emphasizes self-interest, behavioral economics recognizes altruism as rational behavior, and "doing the right thing" is certainly a great reason to work towards a world without racism. Moreover, as you learned in the previous chapter, nations that have not espoused fair treatment for all of their people have historically paid the price. Regardless of motivations, individual actions to reverse the negative effects of discrimination can be much more immediate than waiting for government actions and laws to change things. As US Senate Chaplain, Peter Marshall was in a position to observe closely how government works. He once observed "Small deeds done are better than great deeds planned."

Keys to Prosperity

Rising Above Racism

Harriet Tubman, Sojourner Truth, Richard Allen, Buffalo Soldiers, George Washington Carver, Frederick Douglass, Thurgood Marshall, A.G. Gaston. These names may be familiar to you. If not, put them in your browser to understand how people rise beyond slavery, oppression, and discrimination. By example, they demonstrate keys to prosperity and opportunity for individuals and the greater community.

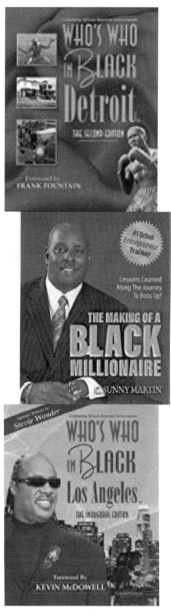

You can discover contemporary examples of rising above racism in the "Who's Who" series of books by Sunny Martin about influential Black citizens from Atlanta to Los Angeles and many cities in between. Martin interviewed thousands of Black leaders and describes success attributes he discovered in the book about his own life, *The Making of a Black Millionaire*. He found that reading books about successful people and creating value in the marketplace by solving community problems are two of the keys to prosperity. When asked by the authors his advice for others to achieve success, Sunny Martin commented, "Six character pillars of *trustworthiness, respect, responsibility, fairness, citizenship,* and *caring.*

- *(Sunny Martin, entrepreneur and author)*

Recognizing the Problem

Historically, the responsibility to dismantle racism has often been ignored and/or denied by white Americans. In some ways, it might be easy to see why. Taking responsibility for something that you feel does not exist, or that you feel you did not cause is problematic. A white person who strongly wishes racism to be a thing of the past may point to laws against it and look at their own life experience as an example to "prove" that it no longer exists. However, an objective "just the facts" approach requires all the facts to be considered.

For example, consider the recently published study by researchers at Stanford University analyzing over 100 million traffic stops. Researchers found that Black Americans are significantly more likely to be pulled over, but when darkness falls (and it is more difficult to see the driver) the likelihood is equalized! Furthermore, the same study reveals that Black Americans are much more likely to have searches performed on their vehicles, even though white Americans are far more likely to be found with contraband when a search is conducted. Myriad studies through the last ten years identify similar disparities in arrests, sentencing, employment and more.

This book is about objective analysis, which requires an unbiased view of the way things are, not beliefs based on the way things should be. In the face of the facts, there certainly seems to be strong evidence of systemic racism. Moreover, while there are many laws against racism and discrimination, analysis of behavior throughout history indicates that laws themselves do not fix such problems.

Even without a look at historical facts, tragic events such as the death of George Floyd while in the custody of police in Minneapolis on May 25, 2020, have shaken the country. The death of Floyd and many others have awakened many white Americans to the realities of systemic racism often experienced by minorities. As a result, citizens of many colors have joined in demonstrations protesting these tragedies. Until then, many members of the majority condemned systemic racism but did not recognize or accept any individual responsibility in perpetuating it.

Keys to Prosperity

Realities of Racism

Dr. Terry Esper is an Associate Professor of Logistics at The Ohio State University. He is an expert in supply chain management (SCM) and issues involving the "last mile" of delivery. In a two-part opinion piece during the pandemic published in CSCMP's Supply Chain Quarterly, Dr. Esper highlights the seriousness of the racism faced by workers in the supply chain.

"For the last 20 years, I've been in the SCM academic community... I not only educate emerging SCM talent, but I also spend considerable time studying strategic SCM issues (like last-mile logistics) and working with several major corporations in the process. And, I must admit...In my many years of observing our industry from these various viewpoints and perspectives, never... never have I ever... been as concerned and fearful for the safety of frontline logistics and transportation workers as I am today."

Unknown to many people, there are several recent cases in which black delivery drivers were harassed by neighbors, chased away from properties after making deliveries, and even threatened and/or detained with firearms, many times while wearing official uniforms and/or driving marked vehicles.

He explains, "...I want to be clear in highlighting that the recent pattern of black delivery driver harassments is not reflective of a new issue. In fact, there have been several examples of such encounters over the years, most of which never captured national attention or sparked much conversation. Yet, the more recent occurrences have emerged at a time which allows us to directly address this issue." Esper continues, "...although my focus is on black men because of the examples we've seen in the media, the thoughts below can easily apply to black drivers of all genders, as well as drivers of other minority groups."

Going beyond the moral repugnance of these events, Dr. Esper delineates the significant costs associated with these racist behaviors. While one potential solution to eliminate these costly incidents is to increase tracking and notifications for delivery, Esper points out that in most cases the recipient of the package is not the offending party. Instead, Esper suggests potential solutions that can change the bad behavior in communities, like empowering drivers to always report these incidents and denying services to persons and/or neighborhoods that mistreat drivers.

Dr. Esper's recognition of both the costs and the behavioral realities surrounding these events is precisely the type of "solutionist" approach that can improve prosperity and well-being for everyone in a nation. To this end, Esper and colleagues Tom Goldsby and Walter Zinn recently published an article in the *Journal of Business Logistics* titled "A challenge in our time: Issues of race in Supply chain management," calling for more research into the causes and potential solutions to the problem of racism in supply chains.

- *(with permission from Dr. Terry Esper)*

If you are having trouble understanding the need for white Americans to address systemic racism, one of America's most influential pastors may be able to help. Tim Keller, author of *The Reason for God*, analyzed why racism is an individual responsibility, in a widely disseminated lecture. "Racism and Corporate Evil: A White Guy's Perspective" (https://www.youtube.com/watch?v=EhJJcTKTVGo) explains why, even though individuals may deny their own complicity, they are part of corporate (group) behavior that practices racial discrimination. Keller describes the behavioral reality that people are usually willing to accept the praise and privilege of groups to which they belong but unwilling to accept guilt and responsibility for the evil their group caused. Oprah Winfrey said it insightfully with the comment, "If you turn a blind eye to racism, you are an accomplice."

A field of study that might shed light on this situation is behavioral sociology, analyzing group behavior to find solutions to problems such as racism. Like George Katona is called the father of behavioral economics, George C. Homans, a Sociology Professor at Harvard, is credited with paternity of behavioral sociology. His books and scholarly articles on the topic "Social Behavior as Exchange" combined psychology and economics to explain how humans behave with each other, emphasizing the need for mutually rewarding relationships among people from diverse groups.

Among the applications is an understanding of causes and cures for racism, including how individuals affect groups. Can just a few individuals change the misbehavior of racial discrimination by their group against members of other groups via anti-racism? Once again, History reveals that the answer is a resounding "Yes." The concept of anti-racism is most certainly not a new one and embracing anti-racism should not be controversial for an objective "solutionist."

Historical Examples of Anti-Racism

One person who effectively employed anti-racism was Eleanor Roosevelt. Ironically, her husband President Franklin D. Roosevelt, is frequently identified as racist for ordering the forced relocation and incarceration of about 120,000 Japanese Americans during World War II. Despite this, Eleanor Roosevelt was an antidote to racism, tolerating no discrimination.

Mrs. Roosevelt did not just talk the talk; she walked the walk. Long before "civil rights" was either a law or national priority, Eleanor Roosevelt demonstrated a concern for minorities. During World War II, the military was still segregated. One of these segregated units was the Tuskegee Airmen, the famed force of African-American aviators. During this time, their funding was in danger of being withdrawn because of the bigotry of many toward Black people, foolishly questioning their "ability to operate complex machinery."

Mrs. Roosevelt gathered the news media, including the primary visual journalists of that era, the "movie news." She went to the base and flew in a plane. However, instead of a white pilot she was advised to ride with by the White House, she flew in a plane piloted by one of the Tuskegee Airmen. Her words about the need to overcome discrimination and bigotry were strong; but her actions were stronger. When millions of Americans in movie theatres across the nation saw her flying with a black pilot, Congress backed down. The Tuskegee Airmen received their funding, and their accomplishments are legend.

 It takes nothing for an individual to join a crowd, but that individual often risks everything to stand apart from the crowd and attempt to lead it in a different direction. This has been especially true with racism. Another example of standing against the crowd was President Harry Truman in an executive order issued on July 26, 1948, abolishing discrimination "on the basis of race, color, religion or national origin" in the United States Armed Forces. The executive order led to the end of enforced segregation in the services and almost led to Truman losing re-election to the presidency.

Southern Democrats rebelled at the civil rights record of Truman and at the 1948 Democratic Convention, all 22 members of the Mississippi delegation, walked out of the assembly. Thirteen members of the Alabama delegation followed. They and other Southerners formed the States' Rights Democratic Party

("Dixiecrats"), which nominated Strom Thurmond for President. Pollsters and many newspapers thought Truman would lose that election because of his stand against segregation in the military. They were wrong.

Truman later stepped in to right some wrongs and get several Tuskegee pilots freed from jail and subsequent court martial proceedings against them dropped. Their purported crime? They had attempted to use the officers club at Freeman Field in Indiana (https://www.youtube.com/watch?v=iTzGjOonsT4). Truman also sought to get airlines to hire some of those black pilots.

In the 1960s, after enormous political bargaining, the United States passed legislation designed to eliminate a century of systemic racism, culminating with the Fair Housing Act of 1968, banning discrimination in the sale, rental, and financing of property. Like many Americans, you might think that this would have abolished discrimination in the sale of real estate. This is obviously wrong if you study the history of real estate and racism in many communities.

The reality of behavior is that people can and do ignore laws. In the years after the Fair Housing Act, the real estate agents in some areas such as suburbs with all-white residents, devised a system to discriminate against minorities. The agent would show the house to any family, as the Fair Housing Act required, but when minority families returned, they would be told, "I am sorry, but the house is in contract." In some suburbs, it was nearly all agents who participated in this type of systemic discrimination. The agents often justified their policy by saying that is what their customers wanted them to do.

Research in *Bulletin of Business Research* and other journals "Attitudes of Affluent Suburbia Toward the Negro Neighbor," disclosed the agents were partially correct. The majority (68%) stated that they should be treated like anyone else. About 10% of residents were blatantly racist and stated that they did not want African-Americans to move into their neighborhood and about 1% said they would do everything possible to keep them from moving in.

However, about 9% of suburban residents said they would go out of their way to make African-Americans feel welcome, and it was from this group that organizations such as the NorthWest Area Council on Human Relations was formed. In response to the overt racism in these communities, they organized white "checkers" to follow up on denials to sell to African-Americans. Council members documented the discrimination – a violation of Civil Rights Law – and organized boycotts and other activities against the firms involved. Similar groups were formed across the country. Some of these boycotts were particularly effective because members enlisted major employers in the area to prohibit new employees from buying from violating firms. Ironically, some of the firms complained vigorously this was "unfair discrimination" against them.

Note that anti-racism is not without costs. In one particular Ohio neighborhood, residents from the 1% who said they would do anything to prevent integration chose to poison pets of Council members, vandalized their homes, and left racial slurs on answering machines of their "activist" neighbors. The first Black resident who moved to that suburb experienced two types of reactions from neighbors. One was a bullet through the front window of his newly-acquired home. The other reaction was so many cookies, pies, and other welcome gifts from neighbors that the new resident finally said, "enough already, just treat us like anyone else."

Behavioral sociology describes reality including examples of how members of the majority community can employ their personal behavior to alter the pattern of racism and historic discrimination. People concerned about racism can confront it at the personal level instead of just supporting and waiting for change at the systemic level. Most *value* systems teach that people should treat their neighbor with love, which may include coming alongside and/or defending those who want to become a neighbor.

Another historical example of anti-racist individual behavior was a Director of Admissions named Robert in the business school of a major university. Like most universities, his duties included making sure admission forms did not discriminate against minority applicants, but he also knew there were few requests for admission to Business School from Black students. Robert was a retired officer with decades of experience in the military, an organization that trains and promotes on merit better than most organizations. Although not perfect (no organization is), the military recruits a higher proportion of its force from Black people (currently 29% of women and 17% of men) than the general population and has a record of promoting to all ranks, including Four Star General and Chairman of the Joint Chiefs of Staff (Colin Powell).

Robert wanted to compensate for the lack of Black people applying to business schools and developed a program to alter that reality. First, he approached one of the largest employers in the state and asked for a large donation (several hundred thousand dollars in 1970) to fund the program. Placing ads on social media or emails to reach prospective students was not an option in 1970, so he recruited a couple of professors interested in overcoming historic racism and together they hit the streets in a low-income, predominantly Black area of the city. They started at a car wash employing a lot of young black workers, approaching young black people with two questions. "Do you have a high school diploma?" When the answer was "yes," the next question was "Would you like to attend the university without cost to you?"

When both answers were yes, he recruited 25 of them to enter the university in classes leading to a business degree. Teachers were recruited and special classes were taught to students within the group using the same content as the curriculum for students that entered through the normal admissions process. The program was below the radar of the rest of the university and most other faculty but resulted in students completing the first year with some going on to get degrees and build successful careers. While the segregated classes and below-the-radar nature of the program were not ideal, and the program certainly did not eliminate systemic racism, it made a difference in the lives of some people. This was done without publicity by a few people that wanted to be effective.

If you are a white reader of this book, you may have done something similar as a supporter of Boys and Girls Clubs, Scouts, KIPP Schools (Knowledge is Power Program) or simply anonymously with friends and acquaintances. Or maybe you have donated to schools to support minority students who would otherwise not be able to attend. If so, you are part of a behavioral solution to race-based discrimination. Homans' research indicates cures to racism begin by developing mutually rewarding relationships with people from diverse groups than your own.

Simply making housing discrimination illegal did not fix the problem. Similarly, making employment discrimination illegal did not fix that problem. Moreover, these laws did not come with a check to Black Americans to compensate for all the high-paying jobs they were barred from, for the promotions they never got because of race, or for income and opportunities lost to the centuries of discrimination. These laws were important foundations for change, but they did not end systemic discrimination any more than speed limits stop people from driving too fast. The lesson is clear: individuals, *through individual acts*, can combat discrimination right now rather than waiting for systemic solutions that will never be effective alone.

Dr. Martin Luther King said that the true battle for equality requires economic repair. A 2019 Yale University study, called "The Misperception of Racial Economic Inequality," found that Americans believe that Black households hold $90 in wealth for every $100 held by White households. The actual amount is $10. The Yale study reported Black Americans have lower incomes overall but save at a slightly higher rate than White Americans with similar incomes. Dr. King observed it is a struggle for equality on all levels, but "Now our struggle is for genuine equality, which means economic equality." An increasing number of voices express belief that Black Lives Matter, but Black Dollars Matter also.

Do you see why a chapter on How to Be Prosperous is important for victims of discrimination, whether it is racial, religious, gender or group identities? And why objective analysis using behavioral study involves tools combatting discrimination in different ways than traditional economics? Society can linger, searching for systemic solutions to racism, but individuals can act now and in the future with practical methods to compensate for the past.

It does not take much to conform to the culture of prevailing groups, but it sometimes requires bold actions to stand apart and lead the culture in a different direction. Systemic solutions to systemic racism are important, but the most enduring resolution to racism happens when individuals choose behavior that is part of the solution instead of complicit with the problem.

Does It Take Money to Make Money?

Some people believe the often-repeated assertion "It takes money to make money." But if you follow the *Dragnet* approach to finding answers, you soon realize the data do not support that assertion because many of the world's highest-income and wealthiest people started with little or no money. The psychological literature has many studies demonstrating it is better to be born above average in cognitive competence than to be born above average in wealth.

Michael Dell, Steve Jobs, Mark Zuckerberg, and Bill Gates were college dropouts and grew their companies mostly with profits instead of capital. Dave Thomas, founder of Wendy's, and Apple's Steve Jobs were both adopted and grew up without the advantages inherited by people who win the birth lottery.

Dave Thomas is the epitome of rags-to-riches, never knowing his birth parents and adopted by a family in which his adoptive mother died when Dave was 10. His adoptive father was unable to keep a stable job, moving with Dave from city to city until Dave dropped out of school in the 10th grade and began working in a restaurant, using that experience to create a successful career as a restaurant entrepreneur in a firm he named after his daughter, Wendy.

These examples and the story of how Sam Walton created the world's richest family by starting Walmart with savings he and his wife accumulated working 25 years for JC Penney and other retailers are the theme of *Saving America: How Garage Entrepreneurs Grow Small Firms into Large Fortunes*, by Roger Blackwell, a book providing excellent examples of moving from poor to prosperous. *Knowledge* and *motivation* are more important causes of prosperity than money or capital.

The research of Dr. Tom Stanley, in *The Millionaire Next Door*, found about 20 percent of millionaires became that way through inheritance. The other 80 percent are first-generation rich, starting with little or nothing. In the U.S. and other countries, the poor do not have to stay poor, and the rich do not always stay rich.

The first female self-made millionaire, as those who understand Black History are aware, was not white. She was Madam C.J. Walker, the daughter of enslaved individuals, who built an empire with her hair care products and understanding of marketing. The self-made millionaire used her fortune to fund scholarships for women at the Tuskegee Institute and donated large parts of her wealth to the NAACP, the black YMCA, and other charities.

Forbes magazine's annual listing of billionaires provides one of the most comprehensive sources of data about economic mobility. In a recent Forbes annual ranking of the world's billionaires, 72 percent are self-made, a proportion that increased from about 55 percent two decades earlier. While other studies of mobility report slightly differing percentages, they all indicate most wealthy people did not start out that way. Six of the United States' 615 billionaires are black in the Forbes' Billionaires List.

You may not recognize the names of black Billionaires Robert F. Smith or David Steward, but you may recognize the names of other black entrepreneurs who rose from poverty to prosperity through athletics, entertainment, and social media. Traditional economics looks to capitalists or socialists for answers about poverty and racial inequality. The *Dragnet* approach of using behavioral economics seeks answers as solutionists.

Books such as *The Millionaire Next Door* and *Saving America* describe how you and others can accomplish upward mobility. It is *knowledge* and *diligence* to apply it, not capital or birth that determines who is poor and who is prosperous for most people. But if you do not understand the cause of poverty, you will not know the cure. KIPP schools have helped thousands of students across the nation teaching two requirements for success: Work hard and be nice.

Findings from behavioral science apply to multiple economic levels, not just the very wealthy. Economist Thomas Sowell in his widely used book *Basic Economics: A Common Sense Guide to the Economy* found that among people born in the bottom twenty percent, 95 percent increase their income during their lifetime and over half make it into the top 40 percent. Sowell's 2020 book

Charter Schools and Their Enemies documents that charter schools, despite opposition from teacher unions, provide competition needed to encourage public schools to improve as well as achieve higher rates of college admission and graduation by poor students. Research by Raj Chetty and Nathaniel Hendren (Harvard); Patrick Kline (Berkeley) and Nicholas Turner (Office of Tax Authority) discloses that the proportion of people born to the bottom 20 percent making it to the top 20 per cent has been mostly constant but in recent years has increased slightly, standing now at 9 percent.

The reality is that even people born poor, values such as *knowledge* and *discipline* in their life can help them rise from the bottom to the top. Of course, this requires the opportunity to acquire knowledge, which data clearly shows is not equally accessible to all people at birth. While this is certainly something to discuss as a barrier to prosperity, it is worth noting that there are sometimes ways to overcome these barriers. Reading books from local libraries was the way out of poverty for famed neurosurgeon Dr. Ben Carson as he describes in several of his books including *Gifted Hands*. Moreover, not everyone has the desire to attend a university to obtain the knowledge from a university degree, but there are many other paths to prosperity.

The life of Sam Walton is a real-world example of how to grow up in a working class family and achieve upward mobility. Walton had a passion to compete, whether it was delivering newspapers and selling subscriptions in his youth or leading his school to a state championship as an underweight quarterback of his high school football team in Columbia, Missouri. He worked at the Columbia *Missourian* and other places to pay for an education at the University of Missouri, allowing him to earn a starting job at J.C. Penney for $75 a month, the beginning of his retail career.

While working for other retailers (and serving a few years in the U.S. Army), he observed the attributes of success. His early experiences led him to say, "There's absolutely no limit to what plain, ordinary working people can accomplish if they're given opportunity and the encouragement and the incentive to do their best."

Sam and his wife Helen lived a frugal lifestyle and made careful but strategic financial decisions, saving enough to open the first Walmart store in Rogers, Arkansas at age 44. He used their savings and his retail experience to open a store with self-service, an innovative concept in 1962. He also mastered ingredients of a successful discount store. By lowering prices, he could sell more volume, allowing him to lower the margin, but because of rapid turnover, earning a higher profit. You can read additional details of his path to prosperity in Sam Walton's autobiography *Made in America.*

In his first store, Walton reportedly gathered employees each Saturday at 7:30 am to plan the store's operations when it opened at 8 am. At those meetings Walton asked employees two questions. One was, "What are our competitors doing better than us?" The other question Walton asked his employees (and many others) was, "What books have you read that would make our firm better managed than other firms?"

Notice that the first question is different than many entrepreneurs who focus on their own firm's attributes and sometimes brag about what they do better than competitors. Firms mastering details of competitors' advantages and incorporating those attributes into their own firm prevent their competitors from gaining significant advantages.

Whether you study competitors with the case method while earning an MBA or learn from others with an MWA (Master at Walking Around), you achieve success by building best practices into your own firm from best practices of all your competitors. Walton did that superbly whether competitors were Sears and K-mart or Harry's Hardware. Subsequently, customers voted with their wallets that they preferred Walmart more than his competitors.

People who read magazines and Internet sources obtain useful data but people who read books obtain conceptual models to interpret data. That worked well for Walton and probably is working for you now if have good answers to that same question while reading this book. When you know what is on a person's bookshelf (or Kindle), you know a lot about what is in a person's head. Long form thinking occurs best by reading books.

If you want to know another attribute of financial success, study people such as Leon Cooperman, billionaire CEO of Omega Investors and investor with Warren Buffet. Why does Cooperman want to make more money? Cooperman's answer is candid and simple: to give it away to charities. Cooperman has vowed to give away his entire fortune to charity, and so every additional dime he earns is one that will benefit others. Many billionaires engage in significant philanthropy, and the motivations to do so are many.

With that said, the data on overall philanthropy for billionaires is less impressive. In 2018, the average household in the USA gave 0.33% of their income to charity. While billionaires in the same year gave a much higher 0.8% on average, this drops to only 0.32% if the top two philanthropists (Gates and Buffet) are removed.

Ways to incentivize (or even force) the wealthy to share more of their wealth are often discussed, but typically come with unintended consequences as discussed in Chapter 8. Regardless, there are other positive examples as well. Billionaire Chuck Feeney successfully gave away his entire fortune of $8 billion in 2020, and more than 200 of the world's wealthiest people have signed the Giving Pledge to give away the majority of their wealth. This brings us back to an important conclusion: people whose primary motivation is to be wealthy often fail. People solving problems for customers better than other firms often become wealthy. A motivation to help others can lead both to prosperity for yourself and the ability to help others.

What happens to people such as Steve Jobs who started with nothing but created a business in his adoptive father's garage? He became one of the richest people in the world, before dying at age 56 of pancreatic cancer. His widow, Laurene Powell Jobs, met Jobs when he gave a lecture at Stanford Business School. Laurene Powell was a new MBA student and sneaked to the front of the lecture and started up a conversation with Jobs, who was seated next to her. They ended up having dinner together that night and a year-and-a-half later they married in a ceremony in Yosemite National Park.

Today Laureen manages the vast fortune of the Steven P. Jobs Trust to help others, with charities such as College Track, a nonprofit organization to improve high school graduation, college enrollment, and college graduation rates for underserved students. She is a founding member of the Climate Leadership Council, probably managing the billions more beneficially for society than if the estate were managed by a government official.

"I never did it for the money," Jobs stated. In fact, Jobs intentionally avoided prioritizing wealth, according to biographer Walter Isaacson, who conducted many interviews with Jobs for his book, *Steve Jobs*. Even after Jobs was a billionaire – married to Laurene Powell Jobs and raising his children – he sought to avoid a flashy lifestyle. "His house in Palo Alto is a house on a normal street with a normal sidewalk – no big winding driveway, no big security fences," Isaacson recalled to CBS's *60 Minutes*. "It was a normal family home." In interviews with Isaacson, Jobs explained that despite his wealth, he did not want his life to be impacted by greed and materialism. "I made a promise to myself," Jobs said. "I'm not going to let this money ruin my life."

For young people just beginning their careers, Jobs issued this advice: "You've got to find what you love," he said in his 2005 commencement speech at Stanford. "Your work is going to fill a large part of your life, and the only way to be truly satisfied is to do what you believe is great work," Jobs explained. "And the only way to do great work is to love what you do."

In short, *motivation to help others* is more likely to lead to prosperity than motivation to be wealthy. This is something you can discover through observation, but also by reading books on entrepreneurship or by studying the economic analyses of Diedre McCloskey.

Personal and National Prosperity

The way to create a prosperous nation is to develop an economy that creates prosperous individuals. What about capital and technology? Aren't they the cause of prosperity? No, McCloskey documents in *Bourgeois Equality*. It is "Humanomics," a more general approach to economic theory that includes inputs from the arts, culture, and other fields of human understanding.

Nations move from Enlightenment to Enrichment when they achieve equality of human *inputs*, not equality of human *outputs*. It is not from technology, trade, or capital that nations become prosperous but from liberty that arises from humans connecting ideas, or to employ McCloskey's vivid language, "when ideas start having sex."

 Key among the characteristics of prosperous people and prosperous nations is the degree to which its *citizens care about and for each other*. Confronting racism is one example of individual caring. The same conclusion applies to individual prosperity. Sometimes it seems it takes a disaster – hurricane, forest fire, or pandemic – to observe a clear demonstration of the care and compassion people have for one another. When it happens, often in the context of faith and religious practices, values which are sometimes just words become manifest in behavior.

Do you know why hamburgers are square at Wendy's? "Because you don't cut corners when it comes to quality," was the belief of Dave Thomas in starting his burger empire with nothing but his own hard work and human abilities – not with family connections, wealth, or college degrees. The simple answer to why some people prosper, as did Dave Thomas, was Humanomics, including behavior based on values. That is why KIPP schools achieve outstanding results by inculcating thousands of students (95% Black and Hispanic) with two values: Work Hard and Be Nice.

Can a nation become a rich nation because of its values instead of its natural resources, technology, and capital? It worked well for the U.S. compared to the rest of the world. It is important to remember that the United States had the same natural resources in its beginning as it does today. Europe had more capital than the colonies, higher levels of technology and much more experience with trade than the U.S.

In 1800, the average income in the U.S. was the same as the average income in the world – $3 per day. By the 21st century, when world income was $30 per day, U.S. average income was $130 per day and continuing to increase, much higher than Mother Britain and most other nations in the world. The reason for prosperity is not resources, technology, or capital. They are the *results*, not the cause, of what happened in the U.S. (and nations such as Canada and other former colonies of Britain). Empirical data demonstrate the cause of prosperity for both individuals and nations is *values*. Values make nations great.

The Problem of Homelessness

Despite the level of affluence in the U.S., poverty persists. One of the most visible manifestations of poverty is homelessness, a problem prevalent in many locations, perhaps no place more visibly than in California when you walk around areas of Los Angeles or San Francisco and compare them with San Jose. Homelessness is rampant not far from some of the highest income areas of the nation. Perhaps you are one of the people who are concerned and want to solve this increasing problem. But if you do not know the cause, you will not know the cure.

The next time you are approached by a homeless person asking for "spare change," you might want to take the time to ask the person how they became homeless. Sometimes, the answer heard is they once were prosperous. There are myriad causes of homelessness, but for some they fell off the career ladder when they fell off a wagon of some type. However, more often the cause has something to do with the person's background.

The way to learn the cause of homelessness is to listen to those who are experiencing it. And perhaps doing something to show you care, such as taking them to a nearby restaurant and buying a meal for them. If you do not want to take time to do that or prefer not to, experienced listeners recommend you give them a gift card enough for a meal at a nearby Wendy's or McDonald's instead of "spare change." People who care enough about other people to become active in acts of caring for other people demonstrate the real values that actually made America great. Moreover, these conversations can provide valuable insight into how people end up on paths that lead to homelessness and/or destructive lifestyles. More importantly, this can help to identify ways that such paths to poverty can be reversed.

The path to prosperity instead of poverty requires changing momentum. If you watch sports, you have likely heard that phrase by sportscasters saying, "the momentum has shifted." Can the same changes happen for people trapped in poverty? Yes, is the answer you will find in *Momentum Power Play: How to Create It When You've Never Had It and Keep It Going Once You've Got It,* a follow up book to *Sociopsychonomics* by Lawrence Funderburke. It is a book with practical methods to change momentum from going down to going up. The methods work so well the book is distributed in prisons and among concentrations of people whose lives have trapped them in poverty instead of prosperity.

Why are some people able to deal constructively with their emotions while others get stymied by them when making difficult decisions? Why are some people able to capitalize on opportunities that others seem to squander? Why are some people who have been dealt a bad hand in life (often through no fault of their own) able to play it out while others get played by it? Those questions are answered in *Momentum Power Play*.

Highly effective solutions to homelessness do exist, but they are not as plentiful as society needs. These approaches are almost always ground up, community based, market driven and most use social enterprise strategies to get to the root and solve the triggers of homelessness. They see homelessness as a consequence of the internal human struggle, not a result of external economic shifts.

One such approach is an organization called Solutions for Change, operating in the epicenter of over 100,000 homeless in southern California, which represents a staggering one-fifth of the nation's entire homeless count. Solutions for Change has trailblazed an innovative design that is changing how people see and act on homelessness. Founded in 1999 by Marine veteran Chris Megison and his wife Tammy, Solutions for Change offers a new way forward. They have won the support of professionals in the field of national systems change who have come alongside of them to help share their model in other places. If you are interested in seeking to be part of the solution to homelessness, Solutions for Change is worth looking into.

Keys to Prosperity

Helping the Homeless

It was a cold, freezing February night when Dr. Pat Angelo felt a command to get into his car and drive downtown with a desire to feed and warm the homeless. He arrived at a homeless encampment on Lower Wacker Drive, and for more than 13 years, Angelo spent four nights a week buying food with his own money from his dental practice and bringing it to about 70 people per night in their makeshift shelters, much like Paul Newman donated profits from his salad dressings to charity.

When a Chicago *Tribune* article called Angelo "The Angel of Lower Wacker," several people came forward to help the "angel" dispense sandwiches and kind words. Since then, the word spread, and at least 30-40 volunteers provide help to the homeless seven nights a week, coordinated by "chief giving officer" Aaron Garza.

"For twenty years", Dr. Angelo reports, "I've been working with people addicted to heroin, cocaine, and alcohol. Most people without homes are addicted. If you diagnose a person as homeless, you might think the solution is to give them a home. But it's not the solution. It's solvable, but not by giving them a home. We stay with them and love them and give them what we can. But for heroin, you have to get them to want to quit, then get them on treatment, then get them out of the environment. If you don't, they're probably going to fail."

Dr. Angelo is diligent about helping the homeless. Perhaps his example will motivate you to help the homeless.

Data excerpted from "Guardian Angel" in Fra Noi magazine, December 2021.

Income and Wealth Are Different

Prosperity involves both income and wealth and it is important to understand what causes each. In Chapter 3, you read why some people earn high incomes and others earn low incomes, especially in the paragraphs concerning the relationship between time and money. People earn high incomes mostly because their time is valued highly, whether because of education or skill.

Sometimes the value of time is influenced by education, but not always. Sometimes high income is earned by people with skills needed by other high-income people. Sometimes people such as Bill Gates, Steve Jobs or Michael Dell earn high income because of high-value products they produce with their knowledge, even though they do not have a college degree. People who know how to write computer code earn $100,000 a year or more, but so do some long-haul truck drivers and landscapers. There is no doubt that people who understand nanotechnology, AI, robotics, 5G and a host of other technologies will earn high income in the future but so will the next Sam Walton and a host of other entrepreneurs. Why people with high incomes become wealthy is a different question.

What you *have* (your wealth or net worth) is not determined by what you *earn* as much as what you *save*. It is easy to find people who earn high incomes, such as sports stars and celebrities or people who win the lottery who end up in poverty or close to it. The reason? They spent instead of saved.

There are also lots of examples of people who never earned high income but end up with enough wealth to live comfortably the balance of their life because they lived by the rule of saving some portion of every dollar they earned. A fascinating example is a man named Ronald Read who worked as a janitor and gas-station attendant. Despite his meager income, at the time of his death Read had amassed a fortune of $8 million. In his will, Ronald Read was able to give $1.2 million to a local library, and over $5 million to a local hospital. How did he do that? Read was an avid reader who saved a portion of his small salary each month and invested it wisely.

How to Be an Einstein at Investing

There is a simple strategy allowing anyone to be a millionaire. It can be stated succinctly in two words: *Start young*.

If you asked Albert Einstein to name the most powerful theory in the world, you might expect him to say, "The Theory of Relativity." He did not, naming the theory of compound interest as "the most powerful force in the universe," calling it the eighth wonder of the world. He added, "He who understands it, earns it… he who doesn't pays it."

If you adopt in your youth the theory of Compound Annual Growth (CAG) – letting appreciation and dividends grow over time – you are almost certain to be a millionaire when you retire. If you put the maximum allowable amount starting at age 20 in a Roth IRA ($6,000, currently) in stocks paying dividends or mutual funds averaging the same return as the stock market the past century (10%), your IRA will have about $6.8 million in it when you reach normal retirement age (67). If you wait until age 30 to start, you will only have $2.47 million.

Whatever amount you have at age 67, and wait another 7 years to retire, you will have double that amount (the Rule of 72). And since most people in reasonably good health at 65 have another 20 years or more of productive life, you probably will want to postpone retirement beyond 67. Put "IRA Calculator" in your browser with your own age, income, and yield to determine how much you need to save now to be able to be prosperous in the future. The power of CAG turns most everyone into a millionaire if they just start young, even with small investments.

Save or spend? That is the question. Those who decide to save in an IRA instead of spending on a variety of fun, but unneeded (and sometimes unsafe) purchases can retire with a million dollars – and perhaps many millions. Many people save whatever is left at the end of the month from their spending. People more likely to be prosperous save first at the beginning of the month and spend what is left over. That approach is described in Andy Stanley, *The Best Question Ever*. *Discipline* is more important that quantity of savings.

What is the tax rate when you take money out of an IRA? Whatever the maximum tax rate (currently 37%) at the time you withdraw funds if you save in a Traditional IRA. What is the maximum tax rate when you withdraw funds from a Roth IRA? Zero. You see why people who want to be prosperous choose a Roth instead of a Traditional IRA. And saving comes before spending.

Warren Buffet in a letter to shareholders described investing as "The decision to postpone current consumption in order to have ability to consume more in the future." This is simply delayed gratification! You can decide to spend on little things now and never be wealthy, or postpone spending on little things, invest the savings in a Roth IRA, and have a million – or many millions – later. CAG is a marvelous tool for becoming a millionaire, and it is available to everyone, even people with incomes as low as a janitor in a public school.

Buffett started his multi-billion-dollar empire when he was a teenager. His first job, at age 13, was delivering newspapers. He went on to start a pinball-machine business in high school, accumulating $10,000 from his business ventures by the time he graduated from college. Sam Walton also started his career with a paper route. Parents who teach their children how to work as teenagers (and save a portion of what they earn) give their children the gift of prosperity as adults.

Values from parents are more valuable than inherited dollars. How prosperous people are as adults is heavily influenced by how well parents teach their children to understand prosperity early in life, one of the reasons children growing up in a home without both parents present to teach those values have to work harder than other children to achieve prosperity.

For you, it may be late to accumulate wealth if you are 50 instead of 20 or 30. But it is not too late to teach CAG to your children or grandchildren or any young person desiring a path to prosperity. If you teach the principle of saving and CAG now to your young grandchildren, they may be able to assist you when you are advanced in age.

A report in *Street Authority* analyzed self-made millionaires and discovered the "7 Secrets of Self-Made Millionaires." Number 1 on the list was the ability to delay gratification. The wealthy concentrate on the future along with their everyday tasks. Rather than spend money today on short-lived pleasure, prosperous people make wise spending decisions with future benefits firmly in mind.

For example: Rather than lease an expensive car right out of college, someone with a wealth-driven mindset buys an inexpensive car (probably used) with the goal that after the loan is paid (even better if they buy one with saved cash) they will drive it a few years longer, placing the normal monthly loan repayment into a savings fund that will be large enough in a few years to buy a nicer car with the money saved. Using these principles, some people never make a car payment after the first one they buy and never make a home mortgage payment after age 50. Despite being one of the richest people on earth, Warren Buffet still lives in the same modest home he bought for $31,500 in 1958.

Avoiding the Opposite of Wealth: Live Debt-Free

Buying on credit typically costs thirty percent more than purchases from savings or cash; often, much more when finance fees are added to interest charges on unpaid balances. A 100%-financed house that costs $100,000 will cost $300,000 or more when paid with no down payment and a thirty-year loan. In contrast, making a down payment of twenty percent from savings with additional payments in the first few years of a mortgage lowers the total cost of the house, allowing consumers to save more, providing funds to afford to buy more in the future.

Whether choosing new cars, new carpeting, or a vacation home, relying on credit instead of cash and savings reduces money available for other purchases and savings. Heavy use of credit increases inequality and shifts wealth from Main Street to Wall Street. If you want to be able to own a lot more goods and services than your credit-burdened neighbors, read books by Dave Ramsey such as the perennial best-seller *Total Money Makeover*.

Ramsey's rules are simple: *Live debt free, spend wisely* and *save* to create financial freedom. Consumers who follow his advice can buy more of everything and live in nicer homes than neighbors living on maxed-out credit cards. Ultimately, debt-free consumers with accumulated savings become part of the prosperous middle class instead of the struggling middle class. In the process, their savings create investment funding to start their own business or invest in the firms of entrepreneurs, creating growth and prosperity for themselves and the economy. *It is not what you earn that determines what you have. It is what you save.*

One of the dangers in redistributing wealth from the wealthy to the poor is that it may reinforce behavior of spending instead of saving. Lasting help to the poor should be structured with the behavioral principle of reinforcing behavior of postponing gratification as a method to move from poor to prosperous. This should also include increasing the ability to earn income with improved job skills. There is reality expressed in the motivational poster "work while they sleep, learn while they party, save while they spend, then live like they dream."

Your job and how well you do it determines your income. Your savings and how well you grow them determine your wealth. Study behavior closely and you discover *economic altitude is determined more by attitude than aptitude.*

Discussion Questions

- Thinking about people you personally know, what are the reasons some are poor, and some are prosperous? What are the determinants of your own income and wealth?
- Which of your activities in your life might be considered an accomplice to racism? Which might be considered antidotes to racism?
- What actions could you be taking now to be more prosperous in the future?
- In your opinion, what are the most important lessons from the life of A.G. Gaston? Why are conclusions identified in the "Marshmallow Studies" at Stanford University important in understanding prosperity? What implications do these conclusions have for making decisions about your future?
- Consider the phrase "It takes nothing for an individual to join a crowd, but often asks everything to stand apart from the crowd and lead in a different direction." In addition to the examples in the text, what examples would you provide from your personal experiences?
- "It takes money to make money," is a statement expressed by many. How would you respond to this statement?
- In the community in which you live, how serious is the problem of homelessness? What can you do to alleviate the problem? What proposed solutions have you seen that might be ineffective?
- This chapter makes the statement income and wealth are different. Why?

Chapter 7

The Ironic Inequality Paradox

The 2020 Coronavirus Pandemic made household names out of statisticians and mathematical modelers because of their ability to interpret data about rates of infection, hospitalization, and death. One statistician in the news was Professor of Statistics Ron Fricker, at Virginia Tech University, who holds a Ph.D. and M.S. in Statistics, and an M.S. in Operations Research. He was Senior Statistician at the RAND Corporation and the National Security Research Division (NSRD), a research center sponsored by the Secretary of Defense. In other words, this person knows numbers.

When speaking about the pandemic, Fricker gave the following advice: "The message I'm trying to get out is, science. Do not be in the optimist camp or the pessimistic camp. Be in the realistic camp." That was sometimes not followed during the recent Covid-19 pandemic with lethal consequences, but it remains excellent advice when studying the topic of economic inequality. Like other topics in this book, remember "Just the Facts." The topic of inequality needs data and science over opinion, optimism, or pessimism. To get started, consider the following question:

Is inequality increasing?

Depending on what you have read on this subject over the years, you may believe that the answer to this question is an irrefutable yes. However, an objective look at the data makes things a bit less clear.

Inequality: For Better or Worse?

There are lots of opinions about inequality, often presented as headlines in news media and political opinions. You may have heard statements such as the following.

"The rich are getting richer, and the poor are getting poorer."

"Inequality is getting worse every year."

"In the richest nation in the world, inequality is immoral."

You can probably think of other comments you have heard about economic inequality, but remember, objective analysis describes reality, not wishes of how things should be.

The discussion of inequality can be divided into two eras, BP, and AP. BP stands for "Before Piketty" and AP for "After Piketty" since publication of his best-selling (2.5 million copies) book *Capital in the Twenty-First Century* by Thomas Piketty and his follow-up book in 2020 *Capital and Ideology*. Both books were translations into English from the original French publications and reported massive quantities of data along with Piketty's interpretation of what those data reveal – increases in inequality in the U.S. and other nations. Between 1960 and 2018 in the U.S., according to Piketty, the proportion of income going to the top 1% rose from about 10% to 22%. Among the remedies proposed by Piketty and his research colleague Emmanuel Saez was a tax of 80% on incomes above $500,000 and a wealth tax imposed annually by every nation.

In *Capital and Ideology*, Piketty goes further than he did in his earlier book, calling for policies that would essentially make property ownership temporary, put workers and owners on nearly equal footing inside corporations, and implement universal capital endowments, universal health care, and basic incomes, paid for by higher taxes on the incomes and estates of the wealthy.

Does that remedy to problems facing non-prosperous people sound too good to be true? You probably know what people usually discover when they see a claim that seems too good to be true.

A closer examination of the Piketty data reveals some flaws in the Piketty analysis. To start, the analysis of the data raises questions as to the true magnitude of any change in inequality. Additionally, focusing on financial capital instead of human capital ignores movement between classes in the U.S, something also occurring in other nations that have increased in prosperity in recent years such as China and Bangladesh.

Questions About Piketty's Analysis

When you dig deep into the inequality data, as an objective behavioral economist would do, there are other problems with Piketty's approach. Top income share estimates based only on individual tax returns, such as those of Piketty and his colleagues, are biased by tax-based changes, major social changes, and missing income sources. These issues are addressed in a paper published in December 2019 by Gerald Auten, Office of Tax Analysis, U.S. Treasury Department and David Splinter, Joint Committee on Taxation, U.S. Congress. Their analysis considers the kind of demographic realities recognized in an objective analysis of income.

Estimates by Auten and Splinter correct Piketty's tax sample to remove dependent and non-resident filers, as well as filers under age 20. Importantly, they also account for increases in the share of single-parent households and changing family size, as well as for falling marriage rates. They also correct for many specific features of how income is reported on individual and corporate tax returns and how this has changed over time. While many improvements have only small or offsetting effects on top income shares, their cumulative effects are significant.

An extended discussion of whether the Auten-Splinter data are more accurate than Piketty is beyond the space (and probably interest of you the reader), but if there are questions in your mind about whether inequality is increasing or staying about the same, you can put the names of Auten and Splinter in your browser and read original papers reporting the data. The bottom line is that Auten and Splinter found the top 1 percent's share of after-tax income rose from 8.4 percent in 1979 to 10.1 percent in 2015, much different than superficial data reported by Piketty. Even more revealing is that when the data are corrected to reflect post-tax data and government transfers, Auten and Splinter find barely any change in the proportion of income received by the top 1 percent since the 1960s, shown in a chart from the *Economist* magazine.

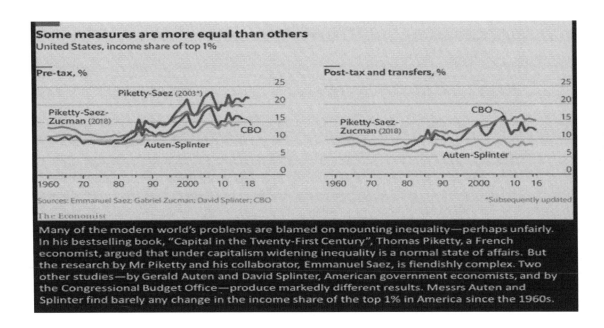

Some measures are more equal than others
United States, income share of top 1%

Pre-tax, %

Piketty-Saez (2003*)
Piketty-Saez-Zucman (2018)
CBO
Auten-Splinter

25
20
15
10
5
0

1960 70 80 90 2000 10 18

Post-tax and transfers, %

CBO
Piketty-Saez-Zucman (2018)
Auten-Splinter

25
20
15
10
5
0

1960 70 80 90 2000 10 16

Sources: Emmanuel Saez; Gabriel Zucman; David Splinter; CBO

*Subsequently updated

The Economist

Many of the modern world's problems are blamed on mounting inequality—perhaps unfairly. In his bestselling book, "Capital in the Twenty-First Century", Thomas Piketty, a French economist, argued that under capitalism widening inequality is a normal state of affairs. But the research by Mr Piketty and his collaborator, Emmanuel Saez, is fiendishly complex. Two other studies—by Gerald Auten and David Splinter, American government economists, and by the Congressional Budget Office—produce markedly different results. Messrs Auten and Splinter find barely any change in the income share of the top 1% in America since the 1960s.

The fundamental flaw in the Piketty analysis of inequality is his assumption that the increasing amount of pre-tax income (and wealth) to the highest brackets (whether 10%, 20% or 1%) is due to their financial assets. It is true that the highest tax brackets over time have received more total income. Piketty attributes that to return on capital, while ignoring the fact that the people in the lowest brackets have also received higher income in tax credits, food stamps, rent subsidies, Medicaid health care and other forms of government transfers. Note the irony here: Piketty argues for wealth transfers to decrease inequality but does not correctly include them in his estimates of current inequality.

When all transfer payments received are counted as income and income reduced by taxes (82% paid by the top forty percent of citizens), income inequality is lower than it was 50 years ago. ("Incredible Shrinking Income Inequality," *WSJ* March 24, 2021).

In addition, there is a significant amount of unreported income left out of any government data. Ambitious people find ways to compensate for low wages, often with non-taxed income or benefits. Not all people are required to file tax returns, and tax returns do not always reflect all sources of income. Since those not required to file returns likely have limited incomes, tax data do not provide a representative view of low-income households.

While income from the underground economy, such as earnings from sales of illegal drugs, sex work, and "running numbers" will never be reported to the government, there are also many other ways income can avoid inclusion in such reports. Also understated are some of the tips of waitpersons and bartenders, casual labor ranging from agricultural workers and landscapers to childcare and home cleaning services and some parts of the "gig economy." These services, often on a cash basis, mostly escape traditional economic data and mostly go to the bottom twenty percent of the work force. With that said, the wealthy may also be able to avoid reporting of some sources of income, but the IRS tends to scrutinize suspicious returns from high earners.

Keys to Prosperity

The Importance of Transfer Payments

Transfer payments such as welfare, financial aid, and government-provided subsidies are often excoriated by those that dislike government spending. But, before criticizing a transfer payment, it is important to consider its costs and benefits. Note that there are many reasons that a person can end up in the bottom end of the income distribution, many of which are beyond that person's control. There are also several industries that are critically important for a nation and its economy. For these reasons, transfer payments by the government are important for the security of both individuals and their nation.

Social welfare systems are often discussed in terms of their large costs, which can be substantial in both the size of payments and the cost of program oversight. Considering the benefits, these systems obviously help people in need, but there are other important benefits to consider. Social welfare programs can reduce homelessness, child hunger, crime rates, and more; most of these problems come with their own significant costs to society. Moreover, these programs reduce the uncertainty faced by the citizens of a nation, which is why they are sometimes called "welfare insurance." Knowing that a job loss or health issue will not cause you or your family to become homeless can be a significant boost to a person's well-being as well as their willingness to engage in transactions and long-term investments in their economy.

Subsidies for certain industries can also be critically important. For example, the existence of domestic production of food and raw materials is necessary for any nation that wishes to be independent of the influence of other nations (let alone the possibility of defending itself in a war). Though costly, subsidies can help to support these critical domestic industries where they might otherwise collapse.

With this said, the defense of any transfer payment should revolve around whether the size of the payments (the costs) is justified by its benefits. Some of the behavioral downsides of such programs are that excessively large welfare payments can reduce productivity and work ethic; some payments will come with a stigma that can harm recipients; and, transfer payments are not always directed at those that need them the most. Moreover, as mentioned earlier, the details of the surrounding policy should be studied carefully to evaluate precisely where and how federal funds are being deployed. A true "solutionist" will ask to see the evidence and consider the behavioral considerations before blindly supporting or rejecting a transfer payment policy!

Capital Versus Value Creation

Another important flaw in Piketty's analysis is the focus on financial capital that ignores the typical cause of high income. In nearly every economic activity, most people attain wealth not by owning assets, but by the market-measured value of what they create and do for others. If they are prudent, they use high income received while younger to accumulate assets to prevent their retirement income from expiring before they do. Workers earn varying amounts of money, depending on how valued they are in markets for their skills and knowledge. Data reveal it is market-based jobs (also called "labor" by economists), not capital that leads to inequality.

In jobs involving the arts, masses of entertainers earn low incomes while Madonna earns $125 million a year and $1.2 billion during her career – because she produces what the market values. But another singer, Robyn Rihanna Fenty has more wealth than Madonna because of Rihanna's "second job" as owner of her own lingerie line, her own beauty line, and recently, her own luxury clothing line based out of Paris. It is no wonder Rihanna wakes up at five in the morning to work on her music.

Other musicians are even wealthier. Jay-Z and Paul McCartney are both billionaires. Rising from project housing as a child, musician and entrepreneur Dr. Dre sold Beats for $3 billion, putting him near the top of the inequality pyramid. Income was not a return on capital for these musicians, as Piketty alleges. It was a result of highly valued *labor* first, followed by wise investment and entrepreneurship.

Most writers earn low incomes, but E.L. James earned $100 million with the book *Fifty Shades of Grey* that might more appropriately be called *50 Shades of Green*. Considerable amounts of income and wealth probably also describe Piketty's move up to an elite income group, not because of his "return on capital" but because of huge royalties from his book and speaking fees he can command around the world. His human capital allowed him to receive a big slice of the inequality pie compared to what his working-class upbringing would normally command as the son of militant Trotskyite parents politically affiliated with the French Socialist Party. "The acorn does not fall far from the tree," as the saying goes, but sometimes it grows taller than the tree from which it fell. And sometimes the soil is more fertile for the acorn in the U.S. than in France.

Most writers do not have the income of James or Piketty or the paradox of an author such as U.S. Senator Bernie Sanders and his multi-million dollar book deal that made the Senator and his wife part of the "1% elite." *Labor* is the new source of economic wealth, not inherited capital. Laptops and word processors replaced factory tools and mining shovels as the key to the upper brackets of inequality as a "laborer."

Athletes with market-measured merit can earn $10 million or more a year – a huge gap between them and most players. Quarterback Tom Brady earned $235 million in salary from the Patriots, plus more than $100 million from endorsements, memorabilia, and licensing before moving on to another Super Bowl championship with the Tampa Bay Buccaneers in 2021. Tom Brady did not inherit wealth from his parents, but he did inherit something much better – *values*. Running home from church each Sunday, working on his grandfather's farm in Minnesota and learning the drive to be competitive and the discipline to be healthy.

Serena Williams did not come from a "wealthy" family, but she has leveraged her amazing skills, work ethic, and determination to earn almost $95 million in prize money throughout her career. Together with earnings from her numerous endorsements, Williams has applied her knowledge of investing to grow her wealth to over $240 million. Those are the behavioral determinants to earning high income, much more than capital to which Piketty ascribes so much importance in his books.

CEOs usually earn much higher income than most workers in the corporation – a major contribution to "inequality" – but CEO jobs in major corporations are not inherited. Piketty's analysis focuses on current income, not how incomes change based on the kind of jobs pursued with the values you read about in the previous chapter.

You can look at the EDGAR data base of the SEC and discover the income (many millions) of the CEO at the world's largest corporation (Walmart). That is the same type of IRS data used by Piketty. EDGAR does not disclose, however, that Doug McMillon's "starting income" 30 years earlier was the minimum wage of a warehouse worker at age 17 or that decades later he had earned an undergraduate degree at the University of Arkansas and an MBA from the University of Tulsa. Moving from poor to prosperous is a solution to the "problem" of inequality but it is more likely to happen from accumulating parental *values* and an MBA than from inherited wealth.

In almost any career path, including engineers, physicians, lawyers, plumbers, painters and welders, a healthy economy will provide opportunities to leverage your skill to create additional value. Small businesses created by highly skilled entrepreneurs can be grown into prosperous businesses by people in any field that is valued by consumers. Achieving wealth is not just about inherited capital, it's about value creation.

So where does this misunderstanding come from? Piketty acknowledges an intellectual debt to British economist David Ricardo who believed wealth is based on scarcity. In Ricardo's time, capital was mostly land and the income from it was "rent." That is why some countries prospered, as you read in Chapter 5. In nations such as France, Britain and other European nations income and wealth were mostly from the economic resource described as land.

However, countries like the Netherlands accumulated wealth differently even with a lack of land. In the latter years of the 1800s and through most of the twentieth century, capital (physical assets and ownership of firms) replaced land as the scarce resource. The value of capital increased, and increasing return on capital, according to Piketty, is the reason for inequality.

The key is that in the current century and the future, capital is no longer the scarce resource. In fact, capital has become so abundant that people with large amounts of capital have difficulty finding investments to invest in for a high return. Softbank, a company founded by Masayoshi Son, Japan's richest person, has invested in a variety of technology firms, some which are bleeding losses in its 100 billion dollar Vision Fund. Accumulated capital produces high returns in today's century only if it is accompanied by skilled humans running firms (the investments).

That did not work out so well with Adam Neumann, ousted CEO of WeWork, one of Softbank's major investments of capital, creating billions in losses. Talk with equity fund leaders and venture capitalists and you quickly learn that the scarce resource is human knowledge, skill, and creativity. Karl Marx believed wealth should be determined entirely by labor, not capital, and in an ironic twist of fate, Marx foresaw what is happening today as "labor" has replaced capital as the source of high income. However, it is not the same type of labor that Marx envisioned. Instead of simple farmers and factory workers, the "labor" with the highest payoff today includes physicians, engineers, programming experts, authors such as Piketty and Sanders, athletes such as Tom Brady and Serena Williams, and celebrities such as Kylie Jenner and Rihanna.

The above is not to say that capital is unimportant in determining prosperity. The most prudent of workers – whether high income or low – also use their income to accumulate capital through their savings. Some countries such as Singapore and Estonia recognize the importance of savings from income by mandating citizens save a significant share of their income, placing it into accounts to protect their income in the future.

It is no coincidence that both Singapore and Estonia, where citizens save at high rates, have been high in total and per capita growth in their economies. The benefit from savings is also the reason for so much attention on Roth IRAs and other methods of converting income to capital as you read in previous chapters of this book. The key is that high income can be earned through labor, and that resulting income can be used to obtain valuable assets. These assets can then be combined with income to propel people into the highest levels of prosperity.

Poverty Versus Mobility

An especially important consideration for inequality is mobility. Even if the top 1 percent and other high-income categories of workers are receiving a higher proportion of total income, it is not always the same people. Low-income people move up (in large numbers) and high-income earners frequently fall out of upper income groups.

About 12% of the U.S. population will rank in the top 1% for at least one year; 39% in the top 5% for at least a year; 56% in the top 10%; and 73% in the top 20%. At the same time only about 0.6% of people stay in the top 1% for 10 consecutive years. Half of Americans who earned more than $1 million in any year between 1999 and 2007 did so only once. Just 6% did so all nine years. ("Who Wants to be a Millionaire" WSJ, April 16, 2019)

Further evidence can be found in the study of where billionaires come from. Data from *Forbes* shows that 84% of the most recent new billionaires in the world are self-made. Over time, the increasing amount of mobility into the highest tiers of wealth has led to the total number of self-made billionaires being around 72% globally. To any objective analyst, this clearly indicates that inherited assets are not the driver of extreme wealth.

Note that once wealth is achieved, it doesn't last forever either. Studies show that roughly 90 percent of wealthy families ($5 million or more) exhaust their estates within three generations. The rate of return on capital may be increasing, but not as fast as the ability to spend it by children and grandchildren. This is a fundamental flaw in Piketty's data and ultimately in his policy recommendations, as people currently in the highest income brackets are not the same people as decades earlier.

Some people are surprised to learn that the nation with the fastest growth in ultra-rich individuals (assets more than $5 million) in recent years was Bangladesh with an average increase of 14.3 % per year between 2010 and 2019 according to Wealth-X. Nations with faster growth than the U.S. in ultra-rich families in those years include Vietnam (+13.9%), China (+13.5%), Kenya, Philippines, Thailand, and New Zealand.

In short, the people earning high incomes today are different people than in the past, and this is because of the mobility afforded by labor (or human capital) that creates value for others, not financial capital or assets. To his credit, Piketty admits this mistake in a footnote on page 25 of his more recent book *Capital and Ideology* but fails to correct the data in the rest of the book.

When human capital replaces nonhuman capital as the path to prosperity, how can a person born to a family in the lower tier of income be a winner in the scarce resource of human abilities and skills? Chapter 4 gave you some ideas for that, hopefully, and education of one type or another plays a key role.

Education: Key Attribute of Human Capital

Education is a major path to closing the gap between the poor and the prosperous. "But poor people can't afford education," is often the complaint of those who seek to eliminate inequality. That objection ignores the reality that education does not have to be expensive. Diligence and tenacity are more important than money for people motivated to attend college, university, or trade school. As discussed in Chapter 6, having parents who teach their children the importance of education is a better path to prosperity than inheriting wealth from them.

People sometimes believe a lot of money is required to obtain a college education. It sometimes does, but it does not have to. People who do not plan well or who make poor decisions about which college to attend pay a lot more than they need to get an excellent education. Tuitions at colleges and universities vary from under $1,000 dollars a year (or zero tuition with the right scholarships) to nearly $100,000 per year. Look for schools with lowest in-state tuition and you will probably see several less than $1,000 a year. You can obtain free online courses from many schools. Websites such as edx.org allow you to access more than 2,500 courses from schools such as Harvard and MIT.

Even at major state universities, it is possible for students from low-income families to receive a Tiffany degree at a Walmart price. At some schools, any student who qualifies for a federally funded Pell Grant also qualifies for a donor-funded grant from the university that assures the student does not have to graduate with student debt. Pell grants, unlike loans, do not have to be repaid.

There is no minimum GPA required to receive the Pell Grant, though a student can lose funding by not maintaining what a specific institution defines as satisfactory academic progress. Typically, this status requires students to earn, at minimum, a 2.0 GPA. Parents may affect motivation to attend educational institutions, but *personal determination* determines who graduates – a behavioral reality to which college faculty can attest.

Other paths include identifying an employer that supports education. The Starbucks College Achievement Plan partners with Arizona State University to offer eligible applicants full tuition benefits through a tuition reimbursement program. If you work for Starbucks for a few years, living at home and studying online, you receive the same knowledge and a degree from a major university as students whose parents pay thousands of dollars for expensive university degrees. But you must work for it. Walmart, McDonald's, Arby's, and an increasing number of firms are adding payment of college tuition as a benefit for working in those firms.

Many students who work part-time or full-time while attending college finish their degree debt-free with no assistance from parents. Some students take ten or more years to complete their education because of their belief in "The difficult we do immediately, the impossible takes a little longer." There are many examples of people who work for years while obtaining an undergraduate degree and later return to school to earn a Ph.D. or professional degree allowing them to increase their income potential even more.

Another benefit is that if you work while in college, you are likely to be more attractive to employers than a student with a 4.0 GPA and no work experience. Employers typically look for "jugglers" – students who know how "to keep a lot of balls in the air at the same time." Recruiters usually give preference to students who have significant work experience without sacrificing grades and campus leadership activities. Once again, determination and delayed gratification are attributes of prosperous people.

Others earn their education through on-the-job training, working for others to hone their skills before launching into their own businesses. Studies indicate that entrepreneurs who start their business after age forty are more likely to succeed than people starting firms in their twenties. Sam Walton was 45 when he opened a small store in Rogers, Arkansas with only the capital he and his wife accumulated as employees, eventually propelling it to become the world's largest corporation and the world's richest family.

Even if you attend a college where the tuition is $10,000 a year, you choose whether to pay $30,000 or $40,000 for your degree because you can usually complete a degree in three years (and sometimes less). All you need to do is take appropriate AP courses in high school, take one extra course per semester (and most schools do not charge extra for that) and be careful about changing majors. That takes planning, of course, but as the saying goes: people who fail to plan, should plan to fail. Note however, paying for three years of college instead of four comes with a warning. If you choose three years to receive a four-year degree, you may not become as proficient at beer pong and other campus diversions!

Beneficial networking is an advantage of prestige schools, but the content taught at expensive schools is not fundamentally different than at inexpensive schools. Attending an expensive university is much like buying a Mercedes, Porsche, or McLaren. If you or your parents want a $200,000 McLaren and have plenty of money not needed for other expenses, it is fine to buy one. But a Ford or Chevrolet will get you to the same place for much less money.

Sometimes individuals who have achieved privilege recognize a responsibility to help those who have not. One example is Pete Kadens, a successful entrepreneur from Toledo, Ohio who pledged in 2020 to pay college tuition, room, board, and fees for Scott High School seniors graduating that year who want to attend a university or trade school. Scott High School is in an area of the city where most students are from low-income minority neighborhoods.

Mr. Kadens said he would also extend the same offer to one parent or legal guardian of each graduating student. Regardless of whether Mr. Kadens' actions were "rational" they certainly provide an example for behavioral economists to consider. While many people will complain about a problem, successful people frequently have the interest and means to take personal responsibility for helping to solve the problem.

A study conducted by Pew Charitable Trusts found that the bottom quintile of income is 57% likely to experience upward mobility and only 7% to experience downward mobility. Perseverance, the determination to obtain education, delayed gratification, and other values are more important than money from parents. Poor students who succeed are those who learn that where there is a will, there is a way. Of course, a key here is the role of a student's environment.

Another behavioral reality is that family stability having two parents engaged during childhood is one of the clearest predictors of prosperity. An ongoing study by Princeton University Professor Sara McLanahan, herself a single parent for a decade, studies the fragility of families and its effects on children. Issues involving stability of the home and the parenting resources of two people working to raise children are key factors in childhood development. Unfortunately, having only one or no parents present in childhood is one of the most reliable predictors of poverty as an adult. Psychology and sociology offer some solutions to that problem, typically involving how *values* shape choices and where those values can come from (e.g., mentors).

In addition to difficulties from family structure, another significant problem in seeking education are the disparities across school districts around the world. Access to a good education in grade school is critical for future success. If you are concerned about income equality, look for ways to encourage family stability and equal opportunity to education, primary, secondary, and beyond. Equal opportunity to income may include schools teaching truck driving, nanotechnology, or biomedical statistics as much as liberal arts. And highest earners may get degrees from the University of Tulsa as well as Harvard. That is part of what McCloskey calls "equality of inputs" as essential ingredients for prosperous economies in *Bourgeois Equality*.

What is Happening to the Middle Class?

Is the middle class shrinking in the U.S.? Yes, is the correct answer. However, the next question is equally important: to *where* is it shrinking?

The answer is the middle class is shrinking because some of its members are moving to the upper income categories and some members are moving lower. Fortunately, the number moving higher is about twice the number moving lower. About forty percent stay in the middle class over the decades. It would certainly be nice if no one moved down, but they do because of a variety of life's exigencies as well as events in the environment in which they live. This can also happen because of poor decisions. In other words, people are not always rational optimizers like traditional economic models frequently assume. Average income for all classes increases over time, but that provides little comfort for those moving to the lower income groups or those whose income remains the same.

According to the Pew Research, the size of the middle class in the United States decreased from 61% of the population in 1971 to 51% in 2011 but has remained steady through the subsequent years. During this same period, the size of the lower class grew from 25% to 29%, and the upper class grew from 14% to 20%.

The data shows that the size of the lower class grew significantly until 2011, but so did the upper class (and by a larger percentage). It should also be noted that even though the poor decreased in the proportion of income they earned, annual income in absolute terms increased throughout the period and beyond. As a proportion of the wealth of high-earners, income has decreased for the poor, but in absolute amounts, income increased for most (but not all) of them. It should also be noted that the increase in the average income for the lower class has exceeded inflation (income has increased faster than prices).

In an ironic twist, the possibility of reaching the rich and the upper middle class can provide motivation needed to move from poor to prosperous. This may even be one of the reasons you are reading this book. One of the common learnings across economics is that people tend to respond to *incentives*. The values that create prosperity should be rewarded if they are to be reinforced, a basic principle documented by hundreds of learning experiments in behavioral psychology.

If income were redistributed from the rich to the poor in wealth transfers as traditional economics (and Piketty) would suggest, the problem of poverty is unlikely to be solved any more than giving fish to hungry people instead of teaching them how to fish. They will be hungry again the next day. The same principle applies to modern jobs. Without the knowledge of how to become prosperous, simply distributing income to the poor from the prosperous does not solve the problem of the poor in the future. Solutions must consider behavior!

The solutions to inequality are behavioral answers, not the overly simple answers from traditional economics. The good news is that inflation-adjusted income of people in the lower income categories is increasing. However, the rule in this book is "Just the facts" and the bad news is that there is a significant percentage of people in the lower income class and they are "losing ground" as the income of the upper class has grown even faster.

The poor still exist in every country and quite possibly always will, but that does not mean people in that category have to stay there. The imperative for public policy is how to encourage and help people to qualify for higher paying jobs so that they can build their wealth. The imperative for individual workers is to obtain knowledge and diligence to qualify for higher paying jobs and to use the resulting income wisely. Believing in equality should focus on equality of inputs, to use the term from McCloskey's books, providing opportunity for upward mobility.

Opportunity for upward mobility is also an attribute essential to improving the total economy, as you will read in Chapter 9. Equal access to inputs, and recognizing the reality of inequality in outputs, is the answer to questions about inequality. As Winston Churchill observed, you cannot make poor people prosperous by making prosperous people poor.

Generating High-Income Jobs

How do you create good-paying jobs? That is an essential question to ask anyone concerned about inequality. An answer that sometimes surprises people is *billionaires*. Say that to some people seeking political office and you may cause a heart attack. But objective analysis of data about billionaires is far more important than opinions or political slogans.

A college dropout who learned how to write computer code as a high school student started a company in Seattle that changed the world. That person was Bill Gates and his mind, not his wealth created a firm with jobs for 150,000 well-paid workers, the majority (60%) in the U.S. His mind and skills made Bill Gates rich, but his abilities also made millionaires out of 12,000 Microsoft employees and several of them billionaires themselves.

What happens to average employees when entrepreneurs become billionaires? That is an important question. The answer is that Microsoft Corp in 2020 paid its employees an average of $119,069 a year. The "labor" that used to be found in factories making physical products is now found in factories making software and clouds, causing the middle class to shrink – to upper middle income.

Another Seattle billionaire is Jeff Bezos. He did not have capital to start Amazon, so he put together a business plan seeking $50,000 investments from 20 of his friends to raise the $1 million needed to implement his plan for a new type of retailer of online books. Bezos was honest, telling them there was a 70% chance it would fail but his mother and his Cuban-born father were among the first willing to take the chance he would succeed. In 2018, Amazon was one of the first firms to raise its minimum starting pay to $15 per hour, but its average across all jobs currently is $102,060 a year. Today, Amazon has over 1,000 of its employees with stock in the company worth over $5 million, according to the New York *Times*.

And what happened to that early investment in Amazon by Miguel Angel Bezos, who adopted Jeff at age 4? Miguel immigrated to the U.S. from Cuba at age 16 to escape Castro's struggling economy. He did not know English when he landed in a Miami refugee camp that prepared him to enter a U.S. high school. If Miguel kept all his stock he bought on the strength of Jeff's vision for the future, that stock today would be valued at $30 billion, an example that helping your son learn the *values of determination and optimism* can pay off in later years. However, Jackie and "Mike" Bezos have not kept all that stock. They did what many billionaires do and gave much of it to charities to help people who started like him but have not reached the same plateau of wealth – yet.

The great irony in analyzing inequality is that more people rising to the top increases the opportunities for poor people at the bottom and people in the middle as well. High income people hire the jobless and pay higher and higher wages to those who are highly skilled to build, decorate, and maintain their homes, and much more. Some immigrants to the U.S. adopt young children and inculcate values of hard work and optimism that help both kids and parents improve their economic status.

The ironic inequality paradox is that the inevitable consequence of increased upward mobility is increased inequality, and the inevitable consequence of increased equality is decreased mobility. Take your choice but understand how good jobs are created – by solving problems for other people. "Doing well by doing good," as the lyrics of a folk song by Tom Lehrer once proclaimed.

Learning from Billionaires

How do executives achieve the high corporate incomes usually disparaged by critics of inequality? An exemplary, but not unusual, answer is illustrated by the story of James Hartigan, former CEO of United Airlines. According to his 2020 obituary in the Wall Street *Journal*, Hartigan was 12 when his father died. The second of 10 children, he had a new mission – supporting his family. While finishing school, he delivered newspapers, worked at a bakery and a drugstore, and occasionally won cash prizes in bicycle races. "My earliest management experience was helping my mother," he told the Chicago *Tribune* in 1985.

His career started as a junior passenger agent and progressed to executive offices. Among other things, he helped develop United's first computerized reservation system and later was instrumental in acquiring routes across the Pacific that created thousands of good jobs at United Airlines. Yes, IRS data report him as one of the top 1%, Piketty laments, ignoring his role in creating thousands of jobs for baggage handlers and passenger agents, producing income for shareholders (which include employees in their 401K and pension funds) and growing the U.S. economy. Did he help or hurt the baggage handlers whose jobs he created and passenger agents which he originated?

In passing, did you recognize the name of David Steward in the previous chapter? Growing up in the small town of Clinton, Missouri (population 9,000), he faced poverty and discrimination, but learned values from poor but hard-working parents. He was motivated to obtain a business degree at nearby Central Missouri State University, a school offering both affordability and excellent education. Graduating when the nation was in a recession, with his family unable to help financially, and with all his possessions in a knapsack, Steward hitchhiked to St. Louis, moved in with his sister. He worked part-time as a substitute teacher until he landed a position with the Boy Scouts of America.

He was offered a marketing and sales position with the Missouri Pacific Railroad Company, the first time the Railroad employed a person of color to sell rail services. Later he joined Federal Express where he learned skills convincing him he could start his own company, making the bold decision to venture out on his own as a young married father of two with little money and a mortgage to pay. Carving out a niche and leveraging his transportation experience, Steward founded World Wide Technology (WWT) which today has revenues over $10 billion, one of the largest private companies in the U.S. and named to the 100 Best Places to Work by *Fortune* for five consecutive years. By now, you probably have put his name in your browser and realize his $4 billion net worth makes him the second richest African American entrepreneur in the U.S.

The data show that Piketty was wrong. It is not financial assets that creates or overcomes inequality. It is human capital, clearly observed in people such as David Steward. Of course, none of this is to say that poverty should not be addressed. Are there solutions to the problems of poverty and discrimination? Yes, and you will find empirically supported answers in books by Mr. Steward, *Doing Business by the Good Book,* and *Leadership by the Good Book.*

Solutions to poverty and discrimination do not require you to wait for government action. You may wonder if there are practical examples that improve outcomes for people with special needs. One such example is LifeTown at the Schottenstein Chabad Center in New Albany, Ohio.

Founded by Rabbi Areyah Kaltman and his wife Esther Kaltman, LifeTown provides services to overcome the inequality of opportunity that exists among children with special needs, equipping them to have better chances for equality as adults. The realistic simulation of life experiences is based on the philosophy that young people, including special needs children, learn best by doing, with role playing and other experiences to learn critical life skills (jobs, banking, mobility, literacy, etc.), and allowing them to learn from mistakes in a safe environment. Staffed by volunteers and funded by generous donors, LifeTown demonstrates that some people light a candle on the pathway to a brighter future in contrast to people who are content to curse the darkness of inequality.

Keys to Prosperity

How a Caring Community Develops Life Skills at LifeTown

LifeTown is a 5,000-square-foot indoor, functioning city designed specifically for children and teens with special needs. Through simulated activities with dozens of specially trained volunteers, students build confidence while learning important life skills, including fiscal responsibility, time management, technology, and socialization.

At LifeTown's campus, sections include a bank, medical and dental clinic, pet store, library, movie theater, restaurant, art supply store, and workshop. LifeTown serves more than 5,600 students per year from 20 school districts in seven counties. It also offers a mentor program matching more than 100 area volunteers with older, mildly disabled students who are preparing to enter the workforce. Unlike the real world, there is no hurry and skills can be practiced in a safe, nurturing environment.

Teachers select each student's LifeTown lessons based on needs addressed in the student's individual education plan. They choose a cohesive, evidence-based model designed to improve competencies in the three transitional areas: personal/social, independent living, and pre-employment.

The program provides financial wellness education that includes education on identity protection, credit scores, interest rates, and using bill payment systems to repay credit card installments, concepts critical for managing finances.

LifeTown is an outreach of The Lori Schottenstein Chabad Center, representing the type of "caring for" and "caring about" described throughout this book. It is an example of what people do instead of relying on government to provide such programs. Do you have something similar in your community where you can volunteer? If not, perhaps you will be the one to start such a program.

One of the most important books written on how to lift people out of poverty is by Clayton M. Christensen, Efosa Ojomo, and Karen Dillon, *The Prosperity Paradox,* documenting the importance of innovation in creating prosperity. The paradox, however, is that innovation occurs most often when individuals have opportunity for upward mobility. Inequality provides incentives and opportunity for upward mobility. It is ironic in the minds of many people, and certainly a paradox, but true that inequality motivates people out of poverty into higher levels of prosperity. This controversial reality is a topic for Chapter 9.

You have been bombarded with a lot of information in this chapter and perhaps some ideas from behavioral science different than traditional opinions you have heard about how to help the poor. The next time people in politics or the media say to you what is good or bad about inequality, remember to confront them with the *Dragnet* approach, "Just the facts, Ma'am or Sir. Just the facts."

Discussion Questions

- Consider what situations might exist where some amount of inequality between two people would be acceptable? In what situations would you find some amount of inequality to be unacceptable?
- The argument of the text is that inequality is irrelevant if everyone has equal access to opportunities to become prosperous. This is because inequality then becomes a choice over people's preferences for leisure, risk, and work hours. However, many opportunities do not afford equal access to everyone. What opportunities in your own life were more difficult to access for you than for others? How might this be improved?
- If someone asks you how to get an education that would help them be prosperous even though they have little money nor parents able to pay for the education, what advice would you give to that person?
- Inequality certainly exists for those with disabilities. What can a nation or your local community do to assist people with physical and other disabilities to achieve a prosperous life? What is your personal involvement in accomplishing this objective?

Chapter 8

Unintended Consequences of

Well-Intentioned Policies

For any person, life is full of decisions. Often these decisions are made to solve a problem or to seek out increased happiness and prosperity. The policy decisions of a nation are typically well-motivated to achieve the same purposes. Consider the last "big decision" you made in your life and consider the following question:

Were there consequences from that decision that you did not anticipate?

Whether big or small, most decisions come with consequences that were not anticipated. These consequences could be positive or negative but should always be considered when making a decision. Objective application of behavioral economics can often help in identifying unintended and unwanted consequences before they become reality. Considering unintended positive consequences is also an important part of the cost-benefit analysis of an action or policy. As you read through the examples in this chapter, perhaps you can identify additional positive or negative unintended consequences with respect to the provided examples.

Behavioral economics, at its core, seeks to describe what happens in the real world when the simplifying assumptions from traditional economic theory fail to describe what is observed. Behavioral economics is therefore a primary tool in objective analysis of prosperity, as the goal is to go beyond simple "established principles" to understand the practical causes and effects of economic *behavior*.

One reason that behavioral economics sometimes provides different predictions and solutions than traditional economic models is because humans are quite different. These differences are not only among humans, but across contexts. In short, people make different judgements based on personality and cognitive style, idiosyncratic variations in the weighting of variables, and factors that may even change how the same person responds in seemingly identical situations.

Among researchers accustomed to designing and interpreting research, this is often referred to as "noise" in results. Fundamental causes of noise and ways to deal with the problem is the central theme of the latest book by Behavioral Economics pioneers Daniel Kahneman, Olivier Sibony and Cass R. Sunstein, *Noise: A Flaw in Human Judgment*.

As you read this chapter, it may remind you of some television ads for pharmaceutical companies who present a narrative about the benefits their products offer for skin problems, cholesterol, depression, or a myriad of other maladies. In the latter part of their ad, they also present the possible side effects or unintended consequences of their products. Those warnings are included because the Federal Trade Commission (FTC) requires companies do that. Sometimes the side effects are very discouraging.

The same process happens with social policies advocated by well-intentioned individuals, but the FTC does not require warnings about the side effects of social and political policies. Objective analysis of how people respond to different situations allows careful consideration of consequences that may be unintended. In other words, people may respond in unintended ways, but this is often predictable. Discussing the "noise" of unintended consequences does not mean the policy should not be adopted, but it does highlight the need for thoughtful consideration of potentially bad outcomes and how to prevent them.

Lessons From Finance

As an example of insights from behavioral finance, consider the value of a share in a public company. Behavioral insights are sometimes different than conventional analyses of share value. In an established public corporation, share value has traditionally been expected to be 15 to 17 times its earnings per share (EPS), commonly reported as Price to Earnings (PE) ratio. That typical PE ratio has built-in assumptions of a reliable record of dividends and modest but not high growth expectations for the future.

Experienced investors call that the intrinsic value of a stock. The actual price in the marketplace is often different, explained by behavioral variables more than financial results alone. If enough people believe growth will be higher than normal, the PE will be higher than normal, sometimes much higher based on psychological beliefs in the marketplace.

One extreme example of the difference between traditional finance and behavioral finance can be observed in the stock of Zoom (ZM) at the beginning of the Coronavirus pandemic. In the latter part of 2019, the stock was selling for $60, even though its earnings were only .08 per share, reflecting an extraordinarily high PE even then. Only a few months after the effects of stay-at-home orders from the 2020 pandemic, the stock "zoomed" even higher to nearly $500, with a PE measured in the thousands instead of the typical ratios for high-growth stocks. The explanation is not based on historical financial numbers but psychological expectations of future performance.

Stocks with high PE ratios are called growth or momentum stocks although normally they do not typically reach ratios as high as Zoom. If you are psychologically an extreme risk-taker, you might buy such stocks hoping to ride the momentum and jump out before a reversal. However, if you are a Warren Buffet-type of investor you look for stocks that are selling below their intrinsic value (usually with normal or low PE ratios) and buy them for the long-term growth and dividends – what Buffet calls "forever stocks."

When you study the stock market realistically, through the lens of behavioral finance, you soon realize that the price of a stock is a combination of both economic and behavioral (psychological) factors. You have probably heard the advice of Warren Buffet, "When the market is greedy, be fearful. When the market is fearful, be greedy." It is a strategy that works well for Buffet and others who heed his advice.

The intrinsic value of a stock is based on its past and projected earnings but the actual or market price is sometimes determined by unintended consequences, behavioral in nature. When something unpredicted happens, stocks with very high PE ratios often plummet. Even well-thought-out and well-intentioned strategies can be upended by an unanticipated event, sometimes called a black swan event. Hence, it is even more important to carefully consider possible unintended consequences of a strategy.

The same caution that may help you prosper in the stock market applies to many other areas of life. When you hear someone expressing an opinion about a well-intentioned social policy, the cautious approach is to say the same thing attributed to the laconic Sgt. Friday on *Dragnet*, "Just the facts." When people offer opinions about why you should vote for someone in favor of a well-intentioned policy, do not let the conversation end without asking, "And what might be unintended consequences of that policy?" Because, for every good idea, there will be unintended consequences. Sometimes, it is called the Law of Unintended Consequences.

Even Great Ideas Have Consequences

Think about the Interstate Highway System, possibly one of the best ventures the government has ever undertaken. It cost $billions, was well-motivated, and one of the most beneficial infrastructure projects the government has accomplished. The list of the positives for the interstate highway system is certainly long, and while it is hard to know the entire list of intended consequences, it is unlikely that the Eisenhower administration considered the benefits of this system on the ease of interstate travel using self-driving cars in the future. Regardless, an eye toward the future would certainly have provided additional support for the construction of interstate highways.

It seemed a promising idea to build Interstate highways through the middle of major cities so that downtowns would not lose the business from the previous patchwork of local highways. One (possibly unintended) consequence often was to divide cities in ways that segregated cities by race and income. This happened in many cities including Columbus, Ohio with the consequence of segregating predominantly African-American areas from the prosperous downtown area.

Keys to Prosperity

How Can a Highway Be Racist?

While at first glance it may seem silly to some to believe that the placement of highways was racist,

148

closer inspection reveals this is almost certainly the case. The National Highway Act was passed in 1956 during the time in which the United States was reforming away from segregated schools but also while Jim Crow Laws were still in effect. During this racially charged period, many individuals with overtly racist views were still in leadership positions around the country. Moreover, a simple consideration of behavior would suggest that these individuals would be highly motivated to use their power to continue the segregation of communities via placement of the highways within their communities.

Even if the placement of the highways was not deliberately done to segregate and/or harm minorities, the placement of the highways most certainly had this effect. Government officials sought lower valued properties, which due to segregation, red lining, and other racist policies, disproportionally affected minority communities. Other leaders even saw the placement of public works as a solution to "fixing" neighborhoods they deemed as undesirable. For example, John Moses, who oversaw public works in New York City during this time, mentioned in a 1956 speech "Our categorical imperative is action to clear the slums." Regardless of how the decision was made, the placement of the highway system tended to destroy and encircle minority communities.

This highlights an important point about diversity in leadership. When decisions are made it is possible that the unintended adverse effects of some actions may not be fully understood by everyone in the room. This explains why diversity is so critical, as the inclusion of different perspectives and experiences can prevent managers and firms from making such mistakes. History has shown that the most successful business leaders are those that can understand how their coworkers and customers will be affected by their decisions. Therefore, improving the diversity of leadership in an organization is not just a matter of principle, it is directly tied to your own ability to maximize prosperity in your decisions.

If the unintended consequences were considered in the formation of the interstate system, the interstate highways could have been placed in locations that did not divide downtowns by income and racial patterns. A different location of the freeways might also have removed affluent citizens' ability to avoid passing through impoverished areas of the city without closely observing them. Considering the unintended consequence might even have created alternative arterial streets that could have avoided stalled traffic on interstates during peak commuting hours, an unintended consequence observable in many cities. The reason for asking proponents of a policy about unintended consequences is because they almost ALWAYS happen.

For every difficult problem, there is usually a simple solution – and it is usually a bad one. Complex problems typically require complex solutions, but you will rarely see complex solutions offered by political pundits and TV personalities. An objective approach to identifying solutions requires consideration of human behavior, and behavior is complex. Therefore, considering the unintended and potentially harmful side effects of social policies is as important for social policies as it is for the FDA when approving new medicines and carefully considering potential negative side effects.

Considering the unintended side effects might lead to avoiding them. Solutions to important social issues need facts not only about the desired outcomes, but facts about and analysis of the unintended consequences. When consumers decide who to vote for, rather than listening only to opinions of one political party or another, improved results are more likely to occur from listening to data – carefully analyzed evidence about behavioral issues. When evaluating social policies, regardless of how well-intentioned the motives, informed voters should always insist, "Show Me the Data!"

In the book *The Logic of Social Inquiry,* Professor Scott Greer shows how to analyze these problems, advocating policy decisions be made *on facts and logic rather than desires and opinions*. When evaluating social policies, Professor Greer explains, decisions should be based on *value-free analysis of empirically derived evidence*. Using those criteria, in the following pages you will see some of the questions that might be raised about unintended consequences of topics affecting many areas of economic and daily life.

Is Anyone Anti-Antibiotics?

The widespread use of antibiotics has led to an example of unintended consequences called superbugs. In 1900, pneumonia and related diseases were the number one cause of death. When Penicillin was introduced in 1928, it was called a miracle drug. Antibiotics were so effective against these bacterial infections that today, these same diseases are barely among the top 10 causes of death. It is hard to argue that antibiotics are anything but a marvel of medicine.

With that said, the behavioral consequences of antibiotics were fairly predictable. Since antibiotics can quickly clear up a bacterial infection, and human beings do not enjoy being ill, the demand for antibiotics from sick people has grown rapidly. This includes people pressuring doctors to prescribe antibiotics whenever they had a cold. Some people want antibiotics before dental cleanings. Antibiotics are also given to livestock to prevent disease and to promote growth. The resulting unintended consequence of the predictable overuse of antibiotics was the eventual adaptation and spread of some strains of bacteria highly resistant to most types of antibiotics.

Each year these drug-resistant superbugs infect more than 2 million people nationwide and kill at least 23,000, according to the CDC. Drug-resistant forms of tuberculosis, gonorrhea, and staph infections are just a few of the dangers now faced as the unintended consequence of one of the most common drugs on the planet. Britain's Health Secretary, Matt Hancock, recently stated that these superbugs are as big an existential threat to humankind as global warming and warfare.

Naturally, it would be foolish to say that antibiotics should not have been introduced. The benefits of antibiotics are critically important. However, the overuse of antibiotics and the subsequent growth of resistant bacteria was a predictable outcome. These dangerous superbugs may have been avoided if the potential unintended consequences had been considered during their widespread adoption, accompanied with education and research to prevent overuse.

Free College Tuition

Consider the importance of education in identifying a path to prosperity, and the statement: "Free tuition for college students is a great idea. I would vote for that." Research on advertising effectiveness found the single most effective word attracting attention to ads is the word "free." Whether selling cars, computers, or clothing, no word sells a wide range of products as effectively as an offer of something for "free." Apparently, campaign managers for politicians are aware of that advertising research.

The motivation for free tuition is admirable. As discussed earlier in this book, the benefits of education and the subsequent valuable skillsets received can be a great strategy for moving from poor to prosperous. Most would agree with the importance of college education, even when people question how to pay for it, and free tuition would certainly remove a significant impediment that some people face when considering college. However, any debate about its merits should also raise issues about potential unintended negative consequences, such as effects on existing colleges and universities.

Increased pressure to attend the most prestigious public institutions would make those universities so competitive that students from high schools with lower abilities to prepare students for college would probably lose out in the admission race at highly competitive universities.

Free tuition to public universities may be welcomed by the parents of middle and upper-income families but could generate the unintended consequence of making it more difficult for students from high schools in lower-income districts to gain admission, probably not the social policy desired by people concerned with the inequality you read about in the last chapter. Moreover, parents with higher incomes can always pay for additional training programs and test preparation that could further stack the deck against lower-income students.

What effect would free tuition at public universities have on private colleges and universities? Given the choice of paying $40-50,000 (or more) at private colleges across America, or free tuition at hundreds of state universities, what would be the choices of millions of future college consumers? Well-endowed, prestigious institutions might not be affected much but for the rest, a new chapter would be written. For many private colleges and universities, that chapter would be Chapter 11.

Studies at Harvard Business School report about half of small, poorly endowed liberal arts colleges are struggling for survival now. If free tuition is enacted as public policy, say "Goodbye" to most of the smaller private schools, and with them, students could say goodbye to the myriad choices in specialty, location, and experience offered by those institutions. "It was not our intention to eliminate private colleges," might be the response of those who advocate free tuition, but likely would be the unintended consequence.

A behavioral element to consider would be student motivation and incentives. As it stands, students that are paying for college have a strong incentive to consider what skills they gain from their degree and how they might create value in the future. While free college education may open more opportunities for students to invest time in studies of other subjects, the reality is that valuable skills are what drive prosperity. If students are not incentivized to seek valuable skills, the resulting education is unlikely to provide a path to prosperity even if it is free.

Another potential behavioral result is that students who pay for college have incentives to work through challenges and finish their degrees to earn higher wages. However, when the students incur no cost to attending college, they lose little or nothing if they walk away. This could have disastrous results for retention and efficiency for college education, as it could lead to a significant drop in the percentage of students that finish their degree.

Perhaps an alternative social policy would be free tuition at all schools, not just public institutions. The unintended behavioral result then would be to shift many students from public to more expensive private institutions. This would further compound the problems detailed above, eliminating the incentive and critical need that currently exists for efficiency and productivity in higher education, not to mention the extreme increase in the cost of such a policy. Probably not the intended consequence of these well-intentioned policies.

Given these considerations, you might expect to see high enrollment rates in countries offering tuition-free college, such as Denmark, Sweden, and Norway. However, the rate at which people obtain higher education is lower in Denmark and Sweden than it is in the United States. A major reason for this lack of college enrollment is the low return on investment from university education. Based on recent numbers, students in America can expect a 65 percent increase in earnings after obtaining post-secondary education

In Denmark, Norway, and Sweden, this earnings boost is much lower. In Denmark, workers with a vocational, educational training degree (VET) earn about $70,798 USD on average a year according to Statistica, compared to $82,620 with a bachelor's degree. Workers with graduate degrees earn more, with a Ph.D. averaging $113,976. Even with free tuition, the costs of living, fees and other expenses are so high that 70 percent of Swedish students still take out loans to attend a university.

From a behavioral perspective, it makes sense that prospective students would be less inclined to pursue a university education if the benefits are significantly reduced. More importantly, application of economic theory predicts that as the number of college degrees grows rapidly, the salary expectations for a college degree are likely to decline (supply and demand). While this decline would then tend to bring balance by decreasing the number of students pursuing a degree, the decline in the value of a college education is an unintended consequence evident in other countries that have enacted such policies.

As you saw in earlier chapters of this book, there are alternatives to paying high tuitions at expensive universities where students can acquire valuable skills that can lead to prosperity. Free tuition might also be a disincentive to gaining work experience that adds to both knowledge and employability of students. Moreover, it may draw people away from trades and other high-valued skill development. This is not to say that solutions could not be implemented to assist students in acquiring an education, but the takeaway here is that reasonable solutions must include a comprehensive discussion of how the unintended consequences will be managed. Clearly, there must be far more to such a policy than simply "free" education.

Forgiving Student Debt

An accumulation of high student debt is a similar problem facing many graduates of undergraduate as well as graduate, professional and specialized schools. The solution suggested by many is for lenders to forgive debts incurred by students. There is considerable appeal to such a well-motivated policy, at least among those who incurred great debt.

The unanswered question is who pays the lender the forgiven amounts of debt? If the debt is government based, there would be support from some to let the government pay the debt, but this means that the debt is covered by the citizens of the country. In other words, those that learned a trade, incurred the risks of starting their own businesses, or worked through college to avoid incurring debt will be responsible for paying off the loans of those who incurred large debts.

According to the National Center for Education Statistics, during the 2019-2020 school year the reported total for tuition, fees, room and board at private non-profit four-year schools was an average of $45,570. At Harvard University, tuition costs $47,730, fees are $4,195, and room and board costs $17,682 for total billed costs of $69,607 before any aid students might receive. In either choice, or the many schools in between, a student can incur substantial debt.

If a student chooses a community college, the reported tuition at public two-year schools is an average of $3,377 and it is more likely the student lives with a family member at much lower costs than students attending expensive universities. Students can then transfer to four-year universities to finish their degrees at significant savings. Is it socially responsible to provide debt forgiveness to students who attend high-priced schools by asking those that attended no school or that worked while at low-price schools to pay for it? It is hard to imagine that a policy designed to improve equity is intended to have this result.

Pointing out these negative outcomes is not to suggest that nothing should be done about student debt. Rather, when unintended consequences for programs such as debt forgiveness are carefully analyzed at the inception of a social policy, the process might shape how social programs could be more effective. Students with excessive amounts of debt could receive partial forgiveness each year they serve in low-paying jobs in rural and urban areas with high concentrations of poverty. Graduates who receive M.D., D.O. or other health care provider degrees often leave school with large amounts of student debt. A debt forgiveness program could be formulated forgiving debt to recent graduates serving a specified number of years in underserved populations where it is difficult to attract qualified health care professionals, funded by taxing high income M.D.s, D.O.s and other providers in rich, urban areas.

Another possibility is to provide debt forgiveness or free tuition only for universities with tuitions below a low amount, perhaps $5,000. Perhaps local community colleges could be subsidized even more to induce students with financial constraints to reduce the amount of debt they undertake. This would provide valuable assistance to potential students who could not otherwise afford a university education and provide substantial pressure on other universities to improve their value proposition to students. Such a policy could create incentives for increased productivity and innovation in all universities without bankrupting the majority of small private schools. An unintended consequence of increased productivity, of course, might be to reduce the average salaries paid to professors, a policy unlikely to generate much support in the academic community!

The reason for considering unintended consequences of well-intentioned policies is to prevent problems that arise when social policies are implemented without considering all the likely behavioral side-effects. Considering unintended consequences at the beginning allows for circumspective solutions that decrease the probability of unforeseen problems.

Keys to Prosperity

Debt-free Education

Problems are catalysts for solutions, especially for leaders educated as engineers, a discipline focused on solving problems. When Dr. Kristina Johnson became President of The Ohio State University, she applied her discipline as a Stanford-educated Electrical Engineer along with her extensive business experience and a research record with 119 patents in her name to her new job as President. Her skills found a receptive environment in a land-grant university that produces more graduates from low-income families than all the top dozen highest ranked U.S. universities combined.

The result was a program described as "The Scarlet and Gray Advantage," based on funding from multiple sources, including student-paid internships and work experiences, state and federal assistance, family resources, and strong support from alumni and donors, accompanied by cost reductions based on increased productivity of university resources.

"Let me be clear," Dr. Johnson commented, "this is not free college, (and) not a free tuition program. There will still be an expected student and family contribution, but we will ask our participating students to contribute in ways that are not career derailing and are instead career enhancing. The goal is to allow any participating student graduating with a bachelor's degree to do so without debt." Participating students commit to taking advantage of work opportunities and a financial literacy program. Dr. Johnson added, "I hope the program will be a model for the rest of our colleges in the state of Ohio as well as nationally."

President Johnson's multi-faceted approach is an illuminating example of identifying solutions that consider (and offset) unintended consequences.

Wealth Taxes

As discussed in Chapter 3, the government is responsible for creating the environment that supports transactions between producers and consumers. Critical functions such as national defense and the protection of property rights require investment, and therefore, taxes are a necessary part of a strong economy. However, the debate about how to raise tax revenue includes many potential tax policies, all with varying consequences for the economy.

You probably remember from the last chapter that a wealth tax is one of the policies proposed by Thomas Piketty in *Capital in the Twenty-First Century*. Taxing billionaires and other rich families a proportion – perhaps 2 to 5% – of their wealth every year sounds reasonable to many and over a decade would eliminate most of the wealth of rich families, a consequence some voters also regard as desirable. This should not come as a surprise, especially given the many potential social programs that could be supported with such a tax. Perhaps a wealth tax could be used for government-paid universal day care for all children under age five. Who could object to such well-intentioned motivations?

Raising taxes on the rich might appear to be a reasonable motive to well-intentioned people especially if the money is used for good purposes, such as loan forgiveness for students, funding free tuition, or universal daycare provisions. The Laffer Curve, developed by Arthur Laffer who received both an MBA and Ph.D. from Stanford, causes some concern, however. It states that if tax rates are increased above an optimum level, then tax revenues may fall because higher tax rates discourage people from investing, working, creating jobs for other people, or paying their taxes. However, the shape of the curve is somewhat uncertain and should be augmented by analysis of how people behave in the real world.

The unintended consequences of a wealth tax could be numerous. Among those results would be the difficulty of valuing assets to be taxed, the creativity and investment stimulated to avoid such a tax, and the possible negative economic consequences, especially effects on people who do not possess highly-valued skills.

Beyond such concerns that arise from theory, there is the empirical question of why most European and other nations who tried a wealth tax have abandoned it. In 1990, there were 12 countries in Europe that had a wealth tax. Today there are only three. Analysts say it did not work for a lot of reasons. Among other things, it is costly to enforce. It pushed rich people out of the country, and the wealth taxes did not raise as much revenue as expected. Furthermore, it discourages investment from other nations. When wealth goes away, empirical evidence indicates, so do jobs and prosperity for both high- and low-skilled workers. The reasons why this occurs were discussed in previous chapters.

Valuation of assets would be easy IF the rich kept most of their wealth in bank accounts, stocks and other easily measured (and tracked) financial instruments. But the wealthy often derive much of their wealth from privately-owned firms and LLCs whose value varies greatly from year to year depending on the economy and which family members manage. Such assets generate widely disparate opinions about their value (just ask divorce attorneys about disputed valuations), and include such oddities as family heirlooms, art collections and (non-income producing) personal property ranging from recreational retreats to designer clothing, rare wines, NFTs, and collectible cars.

Even the IRS has found that the actual value of assets is only about half what is reported in lists of the very wealthy reported by business media. Estimates of how much would be generated by a wealth tax are notoriously overestimated in the empirical experience of countries that have tried to implement a wealth tax. Advocates for wealth tax sometimes refer to the Nordic countries of Denmark

158

and Sweden, which both dropped their wealth taxes because of the problems they created.

The avoidance effects of a wealth tax are probably better estimated by behavioral economists than traditional economists. Misbehaving and "predictably irrational" people highly competent in accumulating wealth are also highly competent in restructuring their holdings and transferring them to areas of the world with no wealth tax. There is a reason very tall buildings full of financial firms and lawyers rise from the predominantly poor surroundings of Panama City, Panama, and other financial centers such as Gibraltar, Belize, and Cayman Islands. These places offer stability, regulation, and opportunity for confidentiality through limited liability and other instruments, to people and entities who appreciate the importance of privacy and anonymity.

People sometimes observe the difference between wealthy people and the rest of us is the wealthy have more money. Another conclusion might also be the wealthy have more creativity in tax avoidance. And sometimes, those methods are even legal.

In short, if a wealth tax encourages people to avoid taxes by moving their wealth to other places, who will create well-paying jobs for people who mow lawns, care for elders in retirement centers, paint houses, repair plumbing and HVAC, answer phones in call centers, serve customers in retail stores, pick and ship merchandise in warehouses, and create cuisine and serve it in restaurants? Who creates jobs for those people? Wealthy people who can afford to pay people for their valuable services as you read in earlier chapters.

Census Bureau data reveal that only about a third of adults in the US have college degrees, and even that is a massive increase since 1940 when the Census first asked respondents about their education levels. In 1940, just 4.6 percent had a four-year degree, and they were mostly male. Since 2014, the proportion of women with 4 years of college or more is higher (35%) than the proportion of males (34%). In recent years women earned 61% of associate degrees, 57% of bachelor's degrees, 59% of master's degrees, and 53% of doctorates, and the proportions for women are continuing to increase. The people with degrees, whether male or female, are the people most likely to create jobs for people without degrees.

Basic economic principles explain that people whose time has high monetary value often associated with advanced degrees employ service workers to save their time. Tax the wealthy more and expect fewer people able and willing to pay higher wages to people without degrees. That is probably not the intention

159

behind well-motivated high taxes on wealthy people, but it is likely to an unintended consequence.

It is certainly reasonable to consider the benefits of a wealth tax (and other similar solutions), but it is also important to understand the potentially harmful results if enacted without serious empirical and behavioral analysis of the unintended consequences of such policies. Once these consequences are studied, such policies might be implemented very differently.

Remember what happened to Rome when the government levied high taxes on the richest citizens? Historians report that the rich families left and took their wealth to other places, opening the gates to barbarians. Though the wealthy may not leave the country, their behavior will certainly change. Without objective analysis of the unintended consequences, you may be opening the door to barbarians unknown.

Legalizing Marijuana and CBD

Well-intentioned policies to legalize marijuana and CBD make it more available to consumers who like these products and may benefit from it for medical purposes. Additionally, states can collect taxes to pay for schools, addiction programs or other beneficial purposes, all good reasons for changes in social policies about the product.

But there are unintended consequences. Traffic fatalities increased in Colorado after the state legalized use of recreational marijuana, an analysis published in 2020 by *JAMA Internal Medicine* found. Since the state opted to legalize recreational use of the drug in 2014, there have been an additional 75 deaths resulting from traffic accidents, on average, annually, the researchers estimated.

"We observed that recreational cannabis laws were associated with increases in traffic fatalities in Colorado but not in Washington state, [perhaps due to] the size of the marijuana industry in Colorado, evidence of cannabis tourism in Colorado and other local aspects," study co-author Julian Santaella-Tenorio told media. According to the author, things such as purchasing limits, sales taxes, ability to grow cannabis at home and density of retail stores could be among the difference-makers. Careful analysis and further study of these variables could potentially reduce the impact of these consequences.

In their analysis, Santaella-Tenorio and colleagues reviewed data on traffic fatalities in both Colorado and Oregon from the Fatality Analysis Reporting System. Their review covered a 12-year period from 2005 through 2017. "People are concerned with the harmful unintended consequences [legalization] legislation may pose on communities," Santaella-Tenorio said. "It is important to conduct policy evaluations studies that can shed light on these effects."

Additionally, there may be other evidence to account for then just the number of marijuana related traffic deaths. There have been a great many studies to investigate whether marijuana is a gateway drug to harder drugs, but results of those studied vary greatly and have not proven it to be a gateway drug. Connections exist between marijuana use and later use of harder drugs, but these connections are not the same as causation (just because a person goes on to take harder drugs does not mean that marijuana necessarily caused it). With that said, progression to harder drugs is significant when other risk factors are present. Genetics, behavioral family history, and environment have a large impact.

You might find it surprising that studies by Dr. Marcus Bachhuber and other researchers found that opiate-related deaths decreased by approximately 33 percent in 13 states in the following six years after medical marijuana was legalized. Thus, it is not clear if legalized marijuana increases the total number of deaths per year.

In studies by the National Institute of Health, published in *JAMA-Pediatrics,* hospital visits and Regional Poison Control Centers (RPCs), Colorado cases for pediatric marijuana ingestion also increased significantly after legalization and at a higher rate than the rest of the United States. The number of children's hospital visits and RPC case rates for marijuana exposures increased between the 2 years prior to and the 2 years after legalization. Almost half of the patients seen in the children's hospital in the 2 years after legalization had exposures from recreational marijuana, suggesting that legalization affects the incidence of exposures. Other studies in the pediatric medical literature report similar results. Certainly, this was an unintended – but predictable – consequence.

More intriguingly, would you expect legalization to lead to an increase or decrease in *illegal* sales of marijuana? Will law enforcement be more likely or less likely to enforce illegal usage laws when legal usage is common? California's governor, Gavin Newsom, declared that illegal growth in California "is getting worse, not better" and redeployed a contingent of National Guard troops stationed on the border with Mexico to go after illegal cannabis farms instead, according to NY *Times* and other media.

It is possible to do research with consumers in areas where marijuana is legal and ask consumers, especially younger and lower-income consumers, where they buy their weed. The answer is often not in legal dispensaries. Why? Because the price is often about a third on the street compared to legal dispensaries. Some people might ask, "How can illegal dealers afford to sell at much lower prices than the legal market?" The answer is basic economics. There are no sales taxes or income taxes in the illegal market, nor do these dealers face quality standards, overhead, and others costs that legitimate dealers must incur.

Naturally, there is an increasing amount of research on the medical effects, both good and bad, from marijuana and CBD programs. Other behavioral results are starting to come into focus, observable in traffic deaths, crime rates, addiction statistics and knowledge gained by studying supply chains of drug dealers. Any area considering social policies of legalization of marijuana and other previously illegal drugs should closely follow these developments and the potential unintended consequences that are reasonable to consider.

Keys to Prosperity

Effects of Prohibition

You may know someone who has experienced financial failure, mental problems or even death because of excessive use and addition to alcohol or other drugs. If the government prohibits the sale of such products, wouldn't that prevent human suffering and increase prosperity? That was the rationale for passage of the 18th Amendment to the U.S. Constitution. banning the manufacture, transportation, and sale of intoxicating liquors, ushering in a period in American history known as Prohibition.

It proved difficult to enforce and became associated with an increase in illegal production and sale of liquor (known as "bootlegging"), the proliferation of speakeasies (illegal drinking spots), and accompanying rise in gang violence and other crimes which led to declining support for Prohibition, leading to its repeal in 1933.

The unintended consequence of Prohibition was the rise of criminal activity associated with bootlegging. The most notorious example was Chicago gangster Al Capone, who earned $60 million annually from bootleg operations and speakeasies. As a result, the annual budget of the Bureau of Prohibition doubled during the decade as it fought back against bootlegging. Moreover, the Coast Guard's budget increased substantially as it attempted interdiction and enforcement, weakened by specialists in illegal alcohol production and corruption of public and law-enforcement officials. Economists who study the effects of Prohibition estimate total expenditures on alcohol grew from less than four million dollars in 1920 to almost forty-five million in 1930.

(Data excerpted from Mark Thornton, *The Economics of Prohibition*)

Immigration Policies

Should the U.S. encourage more immigration? Or less immigration? That is a subject reflecting citizen attitudes which can be investigated with tools from behavioral analysis. Surveys could be conducted among U.S. citizens to obtain opinions, but those surveys should probably be conducted from both immigrants and their descendants and descendants of non-immigrants. The latter category, however, would be a restricted number of original citizens found mostly on reservations owned by Native Americans or, in Canada, Original Nations and other indigenous peoples who lived in Canada thousands of years before Europeans arrived in either the U.S. or Canada. Most people in both the U.S. and Canada today are descendants of immigrants, both countries that prospered economically because of immigration.

The desires of immigrants who arrived during the past few hundred years might create a desire to limit immigration mostly to people with the same ethnic characteristics and values as the existing population, a policy incorporated into the Immigration and Nationality Act of 1952 (The McCarran-Walter Act). That Act included a system of immigration preferences to the families of citizens already living in the United States, a policy still in use today.

President Truman was concerned about how decisions to maintain the national origins quota system would establish racially constructed quotas for some nations. He thought the new law was discriminatory and vetoed it, but the law had enough support in Congress to pass over his veto.

An unintended consequence of immigration restriction is lower growth in the nation's economy. For years, the most pressing problem of business firms in both the U.S. and Canada has been how to attract additional consumers. As you remember from Chapter 3, producers and consumers are responsible for about 70% of GDP. When population growth slows, so does economic growth. In addition to the search for new customers, firms in the U.S. now also increasingly face the problem of how to get additional workers to produce. Even prior to the 2020 pandemic, studies of Small and Medium (SMB) firms reported SMBs were turning down new business because they could not find enough qualified workers, a more fundamental problem than lack of new customers. Immigration could help solve both problems.

The size of a population is determined by three factors: birth rates, death rates (longevity) and net migration. Immigration is more volatile and responsive to political preferences, but birth rates and death rates are both easy to forecast and exceedingly difficult to change. That is why these demographics are sometimes compared to a huge ship or a glacier in the ocean – difficult to alter course quickly once they are headed in a direction.

The "replacement" fertility rate of 2.1 is required to renew the population, but by 2018, fertility declined to 1.72, a record low. It has continued to decline since then and in 2020, the number of people in the normal employee category (16-64) declined in absolute numbers for the first time in history, according to the U.S. Census Bureau. This number would be even lower without the births of Hispanic and Asian babies, now almost 25% and 7% of births, respectively.

All told, about 80% of counties in the U.S. are now declining in population because of the plummeting fertility rate, a reason economic growth is projected to be slower in the future than in the past. As you saw in Chapter 3, U.S. total population growth is now only 0.7% annually and even less, about 0.5%, for citizens under age 65. The fertility rate in Canada is even lower than the U.S. but Canada enacted policies to encourage immigration, giving it a higher total population growth rate than the U.S., currently about 1.4% annually, the highest among G-7 countries.

The Economic Innovation Group advocates an immigration policy that would stop the cycle, proposing entry be made available to skilled immigrants on the condition they go to counties struggling with demographic decline. The idea would be to create growth in the working-age population in those places, increasing the tax base and the demand for housing, and giving businesses a reason to invest. Without such policies, the unintended consequence of limiting immigration is to put the U.S. economy on a path toward the same type of economic decline facing Japan, where a few young people must support many older people living longer and longer.

Remember the lessons you read about Singapore in Chapter 5? Singapore's values made the country rich, including immigration policies soundly rooted in attracting people with skills needed for the 21st Century. The result was growing the nation from 1 million in 1950 to 5,836,602 in 2020. Objective analysis shows that immigration is one of the reasons for its economic prosperity. Not all immigrants to Singapore became rich, of course, but enough to create substantial reality in the popular book and movie "Crazy Rich Asians."

People – traditionally called "labor" by economists – offer an explanation with far more insights than what traditional economists call "capital" as a reason for prosperity. Immigration allowed Singapore to become one of the most prosperous nations in the world, an important fact to consider when you hear people expressing views about immigration policies. When discussing social policies, ask for facts, and you may want to be ready to compare immigration policies in nations such as Canada, Switzerland, and Singapore, as well as Japan. Pundits and dinner guests alike are unlikely to have considered the unintended consequences of overly restrictive immigration policies.

You may wonder about the importance of thinking so much about demographics and policies such as immigration. You can't personally control immigration policies any more than what happens with interest rates or the stock market, but you can control the amount you save for retirement. Boosting your personal savings ratio may bring you closer toward your retirement savings objective considering demographics and future trends.

Keys to Prosperity

Demographics and You

Social Security is a pay-as-you-go system, which means today's workers are paying taxes for the benefits received by today's retirees. However, demographic trends such as lower birth rates, higher retirement rates, and longer life spans are causing long-run fiscal challenges. There are simply not enough workers to support the growing number of beneficiaries. Social Security is not in danger of collapsing, but the clock is ticking on the program's ability to pay full benefits.

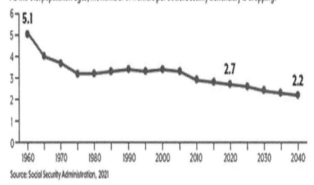

Demographic Dilemma

As the U.S. population ages, the number of workers per Social Security beneficiary is dropping.

Source: Social Security Administration, 2021

It is easy to postpone thinking about the future when you are young, but no matter what the future holds for Social Security, your retirement destiny is in your hands now. The key to future prosperity is to start saving when you are young, saving as much as possible for retirement while you are working.

Don't wait until you have one foot out the door to consider your retirement income strategy.

Mandatory Minimum Wage

Another controversial topic is that of the minimum wage. Poverty is a genuine problem even here in the United States. Research from a multitude of sources confirm that poverty, and especially child poverty, is decreased when the minimum wage is increased. That alone is a significant benefit to society. Raising the minimum wage could also lower the amount of government transfers needed to support those who currently rely on housing and food support to make ends meet, an additional (potentially significant) positive consequence.

The passing of time is a significant factor as well. Few people in the USA would complain that the current minimum wage of $7.25 is too much. Many people might recall working for that much when they were starting their own first job, and subsequently believed this amount was fair compensation. However, the reality of inflation is important to consider and since the most recent minimum wage increase in 2009, prices in the United States have risen more than 30%. In other words, if $7.25 was a reasonable minimum wage in 2009, then inflation alone suggests raising the minimum wage to compensate for the significant rise in prices over that period. A minimum wage increase could certainly be helpful for people working at rates below the new minimums, but as always it is important to understand the potential unintended consequences of a policy.

According to 2020 data from the U.S. Bureau of Labor Statistics, minimum wage workers are mostly young with the majority in the 16-19 age group (think McDonald's and Wendy's). Among workers over age 25, the data report 1.0% are at or below minimum wage. It should also be noted that estimates of workers paid at or below the federal minimum wage are based solely on the reported hourly wage, which does not include overtime pay, tips, or commissions.

For example, a quick investigation of McDonald's website shows that eligible crew have access to $2,500/year as scholarship assistance. Eligible Managers at McDonald's have access to $3,000/year. Participants have a choice for how they apply this funding – whether to a community college, four-year university, or trade school. Given the previous discussion of how impactful education can be in creating prosperity, this is a particularly valuable benefit to both workers and society if they choose to take advantage of it.

Also remember that "minimum wage" is more accurately described as "starting wage." Some firms have 80 to 85 percent of their highest-paid executives having started at minimum wage a few decades earlier. Walmart's CEO Doug McMillon is the poster child for employees who start at minimum wage but do not stay there. That's not unusual at Walmart and many other successful firms. An excellent narrative of how Ron Loveless started as a stockboy at Walmart, born to a welfare-supported family in Hiwassee, Arkansas (population 98), rising through the ranks to become the innovative first president of Sam's Club. You can read the insightful story in his book, *Walmart Inside Out*. It is also an excellent source to understand how corporate culture creates successful firms.

With that said, this raises the question of incentives. What happens to worker productivity when minimum wage is increased? Evaluation of the incentives and subsequent behavior yield somewhat of a mixed result. Naturally, a higher wage would induce people to want to keep their job, and subsequently could result in lower employee turnover and a reduction in training costs.

However, while a higher wage is certainly more attractive, for jobs without significant career advancement opportunities the incentive to work at the new wage is essentially the same – to work just hard enough to not get fired. This is not to say that no employees will work hard, but if you consider the people you have worked with throughout your career, you can likely think of some colleagues that displayed this "doing the bare minimum" behavior. In short, minimum wage increases can be used to increase productivity, but performance metrics that incentivize productive employees should be considered alongside wage increases if increased productivity is the goal.

As an extreme example, consider the Gravity Payments company in Seattle that increased the minimum salary for all employees to $70,000 in 2015. Not only was the company able to increase the salary of many of its workers, the company rapidly increased both productivity and profitability shortly thereafter. As you might expect, this also increased employee retention. With that said, the major driver of this profit increase was the 55% increase in the number of clients that Gravity Payments served in 2015, ostensibly driven by the publicity of the policy. While Gravity Payments did hire extra workers, the firm did not need to increase its workforce by much given the increased productivity.

Gravity Payments had done well to motivate their employees. However, you must be careful to recognize the reality that Gravity Payments was a single firm in a unique situation. If the state of Washington had mandated such a change for all firms, there would have been no publicity and the subsequent growth would not have occurred to compensate for the significantly increased labor costs.

Moreover, the incentive to work harder to stay employed at Gravity Payments would be significantly reduced, given that every company in the state would then pay the same $70,000 minimum salary.

An even more concerning consequence of minimum wage increases is that the incentives that do create significant reasons to work harder, the possibility of a promotion, are diminished when the base pay gets closer to the next highest level. Working hard for a $1 per hour promotion/raise is simply not as attractive as working hard for a $3 per hour promotion/raise. This can also create some anger in those that had previously "worked their way up." Note that this very thing occurred when Gravity Payments increased their base salary, leading to several long-term employees making the same amount as new employees. The CEO of Gravity Payments later admitted the unfairness of the policy to long term workers, and not only offered them an apology, but gave them small raises to let them know that they too were appreciated.

The great irony of higher mandatory minimum wage laws is their effect on the most vulnerable of workers – the minimally educated, people with special needs challenges, and teens contributing to family income in single-parent households struggling with poverty. Mandatory minimum wage laws create pressure to replace such workers with faceless kiosks and robotic French fry cooks and burger flippers.

Note that multiple historic studies have claimed that employment does not always decrease after a minimum wage increase but drawing fair comparisons to show these results is extremely challenging given differences across time and location. Therefore, the validity of these studies can often be questioned. Moreover, many of these studies use older data that may not be relevant given that technology used to replace low-skilled workers has improved rapidly in recent years. Now more than ever, mandatory minimums above the prevailing rate nudge independent restaurants to replace younger, low-skilled employees with automation.

Keys to Prosperity

The Effects of Minimum Wage Increases

Economists have studied the effects of minimum wage increases for decades. One common question tends to be whether increased minimum wages lead to decreases in employment. As often happens, the conclusions have very mixed results, but this should not be surprising. To see this, consider the situation and the resulting behavioral realities.

Put simply, profit is revenue minus costs. When the minimum wage increases, costs for an individual low-skilled worker will increase. This means that some things in this equation must change. First, it is possible that revenue could be increased via a price increase to compensate for the increase in costs. Second, it is possible that the firm could hire fewer low-skilled workers (or give them fewer hours). Note that this requires an increase in the productivity of the remaining workers/work hours. Third, it is possible that the firm could simply accept the lower profitability. Consider that the reason economists throughout history have not been able to pinpoint which of these happens when wages are increased is because the answer is likely "all of the above" depending on the situation.

The outcome of a minimum wage increase will depend heavily on the firm, its location, its employees, and its customers. Firms with high margins and price-sensitive customers may choose to offset minimum wage increases through a combination of accepting lower margins, decreasing the hours for low-skilled workers, or some combination of the two. Firms that have trouble keeping employees and have customers that are less price-sensitive may choose to simply increase their prices.

But firms with low margins and price-sensitive customers may have little choice but to decrease employment (or go out of business altogether). Even the famous paper by recent Nobel winners Alan Krueger and David Card showed an increase in prices after the minimum wage increase in question and mention the difficulties of how price changes can be impacted by the characteristics of the competitive environment.

Unfortunately, they fail to discuss how these same factors could affect their employment results. As mentioned above, there are significant econometric challenges in drawing valid conclusions from such data. A discussion by fellow Nobel economist John Angrist, in his book *Mostly Harmless Econometrics*, points out a serious methodological flaw in the Kreuger and Card analysis that leaves the validity of their conclusions in doubt. Ironically, these three brilliant scholars all won the 2021 Nobel prize together!

Needless to say, firms do tend to find a way to deal with wage increases. A recent article in the Harvard Business Review by economists Qiuping Yu, Shawn Mankad, and Masha Shunko, highlights research showing creative ways that employers can offset losses due to a minimum wage increase. In short, workers are frequently harmed by subsequent changes in scheduling, benefits, and other factors. The authors go on to recommend more well-designed policies to accompany wage increases that could potentially prevent these unintended

> consequences for workers. With that said, the cost
> of the increased minimum wage will be paid by
> someone, and it is unlikely to be only the firms.

Even the non-partisan U.S. Congressional Budget Office estimates that a $15 mandatory minimum law would cause 1.3 million or more Americans to lose their jobs. But this comes with the caveat that this outcome is unlikely to be consistent across the country. A $15 per hour minimum wage might not affect many people in New York City or San Francisco, but in rural America and small towns, it could potentially put a substantial number of firms out of business, often in areas already struggling economically (WSJ, August 12, 2019). Additionally, the firms pushed out of business would predominantly be SMBs. To see why, consider the average annual pay per employee for U.S. businesses relative to their size. According to U.S. Census Bureau data from 2019, the average pay was $44,503 for small enterprises (<100 employees), while the average pay for large enterprises was $63,847 (>5000 employees).

Though it needs to be noted that there are a significant number of exceptions, overall, small businesses tend to pay employees significantly less on average than large businesses. As a result, these small businesses are more likely to be affected by an increase in the minimum wage. In fact, a recent survey of small business owners by the National Bureau of Independent Businesses (NFIB), found that 74% of the surveyed small businesses said that they would be negatively impacted by a $15 per hour minimum wage. Moreover, 89% of those firms said that they would experience less overall profit, 87% stated that they would increase prices, and 58% said that they would decrease the number of their employees.

Higher minimum wages can also prevent small, innovative firms from capturing market shares of large, established firms. There are many reasons that employees might choose to work for a small business that pays less, for example, better work culture, more flexibility, the possibility of growing with a small startup, and the ability to have a greater impact in the company. Regardless of the reason, small firms with lower wage burdens can diminish the dominance of complacent corporate giants by attacking them segment-by-segment. Ironically, the problem of monopolies was the same economic issue that distressed Joseph Schumpeter and his Austrian marginal-revolutionary friends discussing the issue late into the night in Vienna coffee shops more than a century ago. It is unlikely that those seeking to increase the minimum wage are intending to drive an increase in monopolies.

As mentioned in chapter 3, an important key for prosperity is the acquisition of valuable skills. Of course, this assumes that the wages for a particular skillset are determined by the value and availability of those skills in the labor market. Many firms have found it difficult to locate and hire individuals to fill open positions in the wake of Covid-19. As a result, wages for many positions, entry level or otherwise, should be on the rise. As expected, data from the US labor department shows that wages are indeed rising substantially. In other words, the labor market appears to be working. The resulting question is whether or not government intervention via a minimum wage increase would be a better approach than relying upon the market.

A higher national mandatory minimum wage has many benefits and is certainly worthy of consideration as a solution to poverty. However, complex problems typically require complex solutions. Consider the answer to the question: "What would be the unintended consequences for the nation's most vulnerable workers and firms?" If wages are mandated above the market price, is that helpful to the most vulnerable workers whose salaries could go to zero dollars an hour instead of the expected higher rate? This is not to say that increases in the minimum wage are a bad idea, only that the resulting consequences must be considered in the development of such policy. For example, it is possible that any workers who lose their jobs could be assisted in finding new and more rewarding forms of employment, but this requires equal access to educational opportunity, a problem we have already discussed that also needs to be addressed!

Keys to Prosperity

The Rise of the Machines

A common argument against the minimum wage is that human labor will be replaced by machines. Of course, this would only benefit firms if the total cost of the automated "worker" is less than the total cost of the employee(s) it replaces. Naturally, there are differences from industry to industry, but there is historical evidence to believe this is a concern for some employees.

According to a recent study by Oxford Economics, nearly half of the unfilled US jobs in the post-covid recovery are in danger of replacement via automation. As these are jobs are primarily in food service, retail, and manufacturing, it is possible that a minimum wage increase would accelerate this replacement. However, there may be reasons to be concerned even if your current job pays more than minimum wage.

As mentioned above, post-covid wages are on the rise. While this might be good news to workers, the reality is that many jobs in coming decades will be under the same threat for similar reasons. In fact, McKinsey & Co recently forecasted that 45 million US jobs will be automated by 2030, a sobering number.

While there is some question as to how negatively this will impact the total number of US jobs, the reality is that sometime in the future it is likely the demand for US labor may decrease significantly. These forecasts are often used as justification for considering a universal basic income (guaranteed income for all adults in the country).

So, what does this mean for you? If you are in the market for a career change, consider careers that create value in a way that is difficult to replace with a machine. If not, consider how you can increase the value you create for your employer both now and in the future. Finally, regardless of how you feel about a universal basic income now, you may want to consider how the nation will find solutions to a lack of available employment in the future. This may not be so far from now as you might imagine!

Financial Transaction Taxes (FTT)

Where can the U.S. find tax sources for all the programs desperately needed? Taxation of Wall Street is one solution proposed to pay for well-intentioned policies. A Financial Transfer Tax (FTT) on share transfers sounds good because many do not care if Wall Street pays more.

A proposed Financial Transaction Tax would apply to every transaction made in the United States or by a U.S. person, including retail investors. There could be various amounts such as one suggested by Senator Bernie Sanders at a rate of 0.5 percent on stocks, 0.1 percent on bonds, and .005 percent on derivatives. It might be assumed this would focus on the richest, although wealthy people tend to make investments with little volatility rather than frequent trades as day traders and hedge funds often do. This would also tax not just wealthy stock traders, but everyone with a 401(k) or college savings plan.

In a digital age it is easier for transactions to be moved to nations or cities with lower taxes. Some stock exchanges already have FTTs, but many do not, creating competition to historic U.S. dominance. The Chinese cities of Shanghai and Shenzhen are each home to stock exchanges with market caps rivalling Europe's major exchanges. Shanghai stock exchange is China's largest, doubling its market capitalization in the past few years. Most listed companies are large, state-owned companies responsible for China's economic growth. Most investors are pension funds and banks.

Currently, the U.S. is home to the most desirable stock exchange in the world, attracting investment from many countries. Taxes on transactions could have the unintended result of taking jobs from the U.S., moving them to the Chinese markets (including Hong Kong) as well as competitive markets in London, Tokyo, Singapore, and other cities.

The intention is to increase tax revenue, but which shareholders would be the ones paying the taxes? It is easy to think of the stock market as the playground of hedge funds and day-traders, but the reality is most of the stock market is owned by average people in their retirement accounts doing one thing – helping people retire. Seventy-two percent of the value of all domestically held stocks is owned by pension plans, 401(k)s and individual retirement accounts, or held by life insurance companies to fund annuities and death benefits.

What occupation owns the most shares of public companies? People might find teachers a surprising answer, but mutual funds are the primary assets of pension funds, and Teachers Insurance and Annuity Association of America (TIAA) is the largest. Does the average U.S. voter really want the unintended consequence of taxing teachers by reducing yields on TIAA, CALPERS, and state pension funds such as STRS and OPERS? Moreover, according to the Federal Reserve, 52% of households in the U.S. own stocks, and more NYSE individual shares are owned by women than men. Should a well-intentioned social policy be financed by taxing women more than men?

An additional challenge is that policymakers are split on the point of the tax. Is it to raise revenue from members of society or is it a "sin tax" on the finance sector for frequent trading? Voters may support the idea of FTT, but nations fear that imposing a levy on financial trades would push investors to move transactions to other countries, a fear that has stopped many governments from demanding a broad-ranging tax – or supporting it at all. Asian countries take pride in providing competitive tax frameworks for investors and are reducing, rather than expanding, their already modest FTTs. In South Korea, the securities transaction tax on stock trading is being phased out as the government seeks other sources of investment income tax and expands taxation on capital gains. This raises significant questions about the unintended consequences of FTT.

Medicare for All

There have been proposals calling for Medicare for All. A more realistic description of government-provided health care for everyone might be Medicaid for All not covered by insurance or personal funds, but that label has less vote-getting appeal. In the U.S., Medicaid is administered by states, aided by the Federal government, as is health care in Canada, with each Province having its own system, aided by the federal government. In Ontario for example, health care is provided by OHIP but in British Columbia, health care is provided by British Columbia MSP. Like most industrialized nations, Canada now has a two-tier system of free government health care but a private system for people or employers who can afford it.

In the U.S., hospitals receive a reduced rate for Medicare treatment, but currently that applies only to a minority of their patients. With Medicare for all, those rates would apply for all. The unintended consequence could be to put many hospitals out of business, especially in rural areas unless appropriate policies are put in place. This could create even more shortages of health care for the masses of consumers and drive affluent consumers to a private solution as has happened in the two-tier health care systems found in other industrialized countries such as Canada, Britain, Sweden, Australia, and other nations.

Consider the NHS system in Britain to determine what happens to the incomes of health care providers (and eventually supply of providers) as well as availability and delay in access to the masses with the policy of Medicare for all. The data from other countries are readily available and useful in evaluating social policies such as Medicare for all. Government-paid health care in the nearby neighbor of the U.S is described by a Canadian researcher in the accompanying Prosperity Key.

Keys to Prosperity

Medicare for All?

Health care costs disrupt the prosperity of affected individuals and families, causing many to conclude it would be better to have health care costs paid by the government rather than employers or individuals. Many nations do that, and when U.S. citizens consider the issue, they sometimes cite programs of other nations, especially nearby neighbor Canada and Mother England.

When considering such policies, it is productive to examine facts about potential unintended consequences. Consider Canada, where 1.2 million Canadians are on waitlists for critical medical treatment. Patients face a median wait of 22.6 weeks for care from a specialist following referral by a general practitioner. Similar facts are observed in Great Britain's National Health Service. The *Guardian* reported the number of people waiting to start treatment in England recently was at an all-time peak of 5.8 million.

One U.K. man was recently told he would have to wait three years to have a decayed tooth removed. A couple in Northern Ireland learned that their 12-year-old son couldn't have urgent scoliosis surgery for more than two years. The total number of people waiting at any given time for treatment has climbed steadily since 2008. Severe wait times at the National Health Service have led many to turn to private providers, in some cases going abroad for treatment. In these cases, they pay for care out of pocket.

Examining OECD data from 2022, the U.S. was on the higher side for the share of people who sometimes, rarely, or never get an answer from their regular doctor on the same day at 28%. Canada had the highest at 33% and Switzerland had the lowest at 12%. The U.S. was towards the lower end for the share of people waiting one month or more for a specialist appointment at 27%. Canada and Norway tied for the highest at 61% each and Switzerland had the lowest at 23%.

The Fraser Institute, a Vancouver research group, issued a report calculating how much the average Canadian family pays in taxes each year for their publicly provided health care. The total comes to just over $15,000 Canadian for a family of four (about $12,000 USD). Long wait times also affect productivity. According to Fraser, the costs associated with waiting for treatment from a specialist in Canada are nearly $3 billion per year. People in discomfort or pain tend to be less productive. That doesn't include wages lost while waiting ten-plus weeks for an appointment with a specialist or losses realized by family members who quit jobs to take care of loved ones waiting for care.

[Data excerpts from report by Sally C. Pipes, American Institute for Economic Research, December 9, 2021. Ms. Pipes is also author of *False Premise, False Promise: The Disastrous Reality of Medicare for All*, 2020.]

While the statistics and anecdotes in the key above report some comparisons between countries, the ultimate question for U.S. readers to consider is how these reports compare to their own experience with both primary care providers and specialists in their nation. One of the changing circumstances of the health care system in the U.S.in recent decades has been a difference in availability of primary and specialist care. Incentives for higher income have created an increase in supply of specialists compared to primary care, causing adjustments to more care in urgent care centers and other alternative arrangements. Although it is difficult to measure differences in wait times across alternative health plans, consumer reports indicate the Canadian system has less access (and more wait time) for specialists than to primary care.

When care is free, objective analysis of the data reveals that demand soars, causing shortages. Some of this increase will be from people that couldn't previously afford healthcare, a definite positive, but some will also be from people who are simply overusing the system for ailments that do not require a physician. Regardless of the causes of the increased demand, the U.S. is already facing a shortage of surgeons, nurses, and other providers, reported in *The Coming Shortage of Surgeons: Why They Are Disappearing and What That Means for Our Health* by Thomas E. Williams Jr. M.D. Ph.D., E. Christopher Ellison M.D., *et al*. The immediate solution to the shortage has been to import an increasing number of U.S physicians and providers from other countries such as the Philippines, India, and low wage countries, causing provider supply problems for those countries. There are alternative approaches and operational methods to provide high quality care at lower prices such as the Narayana Hospital, described in the next chapter and which you can read about in Clayton Christensen's *Prosperity Paradox*.

The costs of healthcare (in any program) are a significant concern. Solutions as alternatives in Medicare for All include Consumer Driven Health Care (CDHC), the common approach in the U.S. for groceries, cars, and most other services. Switzerland and Singapore offer practical examples of how to make health care costs more affordable and effective than current U.S. health care systems, and more effective than England or Canada, via well-designed government mandates fulfilled by private insurance companies. You can read how Switzerland and Singapore provide health care that is both efficient and affordable in "Consumer-Driven Health Care: Lessons from Switzerland, in *JAMA* (vol 292, No 10) by Dr. Regina Herzlinger and Dr. Ramin Parsa-Parsi. They are also described in the book *Consumer Driven Health Care* by Roger Blackwell, Dr. Tom Williams, and Alan Ayers.

Regardless of the proposed solution to the healthcare problem in the United States, a "Just the facts" approach to Medicare for All discloses alternatives to address the unintended consequences of this well-intentioned policy.

Just the Facts!

As you read through the diversity of social policies described in this chapter, you may have thought of other issues that probably have unintended consequences beyond the ones in this chapter. When voting on candidates expressing views on each of these and other problems, be sure to ask the advocate of well-intentioned policies, what are the unintended consequences? Because there are unintended consequences does not mean proposals for solutions should not be adopted, but it does mean well-intentioned policies should not be adopted without considering their unintended consequences, a process that might improve whatever policy is adopted.

The social policies described in this chapter are sometimes identified with one political party or another, but objective analysis is apolitical, focusing on facts rather than opinions. When discussing policies such as those described above, the best response to most of the issues is "Show me the data."

What type of economic system provides the most effective framework for implementing socially desirable policies? That is a more important question than specific issues addressed in this chapter – and the topic for the next chapter. Are you prepared to park your predispositions and say, "Just the facts?"

Discussion Questions

- What is some proposed government policy that you currently support? Spend some time carefully determining the behavioral effects of these policies and the resulting unintended consequences. How might the effect of these consequences be mitigated?
- What is the "fair share" of income that people in differing income levels should pay in taxes? What are the economic consequences of paying more or less than their "fair share"?
- Of the topics examined in this chapter or others proposed currently, what additional facts or data would you want to observe and analyze to determine both intended and unintended consequences?

Chapter 9

Collectivism or Individualism:

Which is Best?

Consider the following question:

Suppose that that there are two workers, Person A and Person B. Suppose also that Person A and Person B do the exact same job with the same amount of effort and skill. Should they both be paid the same amount?

For many, the answer to this question will strike a chord of equality considerations which will drive your answer. Your answer to this question is strongly related to whether you prefer collectivism versus meritocracy as a means of distribution.

You might be a little surprised at the title of this chapter, perhaps expecting it to be titled "Socialism or Capitalism? Which is Best?" The first problem with discussion of socialist or capitalist nations is there are no pure forms of either one. All nations are somewhere on the spectrum between 100 percent socialist and 100 percent capitalist.

Examples at the Extremes

You might be surprised at that. "What about Cuba?" The government of Cuba owns and operates most industries and most of the labor force is employed by the state with a minimum wage of 225 Cuban pesos ($9US) per month according to Cuba's National Statistics and Information Office, known as ONEI. Cuban doctors earn approximately $60 a month. Cuba is constitutionally defined as a Marxist-Leninist socialist state but even in a socialist nation, there are pockets of capitalism such as in the taxi business, some restaurants (often in family homes), hairdressers, and a few retail operations. However, those businesses are not recognized as legal entities by the Cuban government.

Cuban ruler Raúl Castro has publicly acknowledged that wages in Cuba "do not satisfy the needs of the workers and their families" and complained that some Cubans "have grown accustomed to stealing from the state." Low salaries explain why many people look for jobs in the state food or administration sectors, where they can skim products from the government, or tourism areas where they can have contact with foreigners who have convertible currencies. The possibility of stealing from the government has become more attractive to job seekers than the salaries themselves, experts say.

In contrast, within the United States, which is usually considered a capitalist nation, companies are recognized as a separate legal entity, essentially their own person, with many guaranteed rights like individuals enjoy, but the U.S. is a "mixed" economy. Many enterprises are owned by the government – Federal, state, and local. The Interstate highway system is an obvious example of a government-owned resource, along with businesses such as the U.S. Postal Service, operated by the Executive Office of the government. USPS is a $70 billion business operating at several billion dollars a year in losses competing with for-profit firms such as UPS and FEDEX.

In some nations, railroads are owned by the government and that is partially true in the United States. Amtrak is a for-profit company, but the federal government owns all its preferred stock. Amtrak operates more than 300 trains daily over 21,400 miles of track but only owns about 623 miles of this track. The rest are owned by a variety of other "host railroads," private companies that Amtrak pays to use their tracks.

Universities, public schools, agricultural programs, many hospitals (including Veterans' facilities) and numerous other organizations are government owned. Add airports, research and medical facilities, the military and others to the list and the proportion of government-owned or socialist institutions in a "capitalist" nation is significant.

Keys to Prosperity

ESG in Corporations

Corporations are increasingly judged by their stakeholder concerns including ESG (Environment, Social, Governance). Advanced Drainage Systems provides a variety of innovative and environmentally friendly alternatives to traditional materials, with some of its solutions to water problems used across a broad range of end markets and applications, including non-residential, residential, infrastructure and agriculture applications. The company has undertaken many sustainability initiatives with the goal of "working towards a cleaner, greener tomorrow" including:

1. Keeping 550 million pounds of plastic out of landfills by incorporating recycled materials into the manufacturing process, making the Company the 2nd largest plastic recycler in North America according to *Plastics News*.

2. Decreasing greenhouse gas emissions by 7% through efficiency improvements.

3. Approving $4 million for safety-related capital projects to keep the health and safety of employees paramount; and,

4. Establishing an Environmental, Social, and Governance (ESG) Board sub-committee to

develop and review ADS' corporate citizenship, sustainability programs and ESG policies.

This is a shift from decades past when many companies were perceived as acting only under government duress.

Are such activities compatible with corporate profitability? Apparently so, because if you bought WMS shares at $22, five years later you would have seen your investment increase over 400 percent. "Doing well by doing good" is an effective strategy for both corporations and individuals who care about how corporations solve problems in changing markets. Organizations that pay attention to what is important to their customers and investors often conclude what is good for stakeholders is good for business.

Scott Barbour, President and Chief Executive Officer of ADS, commented he is extremely proud of the progress ADS has made with its ESG initiatives saying, "We treat the problem, not the symptom."

Nordic Socialism

Scandinavian countries are sometimes portrayed as socialist, and sometimes as "Nordic Socialism." The annually produced *Index of Economic Freedom* ranks countries based on several metrics, including "Business Freedom," "Labor Freedom," "Property Rights," and "Trade Freedom." In the 2020 rankings, Denmark came in 8th place among all nations. Sweden came in 22nd. Norway at 28th. All three of these countries ended up in the "Mostly Free" category. The United States actually ranked below Denmark, in 17th place.

Even many politicians in these nations reject the socialist label. Danish Prime Minister Lars Lokke Rasmussen, responding to senators in the U.S., once said, "Some people in the U.S. associate the Nordic model with some sort of socialism. Therefore, I would like to make one thing clear: Denmark is far from a socialist planned economy. Denmark is a market economy."

Sweden is sometimes described as a socialist nation but is more accurately described as an open market economy. Most Swedish enterprises are privately owned and market-oriented with extensive, profitable trading with other countries. It also has strong welfare programs causing some researchers to classify Sweden, not as socialist, but as a "compassionate capitalist state."

Keys to Prosperity

Calling All Compassionate Capitalists

While governments are typically responsible for social programs, implementation of these solutions need not be left to bureaucracy. Firms around the world have the brainpower, platform, and resources to address many of the problems of society. More importantly, firms are beginning to see that they have the incentives to solve these problems as well.

To see why this is the case, consider that consumers' expectations of companies have evolved to include their behavior toward society. Because of this, even the few business leaders that would deny the intrinsic value of corporate citizenship are beginning to see it affect their profit and loss statements.

Moreover, leaving solutions to a government removes a firm's autonomy to affect how they can contribute positively to a situation. When a firm designs and implements a well-conceived solution to a known problem, that firm is likely to benefit. When firms ignore a problem and wait for a government solution, the subsequent changes in policy are more likely to be harmful to their respective industries.

Tuition reimbursement, diversity training, family leave, affordable child-care, and much more are becoming common offerings from companies and can provide shared strategic advantages well into the future. This also highlights how citizens of a nation can easily effect change today. Make it known to firms what you expect in their behavior, and vote with your wallet!

Sweden's strength in the global economy rests on its internationally competitive engineering, mining, steel, and pulp industries, driven by capitalistic firms such as Ericsson, ASEA/ABB, SKF, Alfa Laval, AGA, and Dyno Nobel. Incidentally, Dyno Nobel is a manufacturer of explosive and blasting supplies named for the same Alfred Nobel that serves as the namesake for Nobel Prizes.

The Nobel Prize was founded and is awarded in Sweden and Norway. In many ways, it is a symbol for a tradition of research and development that are important attributes of prosperous nations. Collaboration between science, entrepreneurs, and researchers is key to the type of innovative environment that stimulates globally competitive firms to develop, manufacture and market high-value products. As discussed in previous chapters, this produces prosperity for nations as well as the employees and entrepreneurs within those companies.

Sweden's position as an innovative country serves as an interesting example in this discussion. After World War II, Sweden was in better shape than most European nations. As a neutral country, it did not have to rebuild its economic base, banking system, or infrastructure, as did many other countries.

Sweden achieved an elevated level of prosperity under its mixed system of high-tech capitalism and began to offer an extensive array of welfare benefits in the 1970s. Its universal social benefits were funded by high taxes, predictably causing entrepreneurial talent and capital to move to other countries. This created economic problems by the 1990s and a subsequent impetus to become more market oriented. A special report by *Economist* (Feb 2, 2013) documents how Swedish policies changed between the early 1990s and 2012:

	1993	2012
Government spending as % of GDP	67%	49%
Public Debt as % of GDP	70%	37%
Top marginal tax rate	87%	57%
Corporate tax rate	26.3%	22%
Budget	11% deficit	0.3% surplus

Among the changes Sweden made during this period was inviting private schools to compete with public schools. Sweden now has complete school choice, providing families with vouchers for each child. These vouchers can be used to attend regular public schools, government-run charter schools, or private, for-profit schools, the opposite of what you would expect if it were a Socialist nation. Sweden also changed public employee pensions from defined benefit to defined contributions, meaning that what individuals earn and save during their career determines their retirement instead of a level guaranteed by the government.

Keys to Prosperity

Corporate Responsibility in Solving Societal Needs

"Outcries for corporate sensitivity to human and social needs may soon become a major input into the strategic planning process of all but the most inhumane firms. Executives who once asked why students were not spending more time studying instead of getting involved in social causes now find themselves forced by those same students to plunge headlong into the search for decency and responsibility in the midst of a confusing and sometimes overwhelming environment.

"Profit once reigned unchallenged as the sole rationale for the existence of the corporation and as the basis for strategic marketing planning. In truth, few executives honestly believed profit to be the *only force* worth considering in the firm's operations. Within themselves, executives probably welcome the pressures from outside the firm that have forced them to reveal their innermost thoughts. Thus, they have been able to verbalize their convictions that other motivations are indeed relevant forces that help develop the corporation's strategies. Profit is a necessary but not a sufficient rationale for business.

"Two types of responsibility impinge upon the planning of corporate strategy. The first is social responsibility, which can be defined simply as accepting an obligation for the proper functioning of the society in which the firm operates. Ethical responsibility is the other factor affecting strategic planning. Ethical responsibility is concerned with the determination of how things should be, human pursuit of the right course of action, and individuals doing what is morally right. The basis for social responsibility is derived from the ethical aspect of responsibility."

- *[Quoted from David Kollat et al, Strategic Marketing, Holt, Rinehart Winston, 1972]*

Before they enacted generous welfare programs, Sweden and other Scandinavian countries were economic successes for the same reasons you read about in earlier chapters. Productive economies generating high incomes for workers allow governments to raise tax revenue needed to pay for social benefits. Government benefits did not create wealth in Scandinavian countries, but wealth of its citizens and successful corporations allowed generous government programs. Also note that none of the prosperous Scandinavian countries have minimum

190

wage laws, leaving it the market and industry-level collective bargaining instead of government mandates to establish proper wage rates.

How do Nordic countries pay for their generous government funded benefits that are sometimes proposed for the U.S.? They, like most European countries, levy a VAT (Value Added Tax). If you have travelled and shopped abroad, the VAT is the big tax you pay when you buy products and then save receipts and request refunds when you depart for home. Typical European VATs are 25%+ on top of income and other taxes with top total tax rates in such countries running about 50-60 percent. Something similar has occasionally been proposed in the U.S. called a consumption tax or variations such as the "Fair Tax" as a system encouraging people to spend less and save more, stimulating faster economic growth.

In contrast, corporations in Denmark, Norway, and Sweden have relatively low stated corporate tax rates – 22 percent, 24 percent, and 22 percent, respectively. These rates are only slightly higher than the U.S. current stated corporate tax rate of 21 percent and much lower than the previous stated U.S. rate of 35%. Note that the actual amount paid by different corporations can vary greatly due to tax laws, but the taxes paid by every public corporation are required to be reported to the SEC and available to the public in annual reports and the SEC's Edgar data base.

Another of the Nordic nations, Norway, is a constitutional monarchy, where the King has a mainly symbolic power. The government owns many business enterprises, but the citizens own over $1.3 trillion in stocks through Norway's sovereign wealth funds – about 1.4% of all the corporate stocks in the world. This adds up to about a quarter-million dollars per citizen. This fund was created from the revenues of Norway's petroleum industry and funds the country's generous pension benefits. Fossil fuels have done well for Norwegians, potentially better it seems than how Alaska has managed its oil profits.

Regardless of whether a nation identifies as socialist or capitalist, taxes are as inevitable as death. Without them, there is no way for the government to perform its function. The only real question about taxes in either system is who pays? And how much?

Going forward we will avoid the problems with the terms socialism and capitalism by focusing on the foundations underlying each rather than their various manifestations (Collectivism versus Individualism). While some economists are identified as Socialist or Capitalist, an objective analyst of economics is best described as a Solutionist. Every country lies somewhere between the extremes of fully collectivist and fully individualist, so objective analysis would suggest analyzing those countries close to the extremes.

Rise and Fall of Collectivism

The two key issues in economics you read when you started this book are *production* and *distribution* of goods and services. There are two general approaches to maximizing the efficiency of both production and distribution. One is collective decisions, with one centralized authority or committee deciding what is best for all. The other is market decisions, in which individuals determine production and distribution based on individual contributions to the process and the rewards they receive for their work and responsibility.

The remainder of this chapter includes several pages of history. As you read these pages, though, you may find it helpful to remember the wisdom of poet Maya Angelou, who observed, "History, despite its wrenching pain, cannot be unlived; but if faced with courage, need not be lived again."

Two major nations were early adopters of the collective approach to economics – Russia and China. Two individuals were major contributors to the theory of collective direction of the economy – Karl Marx and Vladimir Lenin. Although Karl Marx was German, he was the ideological founder of its most important adopter, Russia.

Russian Collectivism

The primary source of wealth through most of history was land. If you lived and worked on the land, you probably had enough to eat for you and your family. If you owned the land, you probably not only had enough to eat but if you managed well the land and the people who worked on it, you probably had enough to purchase other things for you and your family. If you owned a lot of land, you could buy a lot of things.

The basis for wealth began to change in the 18th century in Great Britain with the advent of the steam engine, a catalyst for the transition from human power in homes to machine power in factories. By the 19th Century, the transition was also widespread in much of Europe but did not arrive in Russia for 50 to 70 years later than in Britain or Europe. Factories eventually came to Russia by the beginning of the 20th Century although land remained the most important source of wealth.

Russia has more land than any nation, much more (74 percent more than the United States). However, Russian land ownership was different in the 18th century. Almost 95% of Russia's people were peasant farmers who owned no land but paid rent to the country's property owners. Because they farmed specific sections of the land, peasant farmers generally had enough food for their family but little to call their own.

Nearly 75 percent of the land in Russia was owned by the Tsar (or Czar in earlier spellings), considered the richest person in the world. Like Pharaohs in Egypt and Caesar in Rome, the Tsar used the plentiful produce of the land to accumulate jewels, art, and enormous wealth, oblivious to the plight of the poor peasants who farmed the land. If the Tsar had studied the history you read in Chapter 5 of this book, he might have predicted what would happen in his future. By the end of the 19th Century change came to Russia as people with wealth hid it in other countries and thousands of poor peasants flocked to the cities in search of the higher wages of factory work.

A new class of educated professionals also began to emerge, replacing cities stuck in the Middle Ages. Educated in European and British universities, the new Russian middle class returned home and formed secret political clubs to discuss illegal topics such as democracy, socialism, labor unions, and freedom of the press. These groups feared the Tsar's dreaded secret police, as they could be exiled for treason. Revolution was in the air and fighting in the streets.

After two years of battles, the Bolsheviks ("The Reds") emerged victorious with Vladimir Lenin as the leader of the Russian Social-Democratic Workers' Party, dedicated to eliminating injustices from social class differences. On March 8, 1917, tens of thousands marched through the streets of Petrograd (later renamed to Leningrad) shouting slogans of "give us bread" and "down with the Tsar." The next day the crowd swelled to over one hundred thousand as workers, sailors, and soldiers joined in the demonstrations.

On March 13th, thousands of soldiers disobeyed orders and began joining the protesters in the streets. Later that day the red flag of revolution was flying over the Winter Palace. Nicholas II abdicated his throne, ending a 300-year reign of the Romanov family of Tsars. He and his family were eventually executed and the period of 1918 until 1922 began a reign of terror known as the Great Fear. This is undoubtedly another example of the eventual outcome of the mistreatment of a nation's people!

Lenin had formed the Russian Social-Democratic Workers' Party (RSDWP). However, from the start there was a split between Lenin's Bolsheviks

(Majoritarians), who advocated militarism, and the Mensheviks (Minoritarians), who advocated a democratic movement toward socialism. The Red Army, led by Leon Trotsky, fought a civil war with the White Army, composed mostly of people who hated the Bolsheviks. Thousands were rounded up and shot if they were even suspected of being loyal to the Whites. Some estimates put the number of people murdered during the civil war at 50,000. Property and food were confiscated for the use of the Red Army, leading to a mass starvation known as the Red Terror. The White Terror did the same things to suspected communists, especially Jews.

The October Revolution led by Vladimir Lenin was also known in Soviet history as the October Socialist Revolution, the October Coup, the Bolshevik Revolution, or Red October. The main changes brought about by the Bolsheviks were total opposition to private property; nationalization of most industries and banks; and, land was declared social property and peasants were permitted to seize land of the nobility. Lenin promised, "Peace, Land, and Bread," and power to the people based on the ideology of Marxism–Leninism. The implementation of this policy was a centralized command economy with a one-party state to realize a dictatorship of the proletariat. Simply stated, most property and economic resources would be owned and controlled by the state (rather than individual citizens), but all citizens would share equally in economic resources, allocated by a democratically-elected government.

The foundation of the Social Democratic party was *The Communist Manifesto*, written by Karl Marx and Friedrich Engels in 1848 just before revolutions swept Europe. In the last third of the 19th century, social democratic parties arose in Europe, based mainly on the writings of Marx, and were frequently discussed by Austrian economists in those Viennese coffee house meetings you read about in Chapter 2. After Marx died, his friend Engels finished many of his works.

Marx was eloquent about exploitation of the working class perhaps because he was unable to maintain a job himself. He described capitalism as a progressive historical stage that would eventually stagnate and be replaced by socialism. From one of his writings emerged the slogan, "From each according to his ability, to each according to his needs."

The socialism of Marx explains how wages should be determined based on that slogan. If two people have the same job, such as bus driver, the pay of each should be based on their need. If one bus driver has five children to support and another bus driver has only one child, the driver with five children should be paid more, based on need, rather than equal pay for a job. And more generally, the value of labor is the same regardless of the job. The value of an hour or day of a farmer should be the same as a physician, lawyer, machinist, or bus driver. That is how socialism believes an economy's *production* of goods and services should be *distributed*. One important consequence is unequal pay for equal work because pay should be based on need, not ability.

It is difficult to disagree with the morality of the desire to distribute goods and services on need. The ideology has great appeal. Observers who might object to the lofty ideals of such a philosophy are researchers who raise the question of who determines whose needs are most important. Behavioral researchers also raise the question how this method of distribution might affect the quantity and quality of goods and services available to distribute. A fundamental finding from many psychological studies is that behavior that is rewarded is behavior that is repeated, an important consideration in determining how production will function in an economy.

So, how did this work out in Russia? Democracy was supposed to determine who decides how the economy would be operated. When the election results came in, the Bolsheviks had won less than 25% of the seats in the Duma (parliament). Lenin, not believing citizens had made the right decision, ordered the Red Guard to prevent the elected representatives from entering the Palace where the Duma met.

Democracy in Russia only lasted one day and did not return until 1991 when Russians made Boris Yeltsin the first freely-elected president in the history of the country, replacing Soviet leader Mikhail Gorbachev. Most historians conclude Yeltsin was also the last freely-elected president because his reelection in 1996 was heavily manipulated and presidential voting since then has been managed by the people in power instead of the power of the people.

During the semi-retirement of Lenin, Joseph Stalin, a Georgian revolutionary and Soviet politician, rose to power in the mid-1920s as the General Secretary of the Communist Party and Premier of the Soviet Union. Although initially governing the Soviet Union as part of collective leadership, he eventually consolidated power to become the country's de facto dictator by the 1930s. Stalin was ideologically committed to the Leninist interpretation of Marxism, formalizing these ideas as Marxism-Leninism.

In November 1927, Joseph Stalin launched his "revolution from above" by setting two extraordinary goals for Soviet domestic policy: rapid industrialization of the economy and collectivization of agriculture. His aims were to erase all traces of the capitalism that had entered under the New Economic Policy and to transform the Soviet Union as quickly as possible, without regard to cost, into an industrialized and completely socialist state.

Stalin's First Five-Year Plan, adopted by the party in 1928, called for rapid industrialization, with an emphasis on heavy industry. All industry and services were nationalized, managers were given predetermined output quotas by central planners, and trade unions were converted into mechanisms for increasing worker productivity. Many new industrial centers were developed, particularly in the Ural Mountains, and thousands of new plants were built throughout the country. But serious problems soon arose. With the greatest share of investment put into heavy industry, widespread shortages of consumer goods occurred.

The First Five-Year Plan also called for transforming Soviet agriculture from predominantly individual farms into a system of large state collective farms. The Communist regime believed that collectivization would improve agricultural productivity and would produce grain reserves sufficient to feed the growing urban labor force. The anticipated surplus was to pay for industrialization. Collectivization was further expected to free many peasants for industrial work in the cities and enable the party to extend its political dominance over the remaining peasantry. Note that some elements of traditional economic theory might predict success of that plan, but objective behavioral analysis seeks to explain what occurred.

Stalin focused on the wealthier peasants, or kulaks. About one million kulak households (five million people) were deported and never heard from again. Forced collectivization of the remaining peasants, which was strongly resisted by many, resulted in a devastating disruption of agricultural productivity and a catastrophic famine in 1932-33. Although the First Five-Year Plan called for the collectivization of only twenty percent of peasant households, by 1940 approximately ninety-seven percent of all peasant households had been collectivized and private ownership of property essentially eliminated. Stalin's dekulakization program, a program allowing the Soviet government to seize private farmlands, turned them into collective farms and killed millions of people who disagreed with the process.

Financial instability still plagues Russia today, a product of its economic policies as well as power struggles in the Kremlin. Corruption by political leaders runs rampant, as it usually does in countries with collectivist policies. President Vladimir Putin recently called on his finance minister to crack down on regional leaders, arresting three different governors on corruption charges in less than two years' time. Russian media devoted extensive coverage to each arrest, running pictures of cash-laden tables, diamond-encrusted fountain pens and elaborate gifts that the leaders supposedly presented to call girls.

In short, a big problem with collectivism is that someone must be in charge of determining who gets what. In traditional economic theory, this would be referred to as a benevolent social planner (or planners). Unfortunately, history shows that benevolence is a rare trait when few are in control of many.

When the government controls all the economic resources and their distribution, instead of the market, who controls the government? In Russia, the answer is a small group of billionaires called oligarchs. One of them, Leonid Mikhelson, today has a net worth estimated by *Forbes* of nearly $25 billion. Power to the people (and the oligarchs) is part of the problem that causes Russia today to have an economy smaller than Canada, a nation with population about a fourth the size of Russia and natural resources a fraction of Russia's. Remember the data from Chapter 5? Average GDP per person in Russia was $11,585 in 2019 compared to $46,195 in Canada and $65,281 in the United States, based on World Bank statistics.

Keys to Prosperity

The Person of Marx

Karl Marx chose a different key to prosperity than most people, believing he was entitled to be supported by wealthy people, first by his parents who paid for him through his university education and into his adult life. When his father died, Marx sued his mother to gain part of the estate. When that ended, he drained the wealth of his wife's family and later did the same from the wealthy family of Frederick Engels (his co-author in a book that took thirty years to write) for much of the rest of his life.

Marx's family was so destitute, his wife had to sell their personal belongings to pay for food. He signed so many IOUs, that his friends referred to him as "Marx the moocher." According to several biographers, Marx never held a job, causing his wife to write, "Karl, if you had only spent more time making capital instead of writing about it, we would have been better off."

His landlord evicted the family, not only for failure to pay rent, but because of Marx's personal habits. He drank too much, smoked too much, never exercised, and suffered from warts and boils that covered his body, probably from his habit of rarely bathing. His boils and obesity from lack of exercise probably contributed to his death in 1883. The man who said religion was the opium of the masses ended up taking opium for his boils, as well as doses of arsenic.

As for marriage and family, Marx wrote to Engels, "There is no greater stupidity than for people of general aspirations to marry and surrender themselves to the small miseries of domestic and private life." In his letters and essays, he made racist references about blacks and Jews and disowned his daughter for marrying a man of mixed race. His daughter Eleanor died of suicide in 1898 with a mixture of chloroform and prussic acid (allegedly concocted by her husband). His daughter Laura and her husband died by suicide in 1911.

"Communism begins where atheism begins," wrote Marx in the *Communist Manifesto*. "Communism abolishes eternal truths, it abolishes all religion, and all morality."

[Based on excerpts from Paul Kengor, *The Devil and Karl Marx*, 2020]

The China Evolution

One of the largest collectivist political parties in the world is the Communist Party of China. After centuries of domination by multiple dynasties creating high rates of rent and taxes collected by a wealthy minority of village chiefs and property owners, change was inevitable, something you could have predicted from the history of nations described earlier in this book.

The Communist Party of China was founded in 1921, during the May Fourth Movement, which Mao Zedong referred to as the birth of communism in China. After a period of slow growth and alliance with the Chinese Nationalist Party, the alliance broke down and Communists were purged under the leadership of Chiang Kai-shek. The Communists retreated to the countryside and built-up local bases throughout the country, holding them during the Japanese invasion and occupation of World War II and relying on them as headquarters through the Chinese Civil War (1945-49) until the Communist Party of China and Chairman Mao Zedong gained power and proclaimed the People's Republic of China (PRC), in October 1949.

Manufacturing and technology were slow to grow in post-war China and the output of Chinese factories was years behind Western standards. Agriculture received a smaller share of state investment than manufacturing with low growth of technology and productivity. There was some increase in the use of tractors, trucks, and mechanical threshers, but most agricultural activities were still performed by people or animals.

The government decided to create capital in the agricultural sector with an infrastructure program, building vast irrigation and water control systems employing huge teams of farmers. Surplus rural labor also was to be employed to support the industrial sector by setting up thousands of small-scale, low-technology, "backyard" industrial projects in farm units, which would produce machinery required for agricultural development and components for urban industries, and a leap to the final stage of agricultural collectivization – the formation of peoples' communes.

The communes were intended to acquire all ownership rights over the productive assets of subordinate units and take over most of the planning and decision-making for farm activities. Ideally, as traditional economists might predict, communes would improve efficiency by moving farm families into dormitories, feeding them in communal mess halls, and moving whole teams of laborers from task to task. In practice, this idealistic, extremely centralized form of commune was not accomplished in most areas.

Very soon after, it became evident the communes were too unwieldy to be successful, and eventually most governmental responsibilities were returned to local administration. Collectivism failed once again and private plots, which had disappeared into communes, were eventually restored as family farms.

After the death of Mao Zedong, the Communist Party leadership turned to market-oriented reforms to salvage the failing economy. Unlike earlier periods, when China was trying to achieve self-sufficiency, under Deng Xiaoping, foreign trade was considered an important source of investment funds and modern technology. Exports were encouraged and, as a result, restrictions on trade were loosened and foreign investment was legalized, encouraging individual rewards to productive people. The most common foreign investments were joint ventures between foreign firms and Chinese firms.

On July 15, 1971, President Nixon shocked the world by announcing he would visit the PRC the following year. The year of 1972 marked the historic visit of U.S. President Richard Nixon to the People's Republic of China and better relations between the United States and mainland China after years of diplomatic isolation. Nixon probably also hoped his visit to China would gain more leverage in the Cold War with the Soviet Union. Nixon's National Security Adviser, Henry Kissinger, sent overtures to the PRC government and flew on secret diplomatic missions to Beijing in 1971, where he met with Premier Zhou Enlai.

Throughout his visit, President Nixon and his advisors engaged in discussions with PRC leadership, including a meeting with Chairman Mao Zedong, while First Lady Pat Nixon toured schools, factories, and hospitals in the cities of Beijing, Hangzhou and Shanghai with the American press corps hanging on every word and snapping photos at every opportunity. Nixon described his visit "the week that changed the world" and marked China's opening to the world. There are some who say that despite his forced resignation in the U.S., Nixon remains the most popular U.S. president in China and lit a fire to China's economic growth, marking the evolution of the Chinese economy into a more market-oriented economy.

It is important to recognize that while the economy became more market-oriented, China remained collectivist politically. However, the result has been the growth of major firms such as Huawei with 170,000 employees operating in 170 countries. Legally, Huawei is an employee-owned company, but the company's trade union committee is registered with and pays dues to the Shenzhen federation of the All-China Federation of Trade Unions, which is effectively controlled by the Chinese Communist Party.

Some major corporations are state-owned such as China National Petroleum (CNPC), one of the largest integrated energy firms in the world. Others are a combination of public and state-owned corporations such as SAIC, one of the largest auto manufacturers in the world, a partner with General Motors. SAIC-GM, headquartered in Shanghai, now builds and distributes cars and light trucks for GM's Buick, Chevrolet, and Cadillac brands, one of the reasons GM now sells more cars in China than in the U.S. Chinese firms own numerous U.S. firms such as Smithfield Foods, Inc. (which also owns the pork brands of Tyson Foods), a meat-processing firm operating as a wholly owned subsidiary of WH Group of China.

There are numerous private and public businesses in China permitted by the government. Experienced executives report that when you do business with Chinese firms, you probably need a supply of gifts with brands such as Rolex, Tiffany, and other luxury labels to seal the deal. Personal profit drives performance in market-driven economies. Because decisionmakers, rather than the market, are the arbiters of production and distribution, bribes and other perks drive outcomes in collectivist economies.

Growing up on the streets of Hangzhou, a major city in the PRC, Jack Ma learned enough English to become an English teacher and start an online business in 1999 named Alibaba. It went public on the Hong Kong stock exchange and grew to become one of the world's largest retail, e-commerce, artificial intelligence, and venture capital companies in the world, making Jack Ma the richest man in China. Alibaba also sets sales records greater than Amazon on China's Singles' Day, the world's biggest online shopping day.

China had a history of successful traders two centuries before Communism, but the historic visit of President Nixon helped bring that tradition into the 21st century. In 2019 China had over 300 billionaires, according to *Forbes*, putting it second in the world, after the United States. Based on empirical data, the market system produces more prosperity than collectivist communes. Thus it is likely that these billionaires are not coming from communes in China, but from the move to allow for meritocracy in the Chinese economy.

Billionaires aside, what happened to the rest of China? China also has more millionaires (3.6 million in 2019) than the eight largest nations of Europe combined. More importantly, since 1960, China's real income per citizen has increased eightfold.

The number of people living in the middle class in China is now almost as many as the total population of the U.S. If you analyze this data from the behavioral perspective, this can be attributed to hard work and market driven decisions rewarding individual responsibility and meritocracy instead of collectivism. According to the Bill and Melinda Gates Foundation, there are half as many poor people living in the world today as there were in 1960, with China responsible for a substantial portion of them.

The immense issue facing Chinese leadership today, however, is that people who achieve economic freedom often also want political freedom. That makes the massive middle class a problem for its current president, Xi Jinping, General Secretary of the Communist Party of China (CPC), President of the People's Republic of China (PRC), and Chairman of the Central Military Commission (CMC). The conflict facing President Xi in the future of China is probably best understood by examining the current unrest in Hong Kong, which although legally part of China, retains many British influences that made it economically prosperous with a philosophy based on democracy and personal achievement rather than collectivism.

Emerging Market-Driven Nations

At a time when some in the United States are advocating Democratic Socialism as a preferred economic system for the U.S., empirical data reveal what happens to countries that embrace more individualist ideals rather than more collectivist ideals.

The closest to a controlled experiment, the "gold standard" of research methodology, was East Germany. In the collectivism under Soviet domination, East Germany was poor, but a land with potential. Although it had the same language, culture, and geography as West Germany, East Germany was decades behind in both freedom and prosperity, separated by the Berlin Wall.

The Wall finally fell in 1991 not because of losing the debate over Marxist-Leninist philosophy but because of empiricism. East Germans could look across the Wall figuratively and with the aid of television, literally, and see that their West German cousins lived better in every way: more cars, clothing, and computers and most importantly, more freedom. People trying to flee East German socialism were no longer shot by Soviet troops when the fall of the Wall in Berlin proved empirically that the market system of capitalism produces a higher level of prosperity than the collectivism imposed by Soviet socialism.

When the Soviet Union broke apart, it opened the door for growth in other Eastern European countries. Poland was one of the first to see the beneficial effects of a market driven economy. So did the Czech Republic and nations such as Estonia.

On Aug. 20, 1991, Estonia gained its independence after 51 years under the yoke of communism. From its first day of freedom, the new government began market-oriented reforms laying the foundation for a successful transition from socialism to capitalism. The political agenda included monetary reform, the creation of a free-trade zone, a balanced budget, the privatization of state-owned companies, and the introduction of a flat-rate income tax, paving the way for a major increase in living standards.

Purchasing power of Estonians increased 400 percent over the next two decades and life expectancy moved from 66 years in 1994 to 77 years in 2016. Its efficient and attractive corporate tax system helped Estonia to become a worldwide center for high-tech companies, boosting foreign investments and economic growth now higher than its former socialist subjugator, Russia.

Contrast market-driven economies with collectivist economies such as North Korea, Cuba, Venezuela, and empiricism leads to the conclusion that when governments own the means of production and set prices, it invariably leads to a powerful state and creates a large bureaucracy which often extends into other areas of life. The argument in support of socialism is philosophical. The argument against socialism is empirical.

Firms in a market-based economy have incentives to be efficient and produce goods demanded by consumers, creating pressure to cut costs and avoid waste. State-owned firms tend to be inefficient, less willing to reduce surplus workers (especially if they are political appointees) with less incentive to try innovative practices. In a market-driven economy, entrepreneurs and firms are incentivized to seek creative products and invest in new products desired by consumers. There are few incentives for innovation in collectivist economies.

The role of innovation in creating prosperity is documented in the last book written by Harvard Professor Clayton Christensen before his death in 2020, *The Prosperity Paradox: How Innovation Can Lift Nations Out of Poverty* with Efosa Ojomo and Karen Dillon. Christensen and his co-authors provide examples showing how innovation lifts countries out of poverty.

One of those examples is fresh-water wells in Nigeria which work when started by entrepreneurs but generally fail when money to build them is provided by the government or well-meaning NGOs. When water systems are started by entrepreneurs, local people know how to repair them, and profits generated from them can purchase parts needed to keep the wells operating. When the government or NGOs install water systems, they are likely to fail within a few years. Behavioral psychology explains why.

The lesson to be learned from Clayton Christensen and his colleagues is that an economy can never be fully understood, modeled, or controlled as is required in a planned economy. In a market economy, production and distribution is decentralized with decisions made by individuals with both the information and the incentive needed to achieve success. In a collectivist society, the centralized nature of decision-making requires the government to use more generalized information and the incentives for success are not as strong. Wealth, prosperity, and jobs do not come from the government. Jobs are created by solving problems with innovative products created by people incentivized by upward mobility, in much the same way A.G. Gaston did in Birmingham, Alabama, a century ago.

When this process creates wealth for those at the top, it also creates more and better jobs for those at the bottom and products that benefit many, such as the Narayana hospital in India you read about earlier.

In short, a rising tide lifts all boats, but not necessarily equally in a market economy. The creation of prosperity is based on jobs and innovation, both motivated by the opportunity for upward mobility, documented in *The Prosperity Paradox* with examples in some of the world's poorest nations. Wealth and income creation are derived from solving society's needs better in the future than the past. That is why economic prosperity is not a zero-sum game. From this perspective, Schumpeter and Hayek got it right and Keynes got it wrong.

There are problems with market economies, of course. This includes the reality of externalities. These occur when one person's actions affect others in a costly way, but effects are not considered by the person taking the action. For example, consider the global fishery. As each country extracts fish from the ocean, this leaves less fish for other countries but also less fish to reproduce. As no single country is responsible for wiping out all the fish, and every country wants some share of the fish, the predictable result is that global fisheries are overfished. Externalities such as this can result in market failures, and they are typically resolved through some form of regulation by a governing body.

Market failures can also occur due to monopolies and anti-competitive behaviors, which also require laws and regulations. Luckily, many global examples of market driven economies have adopted such regulations to assist the economy in situations when market failures are likely to occur. Regardless, objective analysis from a behavioral perspective suggests that collectivism is not a better alternative. As Winston Churchill once commented, "It has been said that democracy is the worst form of government except for all the others that have been tried." A similar statement could apply to market driven economies.

Collectivist Corruption

Outside of the issues with incentives and information, there is an even greater threat to collectivist economies: the lack of countervailing power by the market. Austrian economists such as Ludwig von Mises recognized the perils of monopolies more than a century ago. When monopolies occur in a market economy, there are two sources of countervailing power. One is the government. In the U.S. and most market economies, there are major government agencies to monitor and regulate some unfair monopolistic practices.

The other (and more effective) countervailing power to monopolies is competition. A tiny store in Rogers, Arkansas started by a man at age 44 and his wife challenged Sears and J.C. Penney and won. Amazon can challenge Walmart, and Alibaba can challenge Amazon. And all those corporate giants have competitors such as Lululemon, Ulta Beauty, Tractor Supply and Duluth Trading nibbling away at their market shares, segment by segment.

With collectivism, there is only one organization creating and operating the monopoly. That organization is the government, and no competitors are permitted to challenge the government monopoly. With collectivism monopolies, there is little or no incentive for innovation, greater profitability, or capital investment. As collectivism restricts the differentiating benefits from individual effort, the incentive for people controlling the government monopoly can be bribes and corruption to benefit the elite with no fear of competition from the market.

"Power to the people" in a collectivist economy typically means power to an elite group of people controlling the government (called the Politburo or similar term) and, empirical history discloses, to the person controlling that elite group. The resources of the economy eventually (and inevitably, history reveals) become the property of the perverse preferences of one person or family supported by oligarchs or other elites who support the Person in Charge. There is good reason for the essay question often assigned in World History courses on the topic, "Power Corrupts and Absolute Power Corrupts Absolutely."

When there is a basis for evaluating and censuring corruption, there is a basis for transferring power from bad decision-makers to others. That can happen when the society is organized as an open society, meaning that the nation believes that there are morals universal to all people regardless of their race, culture, religion, or background. In the United States, that was acknowledged as a part of the nation's foundation, *i.e.*, that all people "are endowed by their Creator with certain unalienable Rights." Among several rights enumerated in the U.S. Constitution are "rights to own private property, and to work and enjoy the fruits of one's labor."

The belief that inalienable rights of humans are *derived from the Creator* is such a formidable obstacle to the Central Planner of a collectivist economy that Communism was wise enough to incorporate atheism into the official fabric of governmental structure. The last thing a collectivist would want is an inalienable, objective standard to constrain the activities of the government. In a collectivist economy, both logic and empirical history reveal that Power to the People evolves inevitably to Power to a Person, whether the name of that person is Lenin, Stalin, Putin, Mao, Xi, Castro or Chavéz.

The major vice of individually driven markets is unequal distribution of prosperity. The major vice of Collectivism is the equal distribution of poverty, except for the elite (and often corrupt) government officials who typically control the economy. When you objectively analyze prosperity from the perspective of behavioral economics based on behavioral realities instead of traditional economic axioms about behavior, you understand why the theoretical appeal of collectivism breaks down quickly in reality.

Incentives inherent in individual rewards and responsibility increase production of goods and services, creating more goods and services to be distributed to everyone, though not equally. The U.S. value system is heavily influenced by the individualism required for survival on the American frontier, according to the thesis of Frederick Jackson Turner in one of the most influential papers ever published by an historian, "The Significance of the Frontier in American History," delivered to the American Historical Association in 1893. A compassionate individualistic or market-driven economy works hard to provide equal inputs for success to its citizens but expects unequal outputs based on their abilities and diligence.

Multiple studies by economists conclude that corruption increases among politicians, bureaucrats, law-enforcement officials, and private individuals with increasing government expansion and intervention in markets. Many of these studies are reviewed by Mark Thornton in *The Economics of Prohibition*, pp 127-138.

The Merits of Meritocracy

When thinking about the importance of individual effort in determining prosperity, reflect on the poem "Attitude," in which Charles Swindoll observes, "Life is 10 percent what happens to you and 90 percent how you respond to it." People live in a variety of economic systems. If you fail to understand the economic system, you face a barrier to your prosperity. The better you understand economic systems, the greater the probability of success from your individual response to them. A major goal for this book is for you to understand the economic systems that confront every individual. The better you understand how to marshal your personal merit, the more you enable your personal prosperity.

Some observers dislike the concept of meritocracy as an enabler of prosperity, despite evidence you read about in books by Clayton Christensen such as *The Prosperity Paradox*. Using evidence from both poor and prosperous nations, Christensen demonstrates that upward mobility is a key to increasing innovations in productivity and producing prosperity for a nation. The importance of meritocracy in contributing to the prosperity of nations is also well documented by Adrian Wooldridge in *The Aristocracy of Talent: How Meritocracy Made the Modern World*.

With examples dating back to classical philosophers such as Plato and historical examples in the U.K., U.S., and other countries, Wooldridge distinguishes "between yesterday's elites who made their money by inheriting it from Daddy (or exploiting the poor) and today's high achievers who made their money by solving difficult problems and thereby improving the state of the world" (p390).

Wooldridge concludes meritocracy provides both a moral critique of the old order and a code of conduct for reformers who want to replace the old ruling class with something better. That is, meritocracy has not always been the standard method of distribution of wealth, as there have been countless systems in the history of the world that do not reward those that create value. When you read many of the Prosperity Keys in this book, perhaps you observed how meritocracy allowed individuals such as A.G. Gaston, Sam Walton, Mary Dillon, and Jeff Bezos to increase prosperity for themselves and others. Did you make notes about how the values and skills of these individuals can be examples to increase your own prosperity?

The hard-working peasants in monarchies of the past would certainly attest to that, and inequities with respect to access to opportunity still exist. With that said, when you evaluate potential changes to your own nation's system of distribution you should carefully consider the notion of meritocracy. Consider if the proposed changes reward those that create the most value, and whether or not these rewards are likely to favor some people more than others.

Whether it is success in sports, arts, business, entrepreneurial endeavors, or other careers, consider your favorite wealthy person. How did they become wealthy? For many the answer will include notions of hard work, creativity, and talent, but consider whether these would matter if meritocracy was not the system of distribution. It is a reality that talent has replaced capital as the key to prosperity, but only if talent can be rewarded. If people save as well as spend, income is converted to capital providing prosperity when income decreases as age increases. Meritocracy in a wide range of endeavors, as Forbes reports, is how 90% of the most recently minted billionaires in the USA started with nothing or nearly nothing, achieving their wealth on talent instead of parents' capital.

This is not to say that the government should have no role in creating prosperity. A pattern for the future can be projected to include a relationship at deep levels between government and private organizations, just as there been in joint projects in the past. Examples include the joint activities to develop technology to land a man on the moon and projects during the 2020 pandemic to develop vaccines "at warp speed." Such joint efforts could be described as *fusion organizations*, combining the strengths, and minimizing the weaknesses of both government and market organizations.

If governments tried to develop Covid-19 vaccines, the result would have been different (and perhaps unsuccessful) than assigning the task to profit-oriented business organizations who accomplished objectives in less than a year that might otherwise take four to five years. But developing those vaccines at "warp speed" would not have happened without funding and regulatory support from the government. And as you read the accompanying Prosperity Key about Narayana Hospital, reflect on the question, would these innovations be as likely to occur if the health care system were owned by the government rather than a for-profit corporation?

Keys to Prosperity

Narayana Hospital: Quality Health Care with Affordability

If you are a health care provider or are concerned about the cost of health care, you may want to study Narayana Hospital (NH) in Bangalore for lessons how to take affordable health care to the people.

Mother Teresa had a profound effect on Dr. Devi Shetty, who was the late Nobel laureate's personal cardiac surgeon in the early 1990s while seeing over 100 patients daily. Most needed surgery but never came back for it. The high cost of cardiac surgery was the reason. Only 120,000 heart surgeries were performed annually when the need was for two million. "It was clear costs had to come down," says Dr. Shetty.

What started as a 280-bed hospital has grown to a 26-hospital network with 6,900 beds across 16 cities employing 13,000 people and 1,500 doctors. Patients seeking affordability previously had to be content with government hospitals, while quality seekers had to spend their way into private hospitals. Dr. Shetty searched for a model that would marry affordability and quality. "I was certain of one thing - charity is not scalable while a sound business model is," he says.

NH's average cost of a bypass surgery is $1,500, significantly lower than earlier years and much lower than other countries. NH's mortality rate (1.27 per cent) and infection rate (one per cent) for a coronary artery bypass graft procedure is as good as that of US hospitals. Incidence of bedsores after a cardiac surgery is globally anywhere between eight and 40 per cent. At NH, it has been almost zero in the last few years. Private equity funds JPMorgan and Pine Bridge have picked up a 24 per cent ownership in NH. They clearly believe NH is creating long-term value for investors.

How did Dr. Shetty manage to achieve both affordability and quality? The NH model leverages economies of scale, building large hospitals and attracting large numbers of patients through innovations such as micro-insurance and telemedicine.

Higher volumes cut per unit cost of surgeries. "Henry Ford taught us this simple principle over 100 years ago," says Dr. Shetty, applying mass production techniques to open heart surgery. "When you perform open heart surgery on an assembly line, not only does the cost go down but quality goes up. Performing a medical procedure repeatedly improves a doctor's skill and reduces errors."

At NH, doctors operate as teams. Each team has a specialist, junior doctors, trainees, nurses, and paramedical staff. "A bypass surgery typically takes about five hours. The critical part, which is the actual grafting, takes only an hour. The specialist does that while harvesting of the veins/arteries, opening, and closing of the chest, suturing and other procedures are done by junior doctors. The preparation of the patient is managed by nurses and paramedical staff. This process leaves the specialist free to perform more surgeries, far more than any hospital globally, and dramatically reducing cost.

Also, frugality is the watchword at NH. Instead of buying all its equipment, it leases some on a pay per use basis, keeping capital costs low. Great emphasis is placed on maintaining equipment and extending its life. Buildings are designed to keep costs low also, with a central buying unit (CBU) and standardized procedures, cutting inventory costs by 15 to 40 per cent with higher quality. NH also adopted technology to aid information flow, cutting costs and enabling management to decide quickly when receiving requests for free or subsidized surgery. NH also mines cloud-based data to raise quality levels and improve efficiency.

- [Excerpted from *Business Today India,* December 20, 2021]

Evaluate a Policy on the Spectrum

Economics is a dynamic process, not a zero-sum game. Individual rewards and responsibility increase *production* which is the key to providing more goods for *distribution* to both the poor as well as the prosperous producers of goods and services. These individual rewards providing the most value are also responsible for creating some amount of inequality. Hence, an economy that is successfully incentivized would be expected to have a distribution of wealth.

Any distribution of wealth guarantees that 50% of people having a "below average" amount of wealth will also have 50% of people with above average wealth. This would surely be inequitable if this was fixed so that the poorest people in a nation could never rise to the top. However, empirical data suggest that there is opportunity for almost anyone of below average wealth to invest in developing their owns skills to create value for others and become more prosperous. In other words, economies that rely more heavily on individual responsibility are unequal but also offer high mobility. How to identify and take advantage of these opportunities is precisely the purpose of this book.

The challenge in assessing the offerings of politicians and pundits is that they will mostly tend to fall somewhere between the extremes. As you saw in Chapter 8, any policy (especially those that seem too-good-to-be-true) has the potential to result in unintended consequences. Always question policies that claim to be simple solutions but ignore the realities of human behavior.

The data show that countries with economies that increase the rewards for individual responsibility and success are more prosperous. In contrast, countries that increase the amount of collectivist programs tend to decline in prosperity. As an objective solutionist, you can evaluate any suggested policy by these metrics. Politicians are well-versed in positioning a policy to appear attractive, but objective analysis can help identify where a policy falls on this spectrum and whether or not the consequences of the policy are likely to be beneficial to the nation. Is a policy likely to increase incentives for businesses to thrive (individualism) or is it likely to decrease incentives (collectivism)? It is also worth considering how a policy can facilitate higher mobility in the distribution of wealth, so that anyone sufficiently motivated can achieve the highest levels of prosperity.

Discussion Questions

- What is the primary appeal of collectivist economic policies such as socialism? What are its major problems?
- The United States is sometimes described as more individually-based in its economic policies than some other countries. Why? What would be your suggestions for improving or changing that in the future?
- Karl Marx is one of the best known philosophers in history. How would you analyze his influence on current policies in the U.S. and other nations?
- If someone asks you whether you are a Socialist or Capitalist, what would be your answer be after reading this chapter? Where would you place yourself on the spectrum of collectivist versus individualist?
- Based on what you have read in this book and other sources, how would you analyze the contributions of the late Harvard Professor, Clayton Christensen?

Chapter 10

Your Personal Path to Prosperity

As you read in Chapter 2, applying behavioral economics does not "throw out the baby with the bath water." Instead, behavioral economics retains enduring principles of economics, sometimes modified by behavioral realities grounded in psychology, sociology, anthropology, and other social sciences. In a similar way, solutions to the problems that you face should not sacrifice the valuable experiences and knowledge that have led to past success. Rather, the material from this book can be used to hone and improve your methods for assessing the world of opportunities around you.

If you have taken time to reflect on the themes of this book, you probably now realize that the path to prosperity, for both individuals and nations, is *values*. For nations, that deduction is well supported by data in the trilogy of books by Diedre McCloskey mentioned in several places throughout this book. Why did Canada, the U.S., Australia, and Hong Kong become more prosperous than colonies in South America and Africa which often had more natural resources than British colonies? Data-based answers to those questions are readily available and summarized below from *Why Nations Fail: The Origins of Power, Prosperity, and Poverty* by Daron Acemoglu and James A. Robinson. Also, in Joel Mokyr's *Culture of Growth: The Origins of the Modern Economy*.

How can nations as small as The Netherlands, Singapore and Switzerland achieve high levels of prosperity with almost no natural resources, but nations sitting on vast resources such as Russia, Nigeria and Brazil attain low levels of prosperity and high levels of poverty? The answer is their citizens' prosperity-inducing *values*. Hopefully you observed examples in previous chapters closely enough to form your own conclusions about which values lead you to personal prosperity.

Knowledge and motivation are more important causes of prosperity than wealth or financial assets. For most people, it is *knowledge* and the *diligence* to apply knowledge that determines who is poor and who is prosperous. *Discipline*, focused *education* and the importance of *personal motivation* and *individual responsibility* determine which nations and which individuals within nations prosper. *Delayed gratification* is an essential value separating prosperous people from poor, a lesson identified in the marshmallow studies at Stanford, applying to many dimensions of life beyond economics. *Frugality* and *savings* are also key values separating prosperous people from poor. So is *cleanliness*. From a national standpoint, *property rights* are also very important, as the incentive to work hard has little value when workers cannot keep what they earn.

It would be nice if society had no poor people, but the empiricism of objective economics discloses that some level of inequality is desirable when those differences are explained by the value created by the individual (meritocracy). Likewise, this means that some percentage of people will always be "below average" in wealth relative to others, regardless of how the standard for poverty is defined. However, in economies that emphasize individual effort and responsibility, people with knowledge and discipline can hopefully rise from the bottom to the top.

In the U.S., about ten percent rise from the very bottom to the very top. With that said, policies that improve the equal opportunity for such mobility are key. For people rising to the top from dysfunctional families, the difference is often *mentors* outside the immediate family showing how and encouraging poor people to rise from poverty to prosperity. If that idea does not resonate with you, go back, and read the books of Wes Moore and J.D. Vance for examples from both white and Black cultures. If you want practical advice on how to overcome prejudice against people rising with a felony conviction, you will find it in a book by Harley T. Blakeman, *Grit: How to Get a Job and Build a Career with a Criminal Record.*

Keys to Prosperity

Making a Difference

Can a firm prosper if it hires people with diverse backgrounds, including formerly incarcerated citizens? Craig Poole, General Manager of DoubleTree by Hilton in Reading, PA says "yes," and demonstrates that principle with a staff including employees with alternative resumes, as well as many colors, ethnicities, and physical challenges.

Staying in the hotel reveals to observant guests that the firm represents DEI (Diversity, Equity, Inclusion) in action. You might also observe highly-loyal employees hugging Poole in gratitude and often exuding praise to guests about a boss who treats them like friend and family. Watch Poole in the lobby greeting hotel guests so pleased with the perfection of nearly everything about the hotel they can't wait to come back. So nearly perfect, in fact, that the property recently won the award for highest level of customer satisfaction in the Hilton chain.

You will also see in the lobby a trophy case containing more than forty awards from hospitality and community groups recognizing the hotel for its unusually high levels of service, restaurants, creativity (with shelves full of books on lobby walls) and cleanliness. Based on metrics of customer satisfaction and high occupancy rates, the conclusion is clear: Prosperity is often achieved by people and firms doing well by doing good.

-   *[Based on interview with Craig Poole]*

If you are a winner in the birth lottery, that is very fortunate for you, but it does not guarantee a prosperous future. For everyone, understanding values that cause and create success provides a more reliable path to prosperity. If you have a choice of what to inherit from your parents, which would you choose? Wealth or values? Study intergenerational mobility and you will probably conclude that prosperous values from parents are more enduring causes of prosperity than inherited dollars.

Individual responsibility tends to yield more prosperous nations than collectivism as you saw in the previous chapter. Practical examples of rising from poverty to prosperity are well-documented in *The Prosperity Paradox: How Innovation Can Lift Nations out of Poverty* by Clayton Christensen, Efosa Ojomo and Karen Dillon. With that said, nations whose economy is built on individual incentives are more likely to *remain prosperous* if they include *compassionate programs to help fellow citizens* along a similar path toward prosperity. This contrasts with oppression by the elite you read about in nations starting with Egypt and continuing through the centuries around the world, where examples of neglect or abuse of the poor eventually lead to problems.

Empirical observation of successful entrepreneurs indicates that *motivation to help others solve their problems* is more likely to lead to personal prosperity than motivation to be wealthy. Empirical evidence reveals that a key characteristic of prosperous people and prosperous nations is the degree to which citizens care about and for each other. Sometimes it seems to take a disaster – hurricane, forest fires, or a pandemic to observe a clear demonstration of the care and compassion people have for one another. When it happens, often in the context of faith, religious practices, or other shared-value systems across people, *values that were words become manifest in behavior.*

Knowledge is the path to prosperity for ordinary people in the future just as much as it was in the past for people with names such as Bezos, Gates, Walton, Steward, Jobs, Gaston, Thomas, and Dell. For some, that knowledge is obtained in schools in which *parents or mentors inculcate values that motivate children to attend and learn.*

Sometimes education is financed by parents but for others it is self-financed by working as a student or working for Starbucks. The same knowledge is available at inexpensive schools, some costing as little as $1,000 a year, as at expensive schools. The founder of the world's largest corporation graduated from Missouri University and its current CEO received his MBA from the University of Tulsa, not Harvard or Stanford, as excellent as those schools are. *Bloomberg BusinessWeek* publishes a list each year of the top-ranked business schools that provide the most full-ride scholarships to their MBA programs, but it is individual initiative and effort that allows people to earn those scholarships.

Expensive and inexpensive universities mostly teach from the same textbooks. Note also that professors at the most expensive schools are usually faculty members at those schools because of their research skills, not their teaching skills. Incentives for effective teaching change as a result. And regardless of what universities are accessible, the same knowledge is also available in books you find in your local library, on the Web, or through online education resources where the cost of obtaining knowledge is much less than at a university.

Is it truly possible for a student to teach herself or himself the knowledge needed to obtain a college education by reading books in the library? Just ask Lashawn Samuel, a 19 year old who walked three miles round trip most every day from his home in a troubled area of the city to a local library to get help with his homework, and it paid off. The Columbus City Schools student told the Columbus *Dispatch* in the Spring of 2020 he was accepted to 12 colleges and universities, and several of them offered a full scholarship, including his number one choice, The Ohio State University. It was not money that created his success in gaining acceptance to college. It was his values. Tenacity can be a more important determinant of prosperity than money.

Successful athletes play with pain. So do successful people – perhaps not the physical pain an athlete faces, but the fear of failure, conflict, or wrong decisions. In athletic arenas, victors sometimes play with painful injuries. In economic arenas, successful workers sometimes play with emotional fears and undertake short-term financial risks to bet on themselves. Making it to the victory lap at the end depends on the depth of vision for success at the beginning and values that underly a journey to the end. "Without a vision, the people will perish," is a Proverbial truth applying to both national and individual prosperity. Do not expect poor people to become prosperous without a vision that shows it can happen, tools to make it happen and the motivation providing diligence to sustain it happening.

If you hear someone concerned about inequality, ask that person (or organization) what they are doing to help poor people gain the vision that leads to prosperity. Vision is more valuable than wealth in achieving upward mobility. As Sun Tsu explained in *The Art of War*, "Vision is the strategy from which victory is derived." That *behavioral* truth applies to nations, organizations, and individuals.

Keys to Prosperity

Accelerate Your Career with a Mentor

Whether you are just beginning your career or ready to take it to a higher level, mentors can accelerate your path to prosperity. An example can be observed in the career of Mary Dillon, Executive Chair of Ulta Beauty.

Mary Dillon didn't inherit wealth. She was one of six siblings in the one-bathroom Chicago home of a steelworker and homemaker and attended nearby University of Illinois in Chicago, paying for her education working as a waitress and cleaning apartments. She chose a business major because "I knew I needed to get a job right out of school." She began her career at Quaker Oats Co, promoted to her first executive role at 27, eventually running the Quaker division for Pepsi. That led to her appointment as Global VP of Marketing for McDonald's Corp and later CEO of U.S. Cellular before selected as CEO of Ulta Beauty.

In an interview with the Wall Street *Journal*, Ms. Dillon described the importance of mentors in her career. They included Andy McKenna, Chairman of McDonald's, Sol Trujillo, an outstanding executive in the telecommunications industry, Anne Mulcahy, CEO and chairwoman of Xerox Corp and Tracee Ellis Ross, Actress and CEO of Pattern Beauty. (From "Mary Dillon, "The Mentors Who

Helped Ulta Beauty's Unlikely CEO Succeed," WSJ, January 29, 2022).

You can understand how to advance your own career by studying lessons learned from people such as Mary Dillon. Understanding the careers of leaders can also accelerate your retirement account by investing in firms with leaders such as her. Don't buy individual stocks without studying leadership of the firm. As one of the authors, I studied her career, checked out the credentials of her (50 percent female) Board of Directors at Ulta, and the increases in productivity achieved after Dillon became CEO (available in reports from Morningstar Research), causing me to buy stock in ULTA – which more than doubled in value in three years. You can find these data in publicly available proxy statements and annual reports for every public corporation on the SEC's Edgar website and financial websites. Don't buy individual stocks without reading their proxy statements. Doing well with your retirement account includes doing your homework before buying individual stocks.

-   *Roger Blackwell*

On-the-job values determine which employees prosper in organizations and which ones do not. Most careers involve other people. You can have great academic intelligence and still lack social intelligence – the ability to be a good listener, to be sensitive toward others, to give and take criticism well. Those are principles developed from *behavioral* knowledge of psychology and sociology, not traditional or Keynesian economics.

The Carnegie Foundation for the Advancement of Teaching discovered a significant fact in their research: in a person's career 15% of one's financial success is determined by one's technical knowledge and the other 85% is due to skills in human interaction and the ability to lead others. Success involves EQ (emotional intelligence quotient) as much or more than IQ.

One of the most important questions facing any employee is, "How do I add value to this company?" In the long-run, *adding value determines what you are likely to be paid.* When you are self-employed instead of working for an employer, the question is the same, but worded a little differently, "How do I add value to customers and potential customers?" Those questions are key to prosperity and hopefully Chapters 3, 4, and 5 gave you answers to apply along your own path to prosperity. In marketing courses, students learn how to create brands, but the most important brand you will ever create, whether as an employee or an entrepreneur, is the *brand called YOU.*

Wisdom is achieved by making decisions, many which turn out to be wrong. There will always be mistakes, even among the most successful entrepreneurs or employees. Prosperous entrepreneurs and intrapreneurs learn from mistakes in the past to make fewer mistakes in the future. That process is made easier and the road to prosperity made safer with *values* to guide personal decisions.

The Value of Values

Values and their effect on behavior have been the subject of research by many scholars in social psychology and other disciplines. One of the pioneers in this research is Shalom Schwartz, Professor of Psychology at Hebrew University, who identified the structure of basic human values and where they come from based on research in 82 countries.

The Schwartz Value Survey is used in consumer behavior studies to measure how values affect a wide range of economic behavior including brand preferences, financial security, enjoyment, self-direction, and other decisions across cultures. Many of the major findings about how values influence behavior and differ from other psychological constructs are described by Sonia Roccas and Lilach Sagiv (eds) in *Values and Behavior: Taking a Cross Cultural Perspective.*

Values can be defined as *shared beliefs or group norms internalized by an individual.* Values have profound effect on national prosperity because they are shared by *groups* of people. The group might be any size from very small, such as a family or a sports team, to very large such as a nation or a geographic area where references are sometimes made to "Midwestern values" or "Scandinavian values." There are values permeating the entire culture of Switzerland such as democracy, privacy, and civility (and chocolate!) but still allowing variations between German, Italian, French, and Romansh groups within the nation.

To be relevant to behavior causing prosperity, regardless of the type of group, the norm for that group must be *internalized (accepted and acted on) by an individual*. Sometimes individuals fail to understand normal behavior in a group to which they belong and sometimes they actively reject a group norm. Your family may believe in values that cause prosperity but if you fail to learn or *accept* those values, they will contribute little or nothing to your own prosperity. In contrast, if your family acts upon values that lead to poverty, they may lead to your own poverty unless you *reject* those values.

Keep in mind that "Internalized by an individual" is the key phrase in understanding the importance of values in determining prosperity. "Norm" of the group is a statistical average, not necessarily the behavior of every individual within the group.

Research on how values affect behavior recognizes two forms of values, *terminal* and *instrumental*. Terminal values are *words* that describe the goals of the group and provide motivation for individuals within the group. *Instrumental* values are the behavior expected or exhibited by members of the group, measured by the actions of individuals within the group. They also determine the teamwork required and associated with accomplishing group goals. *Behavior* is a measure of the group's values, like the comment sometimes made that "the walk matches the talk."

Most of this book is about how values affect personal prosperity as well as national prosperity. Values also affect the prosperity of organizations such as business firms and other groups.

Do organizations with visionary values achieve greater long-term success than other firms? That question was definitively answered in one the highest selling business books of all time, *Built to Last: Successful Habits of Visionary Companies* by Stanford Professors Jim Collins and Jerry I. Porras and follow-on books by Collins, including *Good to Great: Why Some Companies Make the Leap...And Others Don't*. You can also find data to support the importance of values and corporate performance in *The Culture Cycle*, by Harvard Professor James Heskett, a follow-up to the classic *Corporate Culture and Performance* by Heskett and Professor John Kotter. If you want documentation on the criticality of values in organizational performance, you will find it in these and many other books and scholarly articles showing a clear relationship between values and organizational success.

You will also find evidence of the relationship between values and prosperity when you board Southwest Airlines, rent a car from Enterprise, or eat candy from the Mars corporation. These firms have invested heavily in onboarding programs and training that inculcates their values into the minds of their employees.

Keys to Prosperity

Creating Cultural Capital

What is better than corporate DEI (Diversity, Equity, Inclusion) programs? The answer is Cultural Capital. Just as firms sometimes record "goodwill" on their financial balance sheets, Cultural Capital reflects the goodwill generated by meeting needs of people of color and other minorities.

Cultural capital focuses on bringing America together by helping people excel in diverse occupations. It helps overcome poverty that often occurs when people live their lives on feelings and emotions instead of facts and logic. Prosperous people place huge emphasis on education, discipline, and responsibility. DEI is a fleeting endeavor if it does not improve an organization's cultural capital.

- *[Lawrence Funderburke, MBA,CFA, former collegiate and professional basketball player, and Founder of Lane Change U.]*

Your Personal Values for Prosperity

The most important result of reading a book based on solutions for prosperity may be defining how values contribute to your own personal prosperity and the prosperity of your family or of people you care about. That was the harvest of the senior author after studying the topics in this book for more than five decades, resulting in a list of behavioral rules applied to the author's own life. That list is the conclusion of this book, not as a recommendation for what your list should be but as an example of how values affect *behavior*. However, before examining that example, you may have been wondering as you read many of the conclusions in this book about the qualifications of the authors. So, before ending this book, perhaps you would like to know a little more about the senior author and the influences that lead to his conclusions.

The senior author, Roger Blackwell, began life many years ago in the poorest county of one of the poorer states near the rural Ozark village of Humansville, Missouri, named after James Human, a person of African American and Native American ancestry, who settled the area in 1834. In the author's early years, he lived on a farm in Missouri where he learned who prospered more than others, including observations from his farmer relatives about how to discern the farms of families with knowledge and diligence from families lacking those values. And yes, his Saturday night baths as a child were in one of those wash tubs you read about filled with hot water from a nearby wood-burning stove. He survived, without being "thrown out with the bath water."

He learned by the example of his parents how poor people overcame poverty in the Great Depression and World War II. His father worked full-time beginning at age 18 as a teacher in a one-room rural elementary school for a salary of twenty dollars per month. Financed entirely by his minuscule salary and wife's job working in a retail store, his father obtained a college degree after thirteen years of correspondence courses, extension courses on Saturday and summer sessions at the (very affordable) nearby state college.

As a young child, Roger observed his father receive a bachelor's degree, allowing him to begin teaching in a high school and diligently pursue the path from poverty to prosperity, described in a book by Dale Joseph Blackwell, *Farm Boy: Conditions and Incidents in the Early Life of a South Central Missouri Country Lad.*

In high school, at age 16, he began working at a local radio station as janitor where he progressed to higher positions, working full-time while attending college at Northwest Missouri State before transferring to Missouri University to receive bachelor's and master's degrees, all without financing from his parents or accumulating debt himself, demonstrating where there is a will, there is a way for poor people to achieve a college education.

As an undergraduate history major, he was fascinated by courses in European History. You probably observed that interest in history while reading some of the chapters in this book. He also took courses in Economics at the undergraduate and master's level and in his doctoral program at Northwestern University where he received a Ph.D.

The doctoral program at Northwestern prepared him for a career in social sciences by passing doctoral exams in five departments: Economics, Social Psychology, Quantitative Analysis, Business History and Marketing. His doctoral dissertation on price levels in a differentiated oligopoly had co-advisors, one from the Economics Department and one from the Business School.

During his career at The Ohio State University, his primary teaching and research was in the Business School but because of his research in health care economics, he also held a joint appointment in the College of Medicine. That resulted in a book analyzing how to make the U.S. health care system more efficient: *Consumer Driven Health Care*, co-authored with Dr. Thomas Williams and Alan Ayers.

At Ohio State, in addition to his primary research area of Consumer Behavior, he also taught courses in Thanatology (the scientific study of death and the practices associated with it) and for a few years was a member of the Black Studies faculty, reflecting a life-long interest in cross-cultural research, civil and human rights and upward mobility among under-served minority groups.

During his forty years at Ohio State, he taught over 65,000 students and published almost a book a year. The *Consumer Behavior* text which he co-authored was translated into Russian, Portuguese, Spanish, French, Korean and other languages and used in universities and organizations in many countries of the world. Its success as a textbook was the catalyst for him being invited to other countries to teach and do research.

Although Ohio State was his primary locus of research and teaching for decades, experiences as Visiting Professor and Lecturer gave him the opportunity to compare universities in diverse countries. He held Visiting Professor positions at Stanford University, the University of Washington, Guelph University (Canada), University of Melbourne (Australia), University of the Witwatersrand and Cape Town University, teaching in South Africa many times, including a few times in the informal markets of Soweto, a township of more than a million people near Johannesburg.

His understanding of global economics and values was grounded in being a consultant and visiting lecturer on six continents. The diversity of teaching in Saudi Arabia, Turkey, Israel, Brazil, Argentina, Peru, Mexico, Colombia, Germany, U.K., Bermuda, Bahamas, Jamaica, St. Thomas, St. Croix, Haiti, Trinidad-Tobago, Costa Rico, Panama, Japan, China, Australia, Bangladesh, Greece, Italy, France, Spain, Portugal, Norway, Sweden, Philippines, Botswana, Monaco, and Belgium provided a foundation of personal knowledge for the chapters you read earlier about global economics.

Three nations where he studied and taught repeatedly were Singapore, Switzerland, and Netherlands. But you probably discerned that while reading this book, didn't you? In Canada, in addition to Visiting Professor at Guelph, he taught Vistage Executive Seminars in nearly every major city from Fredericton to Vancouver. He knows the U.S. is a remarkable place to teach, work and live, but so are many other nations where the author taught and worked, learning from personal observation what makes some people poor and some people prosperous.

After receiving a research sabbatical for a year at Ohio State, allowing him to travel to numerous nations, conclusions from this research were published in the book *From the Edge of the World: Global Lessons for Personal and Professional Prosperity* and the book (with Salah Hassan) *Global Marketing: Perspectives and Cases.*

After retiring from Ohio State, his understanding of poverty and prosperity was enriched further while teaching General Educational Development (GED) classes almost six years to inmates at the Federal Correctional Institution in Morgantown, West Virginia. There is nothing quite as educational about how people escape (or don't escape!) from project housing in the hood and other dysfunctional backgrounds as teaching former drug dealers and other diverse occupations (including a former Mafia hit man) the subjects of economics, math, government, grammar, and literature. In prison when you teach math, explaining metric conversion of grams to ounces, it is not unusual to be asked, "Is that with or without the bag?"

The author taught students in prison how to obtain a GED and when they leave prison how to get a job, but the GED students in prison taught him even more about the realities of poverty, crime, and injustice. Nelson Mandela was correct when he said no one understands a nation as well as someone who spends time in its prisons.

Instrumental Values for Life

You have read a lot in the previous pages about *terminal values* – the goals that make people and nations prosperous – but how do you translate the words into *instrumental values*, the behavior of everyday life? Midway through his career, the senior author began formulating a summary of how values affect life, which he described as *Roger's Rules for a Successful Life*. In the latter part of his career, he began to reproduce these rules and make them available to students on the last day of class. He also distributed them to audiences where he spoke and to inmates where he taught GED classes.

He has received responses from students and others reporting they posted them on their dormitory walls, office bulletin boards and prison cells. They are reproduced for you on the following page and in his 40th published book, *You Are Not Alone and Other Lessons a Teacher Learned from Parents, Professors and 65,000 Students,* a book describing the events and process that led to the creation of Roger's Rules.

The authors' intention is not that the following page should become behavior you should follow, but the objective is that you come to conclusions after reading this book defining your own values and the behavior that will lead to your own prosperity and success, just as the senior author did after decades of research, teaching and observing people in 39 nations on six continents. Consider the following page as an example of how values affect behavior for *one* person – the author of this book – and perhaps as a template to construct and write your own rules.

The book you have just read is about how people achieve prosperity, especially people who did not inherit it, which is most privileged people in the U.S. After you read the following template, it is the authors' hope you will write your own rules as a practical tool to achieve the prosperity and success that result from your own conclusions about practical values from what you concluded studying Behavioral Economics. Hopefully, your conclusions from this book will lead to prosperity and success in your life. When you do that, you will also contribute to growth and prosperity for the nation.

It is *behavior* that gives value to the study of Behavioral Economics.

Discussion Questions

- What are *your* personal rules for a successful life?
- Have your personal rules for life been influenced by what you have read in this book? If so, how?
- Consider the values of the current and former leaders of your country that you hold in high regard. How important are these values to the prosperity of business and your national as a whole?
- How similar are the values that determine your personal profitability from values that determine the prosperity of a nation? How are they different?
- Consider the role of a business leader. What role should your understanding of values affect your firm's policies?

Roger's Rules for Success

- Treat every individual you meet with respect and kindness.

- When individuals treat you with unkindness or lack of respect, reread Rule #1.

- Help as many people as you can, in as many ways as you can, for as long as you can.

- If you cannot say something good about someone, say nothing about that person at all.

- Love your work. Successful people work for more than for what they are paid.

- Be frugal. Save for the rainy day because rainy days always occur. What you have is determined more by what you save than what you earn.

- Make difficult decisions based on long-term effects rather than immediate gratification. Live to learn, learn to live.

- Eat healthy and exercise regularly. You will live longer, spend less and be happier.

- Lasting success is derived from finding out what God wants you to do and then doing it.

- Love conquers everything else.

- Roger Blackwell

Roger's Rules for Success were given to thousands of students and to audiences where he spoke. The process and events that created them are described in *You Are Not Alone and Other Lessons a Teacher Learned from Parents, Professors and 65,000 Students*. Roger has received messages from people saying they posted these rules on corporate bulletin boards, dormitory walls, government offices, military barracks, and prison cells. Feel free to print a copy to use in your life or organization.

www.rogerblackwellbusiness.com

Index

239

Netherlands
    agriculture in, 79
    art and artists in, 78–79
    culture of prosperity in, 85
    per capita GDP in, 70
    wealth accumulation by, 131
Neumann, Adam, 131
News Nation, 6–7
Newsom, Gavin, 161
Newton, Isaac, 82
Nicholas II (Russia), 193
Nicosia, Francesco, 53
996 workers, 40–41
Nixon, Richard, 200, 201
Nobel Prize, 25, 29, 33–34, 171, 188
Noise, in data interpretation, 33–34, 146
Nordic socialism, 186–192
North, Douglas C., 82–83
Norway
    corporate tax rates in, 191
    Index of Economic Freedom ranking for, 186
    tuition-free college in, 153–154

O

Objective analysis
    apolitical nature of, 181
    of collectivism, 205
    of income, 125
    of inequality, 124, 125
    of Medicare for All, 180
    by news media outlets, 6–7
    of policy proposals, 212
    of price-quality relationship, 22
    of prosperity, 30, 132, 146, 165
    of systemic racism, 99
    of unintended consequences, 146, 160, 181
Ojomo, Efosa, 142, 203, 216
Oligarchs, 197
Online platforms. *See* Internet
On-the-job values, 219
Operation Desert Storm, 73

P

Pandemic. *See* Covid-19 pandemic
Partisanship, in news outlets, 6–7
PE (Price to Earnings) ratio, 146–147
Pell Grants, 134
People's Republic of China (PRC). *See* China
Per capita GDP, 8, 69–70, 80, 83, 85–87, 197
Personal motivation, 89–90, 214
Philanthropy, 110–111
Piketty, Thomas, 124–126, 129–133, 140, 157
Pilgrims and Plymouth colony, 16–17, 80
Poole, Craig, 215
Poverty
    decision-making and, 34, 41, 91
    economic mobility vs., 132–133
    economic principles in determination of, 3
    homelessness and, 113–116, 127
    minimum wage increases and, 167, 173
    overcoming, 89–90, 108–109
    in post–World War I era, 28
    predictors of, 136
PRC (People's Republic of China). *See* China
Predictably irrational behavior, 34, 55, 159
Predictions
    in behavioral economics, 33, 146
    of consumer behavior, 55, 66–67
    demand-related, 25, 26
    of prosperity vs. poverty, 136
    in traditional economics, 7, 26, 34, 146
Price-quality relationship, 22, 23
Price to Earnings (PE) ratio, 146–147
Problem recognition stage of purchase decisions, 55–57
Product differentiation, 59–60
Production. *See also* Gross Domestic Product
    agricultural, 11, 71
    in collectivist economies, 201
    decentralization of, 204
    defined, 11
    efficiency of, 192
    Gross National Product, 8–9

242

Other Books By Roger D. Blackwell

You Are Not Alone and Other Lessons a Teacher Learned from Parents, Professors and 65,000 Students

Saving America: How Garage Entrepreneurs Grow Small Firms into Large Fortunes

Consumer Behavior, 10th edition (Available in multiple languages and Asian editions)

Consumer Driven Health Care

Brands That Rock: What Business Leaders Can Learn from the World of Rock and Roll

Customers Rule! Why the E-commerce Honeymoon is Over and Where Winning Businesses Go from Here

From Mind to Market: Reinventing the Retail Supply Chain

From the Edge of the World: Global Lessons for Personal and Professional Prosperity

Global Marketing: Perspectives and Cases

Contemporary Cases in Consumer Behavior

Cases in Marketing Management and Strategy

Consumer Attitudes Toward Physicians and Malpractice

A Christian Approach to Transcendental Meditation

Strategic Marketing

Laboratory Equipment for Marketing Research

Research in Consumer Behavior

Cases in Consumer Behavior

Acknowledgements

Many people suggested valuable ideas, provided references and data, and read and provided comments on chapters and early drafts of this book. We deeply appreciate the contributions of each of the following persons: Andrea Cummins, Cynthia Kinman, Steve Dunson, John Ely, Sunny Martin, Mazen El-Katib, Ted Griffith, John Gayetsky, Josiah Zimmerman, Sunil Sabharwal, Greg Huddle, John Mariotti, Kent Larsson, Rabbi Areyah Kaltmann, Rabbi Hillel Kapenstein, Craig Poole, Lawrence Funderburke, Rhett Ricart, Loretta Berryhill, Chay Rankin, Dr. David Kollat, Deborah M. O'Brien, Professor Philip Kotler, Professor Mark Thornton, Professor Robert Tamilia, Jayme Hutchinson, Sandra Harbrecht.

The authors appreciate the encouragement and interest received by colleagues at The Ohio State University, especially leadership given to faculty by Dr. Anil Makhija, Dean of the Fisher College of Business.

The authors benefitted from the previous literature on Behavioral Economics. Among influential texts were *Behavioral Economics, 3rd Edition* by Edward Cartwright, Professor of Economics at De Montfort University, and *An Introduction to Behavioral Economics* by Nick Wilkinson, an Economics professor at Richmond, The American International University in London and Matthias Klaes, Professor of Political Economy at the University of Buckingham, UK. A useful introduction to this literature is Philip Corr and Anke Plagnol, *Behavioral Economics, the Basics*. In such textbooks, you will see the terms NM (for Neoclassical Model) to describe Behavioral Economics and SEM (for Standard Economic Model) to describe what is called traditional economics in the book you are now reading. If interested, type "Best books on Behavioral

Economics" in your browser and you will find several of the books mentioned in the book you are about to read.

Most importantly, the authors acknowledge the significance of their families enduring the time commitments of authors while completing the present book. Roger Blackwell appreciates the support of his loving wife, Linda, and her wise counsel based on years of experience at The Ohio State Press. Roger Bailey appreciates the support of his wife Jane Bailey and his amazing children Annabelle and Nathan Bailey.

Finally, the authors express their appreciation to Richard Levick for introducing them to Philip Jan Rothstein and the excellence of editorial assistance of Philip Jan Rothstein, Glyn Davies, and associates at Rothstein Publishing.

Credits

Philip Jan Rothstein, FBCI, is President of Rothstein Associates Inc., a management consultancy he founded in 1984. He is also the Executive Publisher of Rothstein Publishing.

Glyn Davies is Chief Marketing Officer of Rothstein Associates Inc. He has held this position since 2013. Glyn has previously held executive level positions in Sales, Marketing and Editorial at several multinational publishing companies and currently resides in California.

Editorial Advisory Services

Kristen Noakes-Fry

Indexing

Enid Zafran, Indexing Partners LLC

Cover Design and Graphics

Sheila Kwiatek, Flower Grafix

eBook Design & Production

Donna Luther, Metadata Prime

About Rothstein Publishing

ROTHSTEIN PUBLISHING is the premier global content provider in the core disciplines of Business Continuity Management; Emergency Management; Disaster Recovery and Prevention; Information Security; Risk Management; Crisis Communications; Management; and Leadership, Since 1989, we've published an extensive, informational suite of books in these important subjects. More recently we've established ourselves as a serious publisher in the fields of Cybersecurity; Critical Infrastructure; Business Strategy; and Leadership.

Our founder Philip Jan Rothstein, FBCI, is an internationally known management consultant, entrepreneur, publisher, columnist, contributor to 100+ books.

Our authors are globally recognized; several are uniquely distinguished international thought leaders as founders of their respective industries. Most have also been key participants in developing industry standards and best practices. Some are founding fellows of the Business Continuity Institute, as is our publisher Philip Rothstein, who was elected a Fellow in 1994 in recognition of his substantial contributions to the profession.

No matter the company size or your level of expertise, you'll find in Rothstein's publications the most current and practical advice, tools, & tips to protect your employees, facilities, and financial assets, manage your legal & reputational risks and grow your business.

Rothstein Publishing is a division of Rothstein Associates Inc., an international management consultancy founded in 1984.

About the Authors

ROGER BLACKWELL financed his education by working at radio and television stations and a newspaper in Missouri. After receiving his Ph. D. at Northwestern University, he joined the faculty of The Ohio State University where he taught 65,000 students and co-authored *Consumer Behavior*, a textbook used throughout the world in multiple languages and editions, and 30 other books.

He also lectured and conducted research in 40 countries on seven continents, observing in-person why people are poor or prosperous. While a professor, he was on the boards of fourteen public corporations. Currently, he serves on boards of private organizations and teaches seminars about economics in the U.S. and Canada.

ROGER BAILEY was born in Toledo, Ohio, and lived in the economically depressed east side until middle school. After his parents divorced, his mother married a musician, leading his family to move around the country throughout his adolescence (Arizona, Tennessee, Idaho).

Declining to move again, Roger worked on a cattle ranch in Southern Idaho through his last two years of High School. The friendships and different perspectives he gained through these experiences have been invaluable.

After graduation, Roger moved to Northern Arizona and returned to school at the local community college. He continued working full-time at the local hospital while earning his Bachelor's degree and Master of Science in Mathematics at Northern Arizona University, graduating Summa Cum Laude and with Distinction respectively.

A desire to work in a more applied area led Roger to pursue a Ph.D. in Economics at Vanderbilt University and a post-doctorate position in marketing at the Fisher College of Business. As a Clinical Assistant Professor of Marketing, Roger teaches coursework that applies mathematics, statistics, and economics to improve decision-making in the field of marketing. A passionate educator and student advocate, Roger has won multiple teaching awards in his time at The Ohio State University and also serves as Academic Director of the Full-Time MBA program.